ERRATA

The title on page 49 is amended to read
"THE YOUNG COMPANIONS."
Subsequent headings on pages 51,53,55,
57, and 59 are similarly amended.

QUEST
FOR
THE
DAWN

Shoji Kimoto

THE DOUGHERTY COMPANY

Editorial Director: Terry L. Firkins, Ph. D.
Editor, English Edition: Thomas Slattery
Assistant Editor: Cheryl A. McMillan

Quest for the Dawn © 1991 TMS

Originally published in the Japanese language as *Yoake E No Chosen*, Copyright 1979 by Shoji Kimoto.

Prepared and produced by: *The Dougherty Company*
                              A Division of Dougherty
                              Publishing Associates, Inc.
                              12000 West Park Place
                              Milwaukee, Wisconsin 53224

Library of Congress Catalog Card Number: 91-73503

ISBN: 1-878150-01- 4

Printed in the United States

0 9 8 7 6 5 4 3 2 1

Table of Contents

INTRODUCTION

Nearly thirty-five years have passed since Toyota Motor Sales, U.S.A., started its modest operations in a small Hollywood dealership in October, 1957. Back then, our offering to the American market was the Crown, the only passenger car produced by Toyota at that time and one which proved disappointingly underpowered for the vast highway systems of America.

The idea of exporting to the United States had come from Shotaro Kamiya, then president of Toyota Motor Sales Company. It was during his 1956 visit to the U. S. that Kamiya was shocked to see Volkswagen Beetles traveling the American highways right alongside the big Detroit cars. He was also surprised to learn that Volkswagen and other European compact auto makers were aggressively forming dealership networks throughout the country. Having come to Toyota from General Motors Japan, Kamiya had long dreamed of exporting to America, "home of the automobile." It is little wonder that he was greatly interested in the conditions which were creating inroads into the American car market for foreign manufacturers.

The previous year, 1955, had been a watershed for the American auto industry, as all of the "Big Three" -- General Motors, Ford, and Chrysler -- posted record production levels. This glut of cars resulted in an economic downturn the following year, as demand fell sharply and domestic car production was cut by two million vehicles. By the second half of 1957, the American economy was in a full-scale recession. As money tightened, American auto buyers began to shop around for cheaper, more economical vehicles. What they found was the European compact and a European auto industry anxious and ready to please the American public.

Interestingly, about this time the nature of the average American car buyer was beginning to undergo a transformation in tastes and perceived needs, in part due to economics, but also due to a change in image. This added impetus to the invasion by foreign importers. Whereas it was always assumed that Americans regarded economy imports as "the second family car," a 1957 study by *Fortune* magazine revealed that many were being purchased as "the primary family vehicle." Half of the new car buyers surveyed by *Fortune* cited *economy of operation* as the import's main attraction, with only 19 percent citing *low sticker price*. Because gasoline was very inexpensive in the '50s, it was assumed that *economy of operation* referred to the decreased cost of repairs over American-made models.

This change, signaled by increasing reliance on foreign imports, was echoed by similar changes in taste regarding domestically-produced autos. Between 1955 and 1959, for example, AMC Rambler increased annual production from 80,000 to 400,000. None of these signs seemed to worry the "Big Three," who tended to slough off the issue by saying that Americans could always buy used cars if they wanted cheap transportation. In fact, when Toyota's Shotaro Kamiya broached the subject to Harlow Curtice, president of General Motors, Curtice replied: "Within a demand of 5.8 million cars, imports make up 5 percent at the most. Maybe Volkswagen has sold some, but they represent no more than one percent of the total -- five thousand cars at best. Even if this *is* the age of the second car, Americans still always dream of owning a Cadillac. GM has no interest in a market that hasn't reached a scale appropriate for mass production."

Believing that "the key to business success is good timing," Kamiya put aside misgivings about the possible prematurity of his enterprise and questionable outcome of mass-producing for exportation to the United States. As he put it, "If we move now, we have a chance of making inroads into the second car market. If we don't, and European manufacturers continue to increase their market share, to the point that trade restrictions are imposed by the American government, Toyota may be shut out of the American market forever."

Kamiya moved quickly, and in August, 1957, the first two Crowns arrived in Los Angeles. Although well-received, being dubbed "baby Cadillacs," they quickly failed the grueling tests thrown at them by American highways. At average cruising speeds of eighty miles per hour, the Crown's engine roared, power output dropped, and body vibration frightened drivers into believing the car was about to fall apart. This marked Toyota's first lesson in modifying car design to meet specific driving conditions. In Japan, the Crown's engine and suspension were perfectly suited for the country's narrow roads and moderate driving speeds. But in no way did they match the performance and endurance of American-made automobiles. Kamiya was understandably disappointed but remained determined to succeed at exportation: "No matter what happens, we must establish a corporation there. Even if we sell only a few cars, that will be all right, so long as we get a foothold in the U. S. market."

By October of 1957, only two months after the first Crowns touched American soil, Toyota Motor Sales, U.S.A. Inc., was up and running. Most of the corporation's early time and effort were devoted to meeting necessary certification standards, but by July of 1958, thirty new Crowns had arrived in Los Angeles. All told for 1958, nearly 2,000 Crowns were exported to the U. S. from Japan. Priced only $500 above the top-selling Volkswagen Beetle, the Crown was expected to sell well. Unfortunately this was not the case. As the "Big Three" responded to the inevitability of the small car market and began producing compacts of their own, the demand for foreign imports decreased. Orders for new Crowns were canceled. Those already received by American dealers, especially Ford dealers who were trying to recoup their losses from the disastrous Edsel, were simply gathering dust and rain spots in dealership lots. Adding to Toyota's frustration was the competition emanating from one of its own domestic rivals. In 1959, Nissan began exporting the Datsun 210, a compact designed specifically for the U. S. market.

In response to these developments, in 1960 Toyota replaced its poor-selling Crown exports with the Tiara. Little improved over its cousin, the Tiara also was underpowered and poorly designed for the American market. For all of 1960, only 316 Toyotas were sold, compared to 1,640 Datsuns sold by Nissan. As a Toyota engineer reported to his management, "It will take five years before the Crown can meet the American standards." The first moment of true defeat for the budding exporter, however, came in December of 1960, when Toyota Motor Sales halted export of its passenger car to the United States altogether.

With the loss of the Crown and the Tiara, Toyota Motor Sales, U.S.A. Inc. (hereafter TMS, USA) had only the four-wheel-drive Land Cruiser on its list of saleables, a sturdy vehicle born of the Korean War. At the request of the United States Army, in 1950 Toyota had begun experimental manufacture of a heavy-duty jeep for use in combat by U. S. troops during the war. Equipped with a large, high-performance engine, this vehicle rapidly earned the reputation of being fast, maneuverable, and indestructible. In 1956, it was converted for civilian use, introduced to the domestic market and eventually was exported to the United States, at which point it was christened the Land Cruiser. As Toyota Motor Company regrouped for another assault on the American market, TMS, USA, avoided collapse by using the Land Cruiser as a base for developing a dealer network.

As predicted, it took five years for the Toyota engineers to overcome their nemesis of the American open road. For as much as six months at a time, teams of engineers would use American highways as the testing ground for new, improved models. With the Crown as their starting point, by a process of elimination they were able to produce a car that withstood the high speeds and long-distance driving of American car owners.

The introduction of the Corona in 1965 marked a new beginning for TMS, USA, and established the company's reputation for providing dependable, high-quality automobiles. Designed specifically for the American driver, it succeeded in every area where the Crown and Tiara failed. The horsepower rating of its engine was superior to that of comparable imports, it offered an optional automatic transmission, and it was exceptionally fuel-efficient. The base sticker price for a 1965 Corona? $1,860, and that included radio and heater as standard features. Of the Corona, an American automotive magazine said: "The Japanese automobile industry has reached the point where it stands shoulder to shoulder with the European manufac-tures." In no time the car was catapulted into popularity. A sales network consisting of over six hundred dealers sold the Corona and tallied a new Toyota sales record. More Toyotas were sold in the U.S. during 1966 than during all previous years combined.

By the mid-1960s, with Volkswagen leading the way, the import automobile had made a permanent home for itself in the United States. The average import buyer defied classification by age but generally was less affluent and therefore in need of inexpensive transportation. It was growing more apparent that the American buying public was exercising greater personal discretion in its choice of automobile. Quality and dependability were steadily gaining ground on style as primary purchase criteria. This was a trend Detroit chose to ignore. For a long time American auto makers had produced cars with an average life span of three to four years. When the cars "wore out," they were shuffled off to the used car lot and sold to those who could least afford the inevitable repair bills. Since domestic auto makers and dealers were growing fat on new car sales, they had no incentive to rethink their philosophy on long-term dependability.

By 1970, only a decade after Kamiya first met with Curtice of General Motors, foreign imports had doubled their market share in the U. S. to 10 percent. Volkswagen maintained 60 percent of the import segment, while Japanese manufacturers held 4 to 6 percent. This increased penetration by the Japanese was coming mostly at the expense of European small car sales. Toyota continued to increase its presence in the U. S. market by offering a variety of high-quality vehicles designed for the American consumer and by maintaining a sharp focus on marketing. (TMS, USA, was in fact the first importer to recognize the importance of American television advertising.)

Then in the autumn of 1973, world events threw a curve that blanked the auto industry worldwide. With the outbreak of the Middle East War in October, the Organization of Petroleum Exporting Countries, otherwise known as OPEC, turned down the oil pumps and affected the gas pumps around the globe, giving rise to the infamous oil embargo. Overnight the price of crude oil rose 70 percent, and at the end of the year it had virtually doubled. By the summer of '74, it had quadrupled, throwing Japan into nothing short of a state of emergency. Prices of all petroleum-related products soared and created a ripple effect throughout the entire economy.

The Japanese auto industry took an immediate downturn, as the country experienced raw material shortages for steel, rubber, paint pigment, and components for making plastic. In other words, just when the price hike in gasoline was boosting global demand for fuel-efficient compact imports, Japan was being stymied by its own limited resources. Toyota felt like a thoroughbred held back at the starting post. The total number of Toyota vehicles manufactured for 1974 amounted to the same number produced for domestic sale alone two years before. Conservation measures were instituted countrywide to combat this scarcity of resources, which resulted in a marked slowdown at Toyota production facilities. To show the extent to which Toyota was affected by these measures, thermostats were held at the bare minimum and all unnecessary use of electricity was carefully monitored.

One of the positive results of the fuel crisis was the genesis of a new philosophy among Japanese auto manufacturers. Whereas quantity had been the unbending goal from the outset of exportation, emphasis rapidly shifted to quality. When the world would eventually return to normal and its auto industry would be squarely on its feet again, this new emphasis would give Japan a head start on a market that was evolving in the direction of conservation. Due to strict domestic regulations, Japan was already in the process of forging a new technology for emissions control. And the rationing of precious Japanese resources was resulting in a "rationalization" of the Japanese auto industry, as more modern and efficient methods of production went hand in hand with the shift to quality. Those countries less affected by the oil embargo and less toughened by the hardship would find themselves lagging behind in response to the demands of a new conservation-minded world.

Despite strong opposition from Detroit, the United States government moved to enact ambitious energy-conservation measures. One of the first to take effect was CAFE (Corporate Average Fuel Economy), which required American auto makers to achieve an average fuel economy level of 27.5 miles per gallon for passenger cars by 1985. Because the standard "full-size" American automobile was simply too heavy to allow for such radical improvement in gas mileage, the industry responded by "lightening up." Such a move was simply a stopgap. As the "Big Three" scrambled to scuttle excess baggage to meet the CAFE standards, the quality of American cars began to slide. Eventually a toll would have to be paid for the reactive attitude of U. S. auto manufacturers.

Starting in the fall of 1974, the Environmental Protection Agency began making public the fuel performance of all cars sold in America. Japanese cars went unchallenged for the top positions. Moreover, as the Toyota Corona and Celica quickly met increasingly stricter U. S. emissions control standards, as well as posted victories in fuel economy and dependability, Toyota's share of the market steadily expanded. From 1975 on, Japan's passenger car exporters in general experienced sharp annual increases. By the late 1970s, they were adding a net increase of 400,000 units per year. Toyota itself had officially marked the beginning of its ascent in 1975, when it surpassed Volkswagen as the number one selling import, with total sales of 283,909.

The groundwork laid by Toyota's domestic sales program helped TMS, USA, move with assurance to establish an efficient and effective sales network in the United States. In retrospect, it seems humorous that this very efficiency was a source of frustration, as the shipping supply system could not keep pace with the sales opportunities afforded TMS, USA, by the rising demand for Toyota imports in America. In essence, TMS, USA, was capable of selling more cars than they were receiving from abroad. In response to this situation, in the early 1970s Toyota masterminded and put in place its current parts supply system.

Now able to satisfy the growing hunger of Americans for fuel-efficient Japanese imports, Toyota sales steadily increased. It was a phenomenon that did not go unnoticed by America's ''Big Three,'' whose mainstay continued to be full-size cars with poor mileage. That the end of a two-decade run on ''gas guzzlers'' was at hand, however, was dramatically highlighted when sales of compact cars mushroomed to 39 percent of the total U. S. sales for the first four months of 1973. In Los Angeles, the figure went as high as 60 percent. By the end of the first quarter of 1974, American auto makers sat by helplessly as sales slipped 27 percent below the same quarter a year earlier. First quarter profits for the ''Big Three'' followed suit. At Ford, profits were down by 66 percent, at General Motors, 85 percent, and Chrysler came in last with net profit losses of an unbelievable 98 percent.

For the American auto industry, the 1970s stood for a decade-long feud with the government over growing concerns for the environment and conservation. On each of the government's programs, from emissions control to fuel economy, American auto makers resisted by playing a game of ''wait and see.'' Of course, the only ones really paying for this attitude were American car buyers, who continued to complain that their voice was being ignored by Detroit. While Washington and Detroit arm wrestled, Japanese and European exporters moved quietly ahead toward compliance with all of the U. S. government's tightening standards. Many foreign auto makers participated in cooperative research ventures to meet these standards, a practice prohibited by U. S. anti-trust laws. Thus American auto makers were forced into a decade of costly, overlapping research to seek their joint goals of low emissions and higher gas mileage.

In 1981, just as Japanese manufacturers were engaging in voluntary restrictions on passenger car exports to the U. S., the Reagan administration was launched. It was an event which would cause yet another change in the dynamics of the world's automobile industry.

What President Reagan inherited upon taking office was an economic hornet's nest. From the time Japan went off the gold standard, the value of the dollar remained low, and new economic policies failed to alter this situation. From 1971 on, the United States experienced a cancerous trade deficit, as the gap between trade revenues and expenditures widened. Fueled by a sluggish economy, the deficit grew in 1973 to an excess of $10 billion. By 1980 that figure had grown to $30 billion. The slow and steady eight-year increase in the trade deficit was the result of the deterioration in international economic strength of American industry.

In response to the situation, the Reagan administration instituted a policy to loosen the grip of the deficit, to bring about a rebirth of the economy, and to revive the dollar. Several signs pointed to the auto industry as the logical place to begin the revival. As the country's largest industry, the impact of its continued slump was being felt nationwide. The number of auto workers laid off in the summer of 1980 had reached 250,000, and the worsening business performance of the Big Three was showing no sign of letting up. On the verge of bankruptcy, Chrysler was also on the eve of the largest bailout to date by the United States government. By comparison to this depressing situation, the meteoric success of the Japanese auto export industry made Japan a prime target for harsh criticism.

In June of 1980, the United Auto Workers (UAW) brought a suit before the International Trade Commission (ITC) against import auto makers. Following that, Ford began to actively campaign for government limitation of imports. In response to these complaints, Japan posed this counterargument: "The sluggishness of the American auto industry did not originate from imported cars, but from the fact that the American auto makers' responses to the abrupt change of the American market in favor of compact cars had been too slow."

The ITC agreed with Japan's perspective and in November of 1980 disclosed its ruling: "The slump in the American auto industry comes from a general sales sluggishness accompanying changes in the demand structure, in other words, a shift in demand to compact cars, and from recession. The origin does not lie primarily in the increase in imported cars."

Then in January of 1981, the United States Department of Transportation published a report, "The U.S. Automobile Industry, 1980," which stated that the 1973 fuel crisis had changed the unchallenged domestic status of the American auto industry "permanently and dramatically." Transportation Secretary Neil Goldschmidt concluded: "It will take a minimum of five years for our industry to return to full competitive strength. That time is needed to accomplish the structural changes required to meet the market demand for new generation autos at competitive prices."

Though the assumption had always persisted that the American auto industry was at a competitive disadvantage due to the low cost of labor in Japan, the Department of Transportation's report helped to shatter this illusion. Contained in the report was a statement that only approximately one-half of Japan's $1,500 per car cost-advantage was attributable to the cost of labor. Goldschmidt went on to say, "The greatest source of Japanese advantage is structural: process and product technology which yield major productivity gains. U. S. management must commit major resources to matching these productivity accomplishments if our industry is to regain competitive strength."

Asserting that the domestic auto industry was vital to the health of the American economy, Goldschmidt maintained that if nothing was done to spark revitalization, the entire economy would be in jeopardy. He thus recommended that negotiations be conducted with Japan regarding the limitation of auto imports. Subsequent congressional bills calling for industry protection showed that Goldschmidt's point about the long-term necessity of matching Japan's "productivity accomplishments" was missed in favor of seeking a short-term fix.

As tensions over the import issue worsened between the United States and Japan, the Japanese government, particularly the Ministry of International Trade and Industry (MITI), tried to settle the conflict through self-imposed export regulations on automobiles. Their only problem lay in the difficultly of determining precise reduction levels.

The Japanese auto industry insisted that it would practice substantial self-control on exports, arguing that whatever final restrictions were arrived at by MITI should be imposed for only one year. Moreover, it maintained that the ceiling for exports should be set at the 1.82 million mark, which represented the total number of units exported the previous year. After much debate and grueling negotiations, MITI wore down opposition from the Japanese auto industry and announced the final agreement on May 1, 1981: "For three years, starting from April of 1981, we will put into effect self-imposed controls. The number of vehicles allowed for export in the first year of restraints will be based upon an average for the last three years of exportation, or 1.68 million. For the second year of restraints, the previous year's exportation level of 1.68 million will be averaged in and will allow for a 1.65 percent increase. Levels for the third year will be decided after further study."

In response to these limitations, Japanese auto makers began to study more seriously the feasibility of establishing production facilities in the United States. Actually the stage had already been set for this line of thinking. In his February visit to Japan in 1980, the president of the United Auto Workers, Douglas Fraser, had appealed to Japan to build plants in the United States. Eiji Toyoda, president of Toyota Motor Company, responded favorably to the notion and proposed a joint manufacturing venture with Ford. At first, Ford was very enthusiastic about the idea, but cooled as the two companies could not come to an agreement upon the type of car to be jointly manufactured. While Toyota advocated producing a compact car in the Camry class, Ford shied away from upstaging a new compact of its own which was already in the development stage. Both companies made concessions in order to reach a compromise, but in the end negotiations failed.

General Motors seized the opportunity and approached Toyota with an entirely new proposal. Because GM's X-car and J-car compacts had not developed as well as anticipated, General Motors had been forced to reformulate its compact car strategy, part of which involved a joint manufacturing venture with Japan.   Though formal negotiations for the venture between Toyota and GM didn't officially begin until April of 1982, informal talks had taken place the previous year between Seisi Kato, chairman of Toyota Motor Sales, and Roger Smith, chairman of General Motors.   At that time, Toyota was comprised of two separate companies, Toyota Motor Sales and Toyota Motor Company, the latter being in charge of production. As was appropriate for such a joint venture, Kato informed Eiji Toyoda of the seriousness of GM's interest, and Eiji paid a secret December visit to New York for private discussions with Smith.

Prior to that meeting, General Motors had done its homework by sending a team of experts to Japan to make a comparative study of the manufacturing strengths of the Japanese and American auto industries. The study revealed that the U.S. could not possibly compete in the area of compact cars, primarily because of the cost effectiveness of Japanese production systems. Once again, any notions that the Japanese scored better because of low labor costs or pricing advantages from parts suppliers were dispelled. Just as the U. S. Department of Transportation study had confirmed more than a year earlier, the ''edge'' enjoyed by the Japanese was due to overall superiority in manufacturing infrastructure and performance.

In February, 1984, Toyota announced its joint-manufacturing venture with GM, and the New United Motor Manufacturing, Inc., fondly referred to as NUMMI, was born. Utilizing the Toyota Production System, NUMMI was to be an independent company dedicated to production of the Nova, a Chevrolet compact. Excitement over the project ran high, but many details had to be worked out before it could officially get underway. First on the agenda was the division of responsibilities between both partners, an issue that was worked out in lengthy, and often heated, debates. Toyota argued vehemently for control of production, citing their expertise in the complex system of personnel management and manufacturing which they themselves developed. Because it was key to the success of the project, and also because of its comprehensive and integrated nature -- involving every aspect of manufacturing, from parts supply to work flow -- the Toyota Production System necessitated that Toyota have a free hand in the management of the company. General Motors argued for maintaining control of the company's finances.

It was eventually resolved that Toyota indeed would be responsible for policy decisions regarding manufacturing strategy and financial planning, as well as for control of production. General Motors would have an advisory role in the management of finances, with both companies sharing the company's financial burdens equally. The company's president would come from Toyota and would have unilateral authority in the day-to-day operation of the company. The board of directors would exercise the power of approval and be responsible for making announcements concerning changes in company policy.

Though the merger agreement between Toyota and General Motors was of primary importance in efforts to launch the new enterprise, before actual production could begin, agreements also had to be reached with the United Auto Workers (UAW) and with the Federal Trade Commission (FTC). The first of these agreements would prove to be a challenge.

Because General Motors had stipulated that Toyota must invest in kind in GM's closed plants, Toyota had little choice but to involve itself with the plant in Fremont, California, the only GM facility that was completely closed. As Toyota learned later, this plant had been shut down due to severe labor problems, ranging from drugs in the work place to a high rate of absenteeism. For a Japanese company accustomed to a responsible and loyal work force, the Fremont plant presented a difficult challenge from the start. With little warning, Toyota found itself face-to-face with American labor and the UAW.

The first demand made by the UAW was that the Fremont work force be rehired in total before the project could go forward. Toyota countered by pointing out that the unique nature of their labor-management philosophy and their production system would not allow for this. Finally, a compromise was reached whereby the majority of workers would return to work, provided the UAW could guarantee enforcement of a strict absentee policy and also ease the distrust that existed traditionally in America between labor and management. This gave the UAW an excellent opportunity to prove that it could deliver an excellent work force when management provided the right environment, which Toyota was confident of being able to do.

The last remaining obstacle for the NUMMI joint venture was the FTC, which was worried about the implications of a collaboration between the world's number one and number three car manufacturers. (Though Toyota is now number two in the world, at that time it was number three.) In other words, would a marriage between GM and Toyota place the rest of the nation's auto manufacturers at an unfair disadvantage? Though Toyota stressed that the object of the joint venture was to manufacture only one model of car, it still took the FTC almost a full year to arrive at a ruling, which put the entire project in jeopardy. Planning to begin production at NUMMI by the end of 1984, Toyota had hired workers for the long and complicated preparation of the Toyota Production System, and needed FTC approval by February of that same year. Otherwise, the project was in jeopardy of being eliminated.

As it turned out, when the FTC did rule in favor of the GM/Toyota NUMMI partnership, its restrictions were severe. One of the limitations in fact mandated dissolution of the partnership by the year 1996. At that time, either GM or Toyota would be required to assume full ownership of NUMMI, or the concern would have to be either sold to a third party or closed down. It was in the shadow of these restrictions that the project was inaugurated.

From the outset, problems both internal and external to the company hampered implementation of the Toyota Production System. Part of the early external difficulties stemmed from hard-line positions taken by American parts suppliers on the issue of defective parts. As inferior parts began to appear, Toyota proposed to send a team of engineers into the supplier's factory to study quality assurance. At first, this proposal was summarily rejected by suppliers, who insisted that defective parts could be returned and replaced. Toyota remained patient in explaining that a key to the efficiency and profitability of the Toyota Production System was consistency in quality from suppliers. Moreover, they made it clear their motive was not to assume control of the supplier's factory, but rather to work together in a cooperative effort to investigate and pinpoint problems in the supply process. It took two years for suppliers to understand this concept, but when they did, the incidence of defective parts dropped from a double-digit rate to below 1 percent.

Internally, Toyota faced the great challenge of changing the mind-set of the American worker. Under the Toyota Production System, workers have a heavy individual responsibility. A *Standard Work Sheet* is displayed prominently at each work station and serves as a means of visual control, an element essential to smooth flow of work in the Toyota Production System. The concept of *Standard Work* requires that materials, workers, and machines are combined effectively for efficient production, and the worker must adhere to it meticulously. The individual worker is also responsible for correcting any deficiencies in his area of the work flow. Time is not wasted by having a hierarchy of authority on the production floor, and decisions must be made on the spot by each worker. This is why the Toyota Production System is known for trusting the intelligence of its work force and treating workers like thinking individuals, rather than human cogs in an inhuman machine.

By contrast, according to the top-down management philosophy of American manufacturers like General Motors, the worker at that time was identified by a number and was expected to perform a specific function on the assembly line. He was not expected to point out inefficiencies or offer any suggestions for improvement.

With this as a backdrop, one can imagine how strange the new Toyota system must have appeared. Though it was welcomed with great enthusiasm at NUMMI, the radical change in thinking made for a somewhat long and painful learning curve for the American worker.

Toughest of all was the adjustment required of team leaders and supervisors on the production floor. No longer could they simply bark orders and expect the system to work accordingly. Instead they had to listen carefully to the worker, whose direct experience with the manufacturing process made him better qualified to input suggestions for improvements. The entire system depended upon vastly improved communication skills, which meant that workers and supervisors alike had to be retrained from the ground up.

Both General Motors and Toyota had specific objectives they hoped to achieve from this joint venture. GM wanted to learn how to build high-quality small cars by utilizing the efficient and cost-effective Toyota Production System. In the process, it would add a new, well-built car, the Nova, to its Chevrolet dealer lineup.

For Toyota, NUMMI represented a chance to learn whether its production system, which had not yet been tested beyond the confines of Toyota City, could be transplanted successfully. Furthermore, by establishing a manufacturing presence in the U. S., Toyota sought to improve trade relations between the United States and Japan.

As Chairman Eiji Toyoda said, "It's the spirit of competition and cooperation that is the foundation for the growth of the world economy, and this plan for a joint venture is based on that idea. I want this project, as a model of productive cooperation between Japan and the U. S., to succeed no matter what, in such a way that it is helpful to the American economy. I want us from now on to set our sights on GM and to work hard to make ourselves an even better competitor."

A year later, in July of 1985, Toyota announced an entirely new plan for building expansion plants in North America, with Camrys to be produced in the United States and Corollas in Canada. When news of this plan spread, the contest among states and provinces for a berth in the program reached a fever pitch. According to Toyota, the final choices would be based upon several carefully-considered criteria: transportation; labor, parts and energy availability; real estate costs; and the general business climate of the host city. Contest winners were Georgetown, Kentucky, in the United States and Cambridge, Ontario, in Canada.

The entire state of Kentucky rose immediately to the occasion by giving Toyota support in every way possible, including valuable assistance in the screening and hiring of workers. The result was a highly select work force that boded well for the success of the venture. Not only were they predominantly state residents, but they came from higher educational backgrounds and, for the most part, were free of union affiliation. From this point forward the issue of worker adaptability became critical, as Toyota remained unconvinced from its NUMMI venture at that point that Japanese culture and manufacturing philosophy could take root in foreign soil.

At the ground-breaking ceremony for Toyota Motor Manufacturing, U.S.A., President Shoichiro Toyoda gave the following charge:

If you people of Kentucky, the home of the thoroughbred, will pour as much love into Toyota, which is starting here today, as you do into your horses, then I am sure this new company will succeed. I hope you will make Kentucky not only the world's foremost area for producing racehorses but also the world's foremost area for producing automobiles.

Toyota's independent expansion into the United States was met with immediate suspicion and criticism by the American business community. "Aiming at being Number One in the world, Toyota has launched an attack in GM's own back yard," was *Business Week*'s opinion of Toyota's plan for expansion plants in North America. NUMMI came to be seen as an effort by Toyota to soften the territory prior to launching a main offensive from its new Kentucky headquarters. The American joke of the day was that Georgetown, Kentucky, would undoubtedly experience a name change to "Toyota City, USA."

Even Toyota could not refute such an analysis, despite the fact that the American perspective overly simplified an extremely complex issue. Toyota's true objective all along could be best described by the simple phrase "Cooperation and Competition," which it used repeatedly in its negotiations with the United States. What Americans were failing to see was how different Toyota's "expansionist" strategies differed from those of the United States and Europe, who operated according to a "buy out" mentality. The element of "cooperation" entailed utilization of the host work force and a "cultural exchange" philosophy which would work to the benefit of all involved.

In 1990, Toyota Motor Manufacturing, U. S. A. (TMM), was awarded the J. D. Power and Associates Gold Plant Quality Award, in recognition of its production of the "most trouble-free car" in its class, the Toyota

Camry. Without the dedication and teamwork of its 3,650 employees, TMM would never have succeeded in implementing the Toyota Production System in the United States.

TOYOTA'S CONTRIBUTION TO THE U. S.:
THE TOYOTA PRODUCTION SYSTEM

Historically speaking, with the exception of Toyota, Japanese auto makers got their start by importing research and automotive technology from the United States and Europe after World War II. This is not surprising given the fact that America was the world leader in automobile research and technology until the 1960s. After that point, the issues of safety and emissions regulation served to narrow "the technology gap," as auto makers around the world scrambled to meet tighter regulations. Spurred by the new safety and emissions control technology, auto makers experienced an overall upgrade in technology, and the competitive edge became a fine one indeed. What ultimately sharpened the edge for Japanese auto makers was the production system developed at Toyota and later adopted by other Japanese manufacturers.

Dating back to the 1930s, the Toyota Production System was invented by Kiichiro Toyoda, the founder of Toyota Motor Company. Kiichiro had studied the mass-production method employed by Ford and had found it wanting in several respects. Out of the weaknesses he saw there came a method of mass-producing automobiles Kiichiro called "Just-In-Time." According to the Just-In-Time method, parts would not be stockpiled for future use in the assembly process, as Ford and other American manufacturers were doing. Rather, they would be assembled in-line with the demands of manufacturing. This procedure required precision timing in the parts supply program and allowed virtually no room for error.

Kiichiro Toyoda's Just-In-Time concept was fully developed after World War II by Taiichi Ohno, a Toyota engineer. With the company on the verge of bankruptcy due to runaway inflation and a foundering domestic automobile market, Ohno, who was then in charge of the engine machine shop, proposed a plan to raise productivity and still reduce personnel and manufacturing costs. He analyzed each job routine and each machine with the objective of eliminating "waste" in all operations. Using Just-In-Time as his starting point, Ohno developed a system which was opposite from the method most commonly used by American auto makers. Rather than "pushing" materials and components forward on the assembly line, Ohno's system required that they be "pulled" along. Accordingly, workers retrieved what they needed from previous work stations on the line, thus allowing each automobile to be built to accommodate a specific purchase order.

The inspiration for Ohno's improvement upon the Just-In-Time concept was a method used by American aircraft manufacturers during World War II, a method which in turn had come, oddly enough, from the birth of the modern grocery market. It was in large measure due to the supermarket that households no longer needed to store, or "stockpile," food in large quantities. Rather than keeping a five-pound bag of salt in the pantry, for instance, the modern homemaker could now buy a small container of salt and replace it whenever needed. Also meals could be planned on a short-term basis, as opposed to a week or two weeks in advance. Essentially, the major by-product of this new and modern convenience was greater flexibility and variety in meal planning. For the modern grocery market it meant more precise inventory control, as smaller units of food could be moved to the consumer and replaced more easily.

According to Ohno's system, just as the consumer would return more frequently to the market to create individualized meals, and as the market owner responds with greater flexibility and speed to consumer needs, so would each worker on the Toyota assembly line "return to the parts market" of the preceding work station to create an individualized auto. The redundancy factor inherent in stockpiling parts and materials would be eliminated, and manufacturing would proceed with far more flexibility and efficiency. The bottom line, of course, would be greater cost effectiveness and thus higher profits.

While all of this sounds very simple and neat, it actually took Toyota thirty years to perfect its Just-In-Time production method. Not only did its very complex logistics have to be painstakingly worked out, but for all intents and purposes the very essence of the system had to become a state of mind. From start to finish, every facet of the operation had to function as a unified part of an integrated thought in a harmonious brain.

Perhaps it is this last, more philosophical aspect of the system that makes it difficult to understand. Even in Japan, where culture poses no barriers, it is sometimes not totally understood. Where cultural barriers do exist -- say, in the United States and in many European countries -- the system often completely defies comprehension. One thing is for certain, however, the Toyota Production System goes far beyond the practical logistics of manufacturing and effective management of production areas, which is what it represents to many people.

Perhaps the difficulty of understanding this system also comes from the fact that it has been recognized by so many different names. First, it was known in the United States as the Just-In-Time, or *Kanban*, System. Then it evolved into the "Exactly-On Time System," thanks to the interest and a report by General Motors in the early '70s. Though Exactly-On-Time and Just-In-Time seem very similar, the term Just-In-Time captures the nuance closest to its true meaning in Japanese. Whereas Exactly-On-Time connotes a thing accomplished, Just-In-Time dramatizes the urgent sense of process which is ever-ongoing in the fluid stream of manufacturing activity.

Later the term "Lean Production" was coined by John Krafcik in his book *The Machine That Changed the World*. In terms of the actual logistics of the Toyoda Production System, Lean Production comes closest to explaining the advantage created by an endless search for improvement -- in the process as well as the product. It also points to the importance placed upon finding ways of economizing in the work force and seeking greater efficiency in all aspects of the corporate operation. In essence, there are three practical components of the Toyota Production System: Just-In-Time production, *heijunka*, or leveled production, and continuous-flow processing.

Just-In-Time production involves having assembly parts arrive at the appropriate production line at the proper time and in the proper quantity. When Just-In-Time production works perfectly throughout the entire company, excess inventory is eliminated and warehousing is not necessary.

A *kanban*, or special card, is utilized to communicate the type and quantity of a particular part needed for assembly. It conveys information regarding quantities pulled by the subsequent process and produced by the preceding process in order to achieve Just-In-Time production. In other words, it is the heart of an information management system designed to control parts flow throughout the entire production process. *Kanban* is a communications tool within the Toyota factory as well as between Toyota and its suppliers.

In order for the *kanban* system to work well, various prerequisites must be met. Each assembly method must be designed in detail, jobs must be standardized, and leveled production must be executed all in advance of the actual manufacturing process. Without such prior preparation, the *kanban* system cannot work properly. Because highly-sophisticated advanced planning is difficult to achieve for American companies, the *kanban* system has not worked as efficiently as it could in the U. S.

The purpose of leveled production, or *heijunka*, is to minimize fluctuations in quantities of parts withdrawn for use in various sub-assembly lines. According to instructions communicated by the *kanban*, each station in the assembly process withdraws the appropriate part or parts from the station before it at precisely the right time. If any one station works at an unsteady rate or mismanages its parts flow, a disruption is felt throughout the entire system. To avoid such variables in all production lines, including those of outside subcontractors, the utmost effort is made to normalize the flow and thus achieve *heijunka*.

To attain maximum effectiveness, it is necessary to produce and receive components in the smallest lots possible. This differs radically from conventional mass production systems, where large lots are seen as necessary to keep machines and workers operating, thereby avoiding costly downtime.

Under the Toyota Production System, operating with a minimal parts supply allows parts to be conveyed among stations quickly and efficiently and eliminates the need for stockpiling. At work throughout the entire system, from outside parts suppliers to internal sub-assembly, *heijunka*, or Leveled Production, results in a controlled flow of finished vehicles from the final assembly line.

Historically, the development of Leveled Production was greatly influenced by the nature of the automobile market in Japan during the 1950s. Though the market was very "low-volume," it still involved a heavy demand for a wide variety of cars and trucks. As a result, all Japanese auto makers had to modify American mass-production techniques to produce many different models in very small quantities. By necessity, machine tools used by Japanese auto makers had to be general purpose tools, as opposed to the highly-specialized machine tools used by the mass-production system in America. This allowed the Japanese to maintain the high degree of flexibility to alter the manufacturing process at any time to produce a different model, ultimately without altering the production flow. To take this notion to its extreme for the sake of illustration, three different models could roll off the final assembly line one after the other without there having been any disruption in assembly along the way.

As one might expect, quality assurance was tantamount to the success of such a process. Eventually, special mechanisms were built into the production line to prevent defective operation of the machine tools, which eliminates defective parts and thus defective final products. A central part of the Toyota Production System today, this procedure, called *jidoka*, depends upon a series of devices which continuously monitor machinery for manufacturing abnormalities. If and when an abnormality occurs anywhere in the production line, the appropriate worker pushes a button and brings the entire line to a halt. When the problem is corrected, assembly is resumed at the place where it was interrupted.

Jidoka makes it possible to achieve a zero-defect rate of quality *during* the manufacturing process, thus increasing the final efficiency of the system. For several reasons, a similar "in-line" quality rate is impossible in Western manufacturing operations. In American mass production, for example, products are inspected for defects *after* manufacturing. All defective parts or products are then either discarded or returned to the supplier for replacement. The manufacturer's attitude is that he can afford this waste simply because mass production has allowed him to operate in greater quantities at lower unit costs. So long as waste due to defective production never exceeds the cost advantage of mass producing, the manufacturer can earn a profit.

In contrast, the Japanese philosophy maintains that waste is waste, no matter what the cost, and it is this philosophy which drives all aspects of the

Toyota Production System.   One of its major advantages, as *jidoka* demonstrates, is that the emphasis is on the process -- particularly on the efficiency of the process -- rather than on the cost of the final product. When the manufacturing method is totally efficient, cost will take care of itself on every front, from parts to labor, and the assistance of statistical analysis is not needed to achieve zero-defect quality "in the process."

In further departure from the American mass production system, the Toyota Production System requires one worker to perform many functions, a situation which adds greatly to the need for intelligence among the work force. While one of the benefits of this arrangement is economy, the primary reason for its existence is flexibility and quality control. As the work performed at each work station varies in accordance with the type of vehicle being produced at any given moment, each worker must respond quickly to the appropriate change. To allow several workers to coordinate such an effort would be like allowing many hands to operate a single computer key board. The possibility for human error would be infinitely increased and mistakes would thwart all efforts for perfection in manufacturing. In order to make this very complex "multi-model" production system work smoothly, immense amounts of time and planning are devoted to the arrangement of machinery on the factory floor. As the manufacturing process changes from car to car, the worker must have extremely easy access to a variety of machines.   Work at each process goes forward only when the worker completes his given jobs within a specific time frame, or "cycle time," determined by the nature of the model under construction. This aspect of the Toyota Production System is called "multi-process holding."

Multi-process holding is essentially a Japanese phenomenon. In American and European companies, work responsibilities are carefully defined and enforced by the various trade unions present in any given factory.   As a result, a worker is neither required nor allowed to handle machinery and work operations outside his specific job description. This is not true in Japan. There a company is served by only one union, and workers are permitted to do a wide variety of jobs within a given system of seniority. Without this unique form of unionization, the Toyota Production System never could have reached its present level of efficiency and success.

Another element of the historical environment leading to Toyota's development of a system for intelligent, cost-effective use of its labor force stems from the postwar era. Following World War II, the Japanese economy was caught in whirlwind inflation.   Investment capital to fuel the postwar reconstruction had dried up. The bottom had fallen out of the consumer market, and labor unrest began to plague manufacturers in nearly every sector of the country.

Toyota was no exception. A company-wide belt tightening and layoffs sparked a strike that neither labor nor management wanted but were helpless to thwart. Negotiations to end the strike were then begun on the eve of a full-scale return to manufacturing, as the United States fueled the economy by ordering military vehicles for the Korean War effort. Out of these negotiations came two major concessions from Toyota management: lifetime employment for workers and a wage scale based upon seniority, as opposed to job responsibility.

The impact of these concessions was immediate. Overnight, labor became a fixed cost, on par with machinery and tools. There was one essential difference, however. Whereas machinery could be depreciated and replaced as it wore out, the price of maintaining a work force for life appreciated, as cost of living adjustments and seniority took effect. Toyota's answer to this situation was to further perfect its production system by adding the element of "multi-process holding." Great emphasis was placed upon the continuous enhancement of workers' skills and multi-purpose functions, which led to even more lean production and a further departure from the mass production philosophy of the West.

As these various elements of the Toyota Production System matured into a harmonious system of manufacturing, the company prepared for a full-scale trial run. In 1971, Toyota announced that the Celica would be manufactured entirely on a customer order basis. The news sent shock waves of surprise throughout the world's automobile community, including many of Japan's auto makers, who were still using mass-production methods. Having developed a total mindset about the virtues of mass production, manufacturers other than Toyota could not imagine a system where cars were to be "customized for the customer."

From its crude beginnings in a small pilot plant in Japan, through its evolution and perfection due to a homely observation about a new grocery market phenomenon, Just-In-Time was on the eve of revolutionizing a system of manufacturing that had awed the world for three-quarters of a century. Toyota was indeed throwing down the gauntlet to Ford's mass production method, and the world was about to experience the advantage of "full choice" manufacturing.

Even in Japan, many of the country's auto makers were left shaking their heads, as leveled production and "full choice" manufacturing had seemed to elude everyone but Toyota. After this 1971 announcement, Toyota would put further distance between itself and its fellow domestic competitors simply because the dynamics of the "full choice" method were so difficult to fathom, let alone put into manufacturing practice.

The backbone of the "full-choice" system was, and still is, a daily order system. Each day the factory receives a detailed order based upon the exact numbers and types of vehicles requested by dealers throughout the country. Because there is a strictly maintained lag time of four days between reception of orders and actual fulfillment by the factory, all orders are very current.

This cuts the total fulfillment time from the old standard of twenty days to eight days, the time it takes for a car to be registered in Japan.

For this system to function properly, parts from outside suppliers and internally-produced parts must be delivered Just-In-Time according to vehicle orders. Each day the *kanban* are arranged by computer to communicate the precise sequence of manufacturing and parts supply needed to fulfill the day's order. This system is used to coordinate all sub-assembly lines, so that vehicles are being assembled in the same order in which they will be received for final assembly. From start to finish, from the time an order is recorded for a single vehicle until the moment that vehicle rolls off the final assembly line, its progression is constantly monitored. Like the spokes of a wheel, the components of each vehicle converge in a precise and logical fashion toward the hub, and this hub is a newly-minted automobile.

With the success of the Celica and greater recognition of Toyota's departure from traditional mass production methods, both fear and curiosity led the auto industry of the world to want to know more about the Toyota Production System. Toyota showed a willingness to share its technology, but two questions quickly arose concerning the possibility of transplanting the system to other countries and cultures. At issue were the subcontractor system and labor practices unique to Japan. Especially in America, where independence and individualism are seen as the cornerstones of the country's creativity and progress, these questions loomed even larger than in other areas of the world.

Eventually, however, the teamwork and cooperative spirit upon which the Toyota Production System was conceived began to find its way into the American automobile industry. Three factors contributed to this change: advancement of Japanese parts suppliers into the U. S., following the establishment of Japanese auto plants there; increasingly inefficient in-house parts production among American auto makers, which resulted in a growing dependence on outside suppliers; and experimentation by American auto makers with the Japanese-style infrastructure for parts supply.

In America, Toyota worked with many American parts suppliers to facilitate implementation of the Toyota Production System. The progress made by these suppliers has been so encouraging that by the mid-1990s, Toyota anticipates that half of all Toyota vehicles sold in the U. S. will be manufactured locally. It is becoming increasingly apparent to all involved how crucial the parts supply component is to the whole system, so efforts to reach the highest quality standards among suppliers are continuously ongoing. The final objective is to bring to the American parts supply industry the same high level of quality and profitability enjoyed by Toyota suppliers in Japan.

On the issue of labor, Toyota has worked hard to implement Japanese labor philosophy and practices at NUMMI and is heartened by the progress, especially in light of the fact that NUMMI's labor force is unionized. Whereas in Japan, where labor is viewed by management as an important source of input regarding process and product improvement, thus bringing management and labor closer together, in the United States an air of distrust between employer and employee severely hampers the teamwork necessary for success of the Toyota Production System. Progress is being made, but more must be done to overcome these barriers so that the knowledge and valuable input of the American worker can make their rightful contributions to the system.

The level of success attained at NUMMI resulted from adoption of the multi-purpose job classifications required to accomplish "multi-process holding" and "full-choice" order fulfillment. The UAW was cooperative in reducing the more than one hundred different job classifications in place under the old system. Reasoning that NUMMI was a uniquely new manufacturing venture and therefore not bound by the work rules and rigid job classifications enumerated in its old contract with General Motors, the UAW cut its job classifications to just four. Without such a radical change, implementation of the Toyota Production System would never have been possible.

It is this type of cooperation and progress that bodes well for further attempts to transplant Toyota Production System philosophy and technology in other areas of America and the world. With greater cross-cultural understanding and international cooperation among the world's manufacturing community, the day will come when a system of even greater efficiency will evolve from Toyota's improvement upon the mass-production system.

THE FUTURE OF TOYOTA

What we are doing at NUMMI and TMM are all part of the globalization of Toyota. It is experiments such as these that have made us realize what key global and local issues must be addressed as Toyota expands. Internationally, we must deal with trade imbalances, protectionism, resistance to foreign investment, changes in rules governing international trade, and concern for the environment. Locally, we must integrate our operations abroad with the needs and expectations of host communities and countries. This second goal can be achieved in two ways: greater localization of operations through management of the entire automobile manufacturing process, and increased focus on our efforts to become valued members of the host community.

Localization means that Toyota must expand employment opportunities for Americans and offer fair opportunities for advancement. It also means integrating the entire manufacturing process with the community, from development to final assembly of the product. A fruitful exchange of culture and technology is paramount to improving the communications process between Japan and the United States. Without this, Toyota cannot become the good corporate citizen it desires to be. As Dr. Toyoda himself put it:

> If we are not actively working to bring about reconciliation and conscientiously acting as good corporate citizens, we will be isolated from the local people. Actually, there are cases, even in Japanese companies, of Japanese acting as groups. But isn't this running counter to globalization? I think it's especially necessary for us to act as good corporate citizens abroad. Within this homogeneous country [Japan], communication flows comparatively smoothly, but abroad, we must make a certain effort, and there is a cost in that.

Much time and understanding are needed to develop harmonious relations between two countries. That is why the answers to complex cultural issues cannot be ''yes'' or ''no,'' as is often the custom among Americans. It is my belief that a third answer will be necessarily more productive, and that answer is ''wait.'' Unless both sides of the Pacific are patient with each others' differences, efforts toward a true cultural understanding will be constantly frustrated. Time is needed for study and familiarization before true interdependence, trust, and respect can be achieved. This exchange should be equal. Just as Toyota needs the American market to sell its goods, America can benefit from the high quality of Toyota products and contributions Toyota can make in creating new jobs for the American people. As Dr. Toyoda has always said, Toyota must ''enrich society through the automobile.''

Toyota's philosophy is not to compete for smaller and smaller pieces of ''the automobile industry pie,'' but rather to expand the pie. The prosperity which comes from satisfying the demands of the local market in turn increases the demand. As the market expands and further prosperity follows, the demand increases proportionately, until more and more people experience the benefits of the automobile. As Dr. Toyoda points out, ''Among the five billion people on this earth, only one third of them have reaped the benefits of the automobile.'' Only through international cooperation and mutual prosperity can the second two-thirds of the world improve their lot. And this does not eliminate the factor of healthy competition among the world's auto makers along the way. According to Dr. Toyoda:

> If we can make a good car, our rivals will work hard to make a car that is just as good, and they'll catch up with and surpass us. Then we will catch up with and surpass them. In this way we will compete with each

other and, through gradual refinement, a better car will be made. I think that's a good thing. That's what competition is. Competition in which you fight with each other is worthless, but if you do it in such a way that doesn't happen, then competition is a good thing. It's competition and cooperation. That's coexistence and mutual prosperity.

To participate in the globalization of Toyota, to contribute to Toyota's future growth and prosperity, we must first understand the past: the birth of Toyota and its corporate philosophy, and its development as a global corporate entity. Our story began more than one hundred years ago with Sakichi Toyoda, whose quest was to do something for his country. Declaring that "unless I do it, Japan will not be able to catch up with the rest of the world," he invented the automatic loom. But his dream was to someday build an automobile. His son, Kiichiro realized this vision, and built an automobile fifty years later. But Kiichiro's dream was to build a Japanese car for the masses: "Because it is such a difficult task, I have made up my mind that I definitely must do it." Unfortunately, Kiichiro didn't live long enough to see his quest fulfilled. But Eiji and Shoichiro Toyoda fulfilled it for him.

The human struggle to overcome obstacles to accomplish goals: this is what has made Toyota what it is today. Toyota's corporate characteristics lie in the history of the Toyoda family, the family's leadership of the company without regard to their control of the stock, and the roles achieved by the excellent non-family leaders of the company. In other words, it is a story of how Toyota made use of its human talent. It is the human drama of this story that is captured by Mr. Kimoto in *Quest for the Dawn*, a biography of the founders of Toyota, Sakichi and Kiichiro Toyoda.

Yukiyasu Togo
October, 1991

QUEST
FOR
THE
DAWN

Chapter
1

ESCAPE FROM THE THICKET

"Ah, Kiichiro, there you are!"

A middle-aged man, standing in the half-opened sliding door that led from the eight-*tatami* (mat) room at the front of the house into the adjoining ten-mat room, frowned at the sight of the man sitting cross-legged and leaning over a low table.

"Have you been drawing that stuff again? Do you have to be designing machines, even when you've just returned from your father's memorial service?" he scolded.

The man standing in the door was at least six feet in height, which was quite tall for a Japanese man of that time. He was lean and solidly built, with very good posture. This newcomer cut a dignified figure in his mourning coat, a dark necktie knotted firmly under his high collar.

The seated man did not answer. Nor did he make any move to look up. He was bent over a large notebook on the table, drawing what appeared to be diagrams of machine parts.

The ten-mat room the man was working in was simple and large. Its size was typical for a rural dwelling where rooms were generally more spacious than those found in modern houses in the city. This particular room, however, seemed unnaturally empty due to the absence of decorative objects. The only item of furniture was a large, round red-lacquered table placed at the center of the room.

The man drawing diagrams at the table appeared to be about ten years younger than the man standing in the door. He too was dressed in mourning attire, but had tossed his jacket off to one side. The top buttons of his vest and his shirt were undone, and his necktie had been loosened. He was sitting cross-legged on a large pillow, slouched over his drawings. One sleeve was rolled to the elbow. His casual appearance was in direct contrast to that of the other man.

Looking down as he spoke, the man standing at the door seemed to have recovered from his irritation: "The service went without a hitch, and I'm thinking of heading back to Nagoya. Why don't you come back with us?"

Without looking up from his work, the second man muttered a half-hearted "Uh-huh." He seemed to have little time for this person on this dreary early November day.

The year was 1931. The afternoon sky was cloudy and oppressive, threatening to rain on the rustic village where the old country house was located. This was the site of the old Toyoda family residence. The village was Aza Yamaguchi, located in Washizu (now Kosai City) in Hamana County of the Shizuoka Prefecture. The two men had come to this village about two miles from Lake Hamana to attend a memorial service.

On October 30 of the preceding year, Sakichi Toyoda had died at his Nagoya estate in Kakuosan at the age of sixty-three. He had lived a productive life as an inventor and was well-known for the numerous innovations he had made in power loom design. It was Sakichi Toyoda who had perfected Japan's first automatic loom, recognized around the world as the finest loom of its kind.

Sakichi's funeral had been held on November 4, 1930, at the Kyoka Hall in Shin-sakaemachi, Naka Ward, Nagoya. Built with generous donations from Sakichi himself, the hall had been filled with those who knew, loved, and admired him. Attendance was in excess of three thousand people.

On October 30, 1931, one year after Sakichi's death, an anniversary memorial service was held at the main house of the Toyoda family in Choheimachi, Higashi Ward. A short time later a ceremony for the internment of Sakichi's ashes was held at the family cemetery at Kakuosan. Following the practice of the Kenbon Hokke sect of Buddhism to which the family belonged, a portion of Sakichi's ashes was to be buried at Myomanji, the sect's main temple located at Kyoto. The final portion was to be buried in the Shojuin of Myoryuji Temple in Sakichi's hometown of Washizu. It was this last service in Washizu which had just taken place.

Though the service was planned for members of the immediate family, it was attended by other relatives, friends, and executives from Toyoda Spinning and Weaving and Toyoda Automatic Loom Works. Thus, the gathering was much larger and more lively than anticipated. Most of the attendees dropped by the old Toyoda family home to pay their respects after the service, but at last they had all departed. Only the immediate family and a few close relatives remained. Now the house was quiet again.

"Well, what are you going to do?" demanded the man standing at the door.

"I'll stay here for two or three days," replied the other man absentmindedly, still absorbed in his drawings. He was Kiichiro Toyoda, son of the man whose ashes had just been buried. Born in 1894, he was now thirty-seven years old.

"Oh, I see," nodded the man at the door. He made no further effort to communicate. He knew Kiichiro well enough to realize that no one could get through to him when he was preoccupied with his sketches. This tall man turning now to depart was Risaburo Toyoda, husband of Kiichiro's half-sister, Aiko, and president of Toyoda Automatic Loom Works. Born in 1884, Risaburo was ten years older than Kiichiro.

"Hey, Aiko, Kokichiro, we're going home!" Risaburo shouted, looking over his shoulder in the direction of the back rooms.

Immediately, Aiko came in from the parlor with her oldest son, Kokichiro. She had changed from her black ceremonial kimono to subdued everyday wear and was ready for the return trip home. Behind her Kiichiro's wife, Hatako, stood ready to see the party off. She was still wearing her funeral dress.

"We'll be leaving then, Kiichiro," Risaburo said.

When he had come into the room, Risaburo had left the sliding door open, and now Aiko knelt decorously at the doorway and bowed formally as she paid her respects.

It seemed to Kiichiro that when Aiko appeared, the gloomy day and gloomy room suddenly brightened. Aiko was five years younger than Kiichiro and had just turned thirty. She was small, with a lovely round face. In Kiichiro's eyes, her white, fine-textured skin always seemed to glow.

Ten years before, in the autumn of 1921, Kiichiro had toured the United States and Europe with Risaburo and Aiko, then still newlyweds. Kiichiro was fresh out of the university. At the time of their tour, Aiko was a slender young girl, and as she mingled with the larger-framed western women, she had looked especially pretty.

The memory always stayed with Kiichiro, but Aiko seemed even more radiant now. As she entered her thirties, she had a calm, womanly nature which was a constant source of pride for Kiichiro.

Kiichiro's wife, Hatako, waited humbly at the door. She was two years younger than Aiko and somewhat less striking due to her slightly protruding forehead and prominent cheekbones. But her bright, clear eyes revealed the gentle quality of an innocent girl. The youngest of three daughters in a household of nine children, she had been born to the Takashimaya Iida's, a prominent Kyoto family. Her sedate upbringing in a home nurtured by two-and-a-half acres of garden, had bred in her an open, tranquil heart. She had the rare quality of being able to brush aside people's ill-will and absorb only the good.

Kiichiro acknowledged the departure of his sister and nephew and then turned again to his sketches of machines. Impatient to leave, Risaburo had already put on his shoes and gone out into the front garden to call for the driver.

When he returned to fetch his wife and son, Aiko smiled. Then she looked from Risaburo to Kiichiro, aware of the striking contrast between the two men. While Risaburo was aggressive and authoritarian, Kiichiro was reticent and introverted. Recently he had become even more so, as the preoccupation with his mechanical drawings intensified. The only time he became animated was when the topic of conversation turned to technology. Whether standing in an entryway or lounging in the living room, Kiichiro would fall into deep conversation for an hour or two, oblivious to time and place. Or when his mind sparked with a new idea he would drop what he was doing and begin to sketch on whatever was available, even toilet paper.

Without a moment to waste, he would then compose a letter and send it to the engineers who worked under him. Kiichiro was compulsive about his ideas. Even though he had returned home for the burial of his father's ashes, he was not to be deterred from his passionate pursuit.

"Well, take your time," said Aiko, always sympathetic to her brother's interests.

She put on her leather sandals and walked from the house through the front garden. As she reached the gate, she saw the young employee of Toyoda Automatic Loom Works who had accompanied them, bowing deeply before Risaburo, his face drained of color.

"What's the matter?" Aiko asked, looking up at her husband affectionately.

"That hired car driver has gone off somewhere. Here I am, the president of the company, ready to go home, and that insolent fool's not here waiting for me!"

"Oh dear. It's still quite a while until the time you said you wanted to leave. It's because you're in such a hurry that...."

"Shut up!"

A blue vein stood out on Risaburo's high, proper forehead. With the gold rims of his glasses flashing, he roared in the dialect of the Kyoto-Osaka area. It was telling that he had lived in Nagoya for ten years as the "adopted son" of the Toyoda family and had not yielded an inch to the native dialect.

"I'll go and get him right away. I think he's at a noodle shop near here," said the flustered employee. After bowing repeatedly to Risaburo and Aiko, he hunched his shoulders and ran off awkwardly.

Risaburo turned to Aiko and said, "Let me know as soon as the driver gets back. In the meantime, I have something I want to talk to Kiichiro about." He marched across the garden with a firm stride developed from playing golf (at that time a rare sport).

Planting himself at the table opposite Kiichiro, Risaburo abruptly started talking in a severe tone.

"What in the world are you drawing? What are you going to build this time?"

"Before this, you built an engine. You put up a board wall in a corner of the factory like it was a big secret, and inside that, you made a pile of junk. It took a year to build an engine by yourself."

"Does that engine run?" asked Risaburo.

"It runs," Kiichiro answered. "But it's just a toy. If it didn't run, I'd be in trouble."

Aggravated by Kiichiro's flippant response, Risaburo growled, "I won't have you talk to me that way.

"Kiichiro, you said you want to build a car, didn't you? Isn't that true?"

This was the first time Risaburo had asked Kiichiro directly about automobiles, and he spoke as though he wanted to settle the matter once and for all.

"I don't know. I didn't say anything like that," Kiichiro replied.

"Oh no? Then what's this?" Risaburo asked, pointing to the rough pencil sketch Kiichiro continued to work on as Risaburo spoke. Earlier Kiichiro had been working out a problem with gears, but now he was focusing on a series of strange, box-like figures.

Hatako appeared with tea, but a glare from Risaburo set her trembling. Putting the cups down on the table, she quickly exited.

"I wonder what it'll be. In any case, it's another toy," said Risaburo.

Kiichiro looked up for the first time. His eyes beamed behind thick, black-rimmed glasses. With his relatively broad neck and fleshy face, Kiichiro couldn't be called handsome. He did, however, have attractive teeth, and when he smiled, he looked very genial.

"Come on, Kiichiro. This is important, so don't play dumb. In one year, all by yourself, you built a little, four-horsepower gasoline engine; a Smith motor or something. And haven't you recently been going around to factories in Tokyo, Osaka, and Kobe, asking questions and saying you're going to build an autobike or a bike motor? Then there's this sketch. That's the shape of an auto body. Of course it is. On top of that, I've heard a rumor that you said you want to build cars. It sounds to me like you don't want to build one or two for pleasure or research, but rather that you want to start manufacturing automobiles as a business. So I can't help but be worried."

Kiichiro seemed to have no interest in Risaburo's comments. He had returned to his drawing and made no attempt at a reply.

"You know, Kiichiro," Risaburo continued, his voice taking on a more confident tone. "The Toyoda family business is, of course, based entirely on Dad's inventions. He worked hard and never gave in to trouble or poverty. He invented the power and automatic looms, and they became the foundation for the prosperity of the Toyoda family and of all the related Toyoda companies. I'm deeply grateful for that. No one is more grateful than I. But in my position, I just can't stop there. I have an obligation to guard this enterprise carefully and to expand it even further."

As he spoke, Risaburo nodded in a way that emphasized the heaviness of his perceived obligation. After all, according to tradition, he was the head of the Toyoda family, and therefore had total responsibility for looking after his brother-in-law and making a success of him.

Today that arrangement would be different. As the eldest natural son, Kiichiro would be considered head of the Toyoda family and Risaburo would be nothing more than a brother-in-law. But the civil code at that time specified that the oldest male in a single-family registry was the family head. Risaburo had entered the family registry as an adopted son-in-law and, being ten years older than Kiichiro, had assumed the responsibility of family patriarch following Sakichi Toyoda's death.

Risaburo took his role very seriously, often being somewhat autocratic in his demands for obedience. This naturally kindled a secret resistance in Kiichiro.

"I always think I have no right to stop you from immersing yourself in inventions the same way your highly praised and famous father did. Instead I realize that I have an obligation to encourage you and to help you perfect your research and inventions."

Risaburo continued to nod with self-importance as he spoke. "Still, there's a limit to things. Setting aside the question of other inventions or businesses, automobiles present a difficult problem."

Looking up slowly from the sketch that was taking on a clearer semblance of an auto body, Kiichiro said, "It's nothing like that. I didn't say that."

He spoke softly, seeming to agonize over his words. Someone must have told on him. Branching out into the automobile industry had in fact been his desire for some time, but Kiichiro had been very secretive about it. Now Risaburo was speaking as though he knew everything about the plan.

Kiichiro's interest in automobiles dated back to his university days. When he later traveled abroad with Risaburo and Aiko, the many cars he saw in the United States and Europe further deepened his interest. But the real genesis of Kiichiro's passion could be traced all the way back to his father. In his later years, Sakichi often talked about his dream of manufacturing automobiles. Circumstances simply worked to strengthen this vision in Kiichiro.

The year was 1929. Kiichiro had gone to England to facilitate the sale of his father's automatic loom patent to Platt Brothers of Manchester. Because the English had come to prefer the automobile over other transportation, the automobile industry there was burgeoning. And Kiichiro didn't miss an opportunity to get thoroughly acquainted with it. Entrusting the patent negotiations to the officials from Mitsui Trading Company and Toyoda Automatic Loom Works who had accompanied him, he spent most of his time in England visiting automobile factories.

Fortunately, negotiations with Platt Brothers went well despite Kiichiro's absence. As soon as Kiichiro returned to Japan, Risaburo imposed upon him to concentrate his sales efforts in the United States.

"But," objected Kiichiro, "our looms won't sell at all in the United States. They already have excellent looms of their own."

"No, they'll sell. They'll definitely sell. So go there and sell them."

Risaburo's persistence won out, and Kiichiro was soon off to the United States. His enthusiasm for sales was little better there than it was in England. Kiichiro promptly turned negotiations over to Mitsui's veteran employee, Tsutomu Furuichi, and spent the entire time visiting automobile and car parts factories.

In the United States, Kiichiro recognized that the automobile was already an indispensable means of transportation for the general public. His writings from that period clearly reflect his concern for Japan's sluggishness in adapting to this new trend:

In Japan, the automobile industry still hasn't gotten off the ground. At the beginning of the century, automobiles were nothing more than decorative luxury items owned by a fraction of the privileged class. When trains and streetcars were destroyed in the Great Tokyo Earthquake of 1923, the practical value of the automobile was recognized at last, and after that, domestic production began by slow degrees. Still, it's a primitive, almost manual industry, and only about a hundred cars are produced annually. In comparison to the assembly-line production made possible by the conveyer belt in the United States and Europe, Japan's industry is crude and insignificant. In the West, the highly developed parts industry also helps tens and hundreds of thousands of cars roll off the assembly lines each year.

Every time Kiichiro toured a Western factory, he was filled with admiration. Here, Japan had touted herself as one of the five major world powers since the end of World War I. But if one were to gauge Japan's power on the basis of her automobile industry alone, she would be no match for any of the advanced nations of the West:

Considering how widespread the automobile industry in the West has become, it's clear that for Japan to emerge as a modern industrial nation, a full-scale automobile industry is absolutely necessary. Without it, the establishment of Japanese industry as a whole cannot be realized. Under the current conditions in which almost 100 percent of the domestic market is occupied by Western cars, we have to better them, no matter what it takes!

Kiichiro was deeply committed to this ambition. Even the buses and taxicabs that had been used in greater numbers since the Great Tokyo Earthquake, were almost all imported from the West. It was clear that the giant automobile industrialists of the United States were ready to seize upon Japan's rapidly increasing automobile market. Their opportunism went beyond wanting to export finished cars to Japan, and aimed at monopolistic control of the Japanese automobile market into the distant future. There was clear evidence that the groundwork for this control was already being laid.

In December of 1924, Ford had rented a warehouse at Yokohama Dock on the Koyasu waterfront in Yokohama and had built a temporary factory there. The following February, the firm established Japan Ford Motor Company, Inc., capitalized at four million yen. All machinery was shipped from the United States. When the factory was completed, the new operation began producing Fords in Japan by means of the so-called knock-down system. Under this system, all parts were brought from the originating country and assembled by local labor. To the extent that parts took up less space than assembled products, this meant lower shipping fees. In addition, labor costs were much lower in Japan than in the United States, so this approach proved far more profitable than exporting the finished product. And of course, all profits went to the American companies.

Then in 1927, Ford built a private assembly plant of almost 17,000 square yards in Moriya-cho, Kanagawa Ward, Yokohama. Annual production reached seven to eight thousand passenger cars and trucks. These were the famous "Model T's." That factory was equipped with a modern conveyer system, and in anticipation of future growth, Ford doubled its working capital to eight million yen.

Two years later, General Motors responded to Ford's aggressive investment in Japan by establishing a base of operations in Osaka. General Motors rented a spinning factory and warehouse in Taisho Ward from the trading firm, Toyo Menka, and built a plant of over 19,000 square yards.

Not long after, General Motors established Japan General Motors Company, Inc., capitalized at eight million yen. By the middle of 1927, the new facility began assembling and marketing General Motors cars under the same knock-down system used by Ford. The focus of manufacturing was on Chevrolet passenger cars and trucks, but Oldsmobiles, Pontiacs, Buicks, and the now defunct Oaklands were also assembled. The combined annual output was approximately ten thousand vehicles.

The effect of Ford's and General Motors' efforts was noticeable almost at once. Every road in Japan was dominated by American cars. The more Kiichiro saw of this situation after his return from abroad, the more impatient he became.

Until the end of the Meiji period, the power looms used for weaving cloth for people's clothing were almost all imports. As a result of Sakichi's laborious improvement and invention, not only have we switched completely to domestically made looms, but we are even doing a flourishing export trade with other countries. Although the automobile industry is incomparably more complicated than spinning machines and looms, we ought to be able to do it if we try. Just as with looms, we'll drive Ford and General Motors out of the Japanese market someday, and every road in Japan will be full of Japanese cars -- Toyoda cars!

Kiichiro burned with a secret desire to see this become reality. Yet his plan was not complete enough to be shared with others. Moreover, he lacked confidence in his ability to build what constituted the very heart of the automobile -- its engine. Oddly enough, his hesitancy was directly connected to his self-image as managing director of Toyoda Automatic Loom Works.

Had Kiichiro been a typical managing director with a background in law or economics, as Risaburo was, he could have simply delegated research and production of the automobile to a talented company engineer. Because he was an engineer himself, however, Kiichiro felt his knowledge of automobile technology should properly be better than anyone else's on his staff. It was with the goal of gaining superior proficiency that Kiichiro had built with his own hands the four horse-power Smith motor alluded to by Risaburo.

I just don't have the confidence yet to tell Risaburo about building cars, thought Kiichiro. *Who in the world could have told him about it?*

Kiichiro then recalled he had casually revealed his dream to Risaburo Oshima, the director in charge of production at Toyoda Automatic Loom Works. Oshima had long been a trusted friend of the family and favorite of Sakichi. Kiichiro had also disclosed his plans quite explicitly to Tojiro Okamoto, a manager at Toyoda Spinning and Weaving. Okamoto, too, was a trusted confidant, having been appointed head clerk of the company by Sakichi, who had full faith in him.

Both Oshima and Okamoto were fair and honorable men. Certainly they would not have gone to Risaburo before Kiichiro and told him about an idea that was only at the germ stage in Kiichiro's mind.

Oh, the "o-mame." They must have talked, thought Kiichiro. Then he grinned at Risaburo.

"What's so funny?" asked Risaburo.

"Oh nothing. If you get upset, your blood pressure will go up like Sakichi's."

"Don't be stupid!" quipped Risaburo. He smiled wryly to signal he was not totally in the dark as to Kiichiro's intent. Yes, it was the *o-mame.*

The *o-mame* were in their earliest training to become *geishas*. Even younger than the *maiko*, they were still in elementary school and only helped with entertainment at banquets.

At that time, the *geisha* quarters was the place for the business world to congregate. Even if a banquet was held at a first-class restaurant, it would usually be followed by a second party at a *geisha* house. In fact, important business transactions were often carried out amid the pleasant and relaxed environment of the *geisha* house. From Sakichi's day on, the Toyoda family's house of choice had been Yayoi. Suzu Suzuki, the proprietress, had been entrusted by Sakichi with Kiichiro's social life, and she served somewhat as a surrogate mother to him.

Several years older than Kiichiro and affectionately known as *O-su*, Suzu was petite and slender, with a cleverness equal to her beauty. When fully attired in her finery, she was as beautiful as any *geisha* in Nagoya. Yet she was always humble and faultless in her role.

Two weeks earlier, Kiichiro had visited Yayoi. As usual he had been met by *O-su*, who greeted him with a large notebook and several pencils. Then he was taken into a *tatami* room by ten *maiko* and *o-mame*. It was customary for a person of Kiichiro's stature and class to indulge in such social pleasures. He was the son of the Toyoda *zaibatsu* (or large financial cartel), which had become very influential in the Nagoya area through the development of the automatic loom.

But Kiichiro had more serious things on his mind than young, charming *geisha*. For him there was nothing but thoughts and sketches of machines. The *geisha* knew this and almost never approached him with entanglements of love.

Normally when Kiichiro came to Yayoi, he would be surrounded by innocent *maiko* and *o-mame* who frolicked about noisily to their heart's content. Kiichiro seemed to enjoy their energy and never objected to these antics. Through it all he remained quiet and taciturn, absorbed in his sketches of automobile parts, which he recorded in the notebook *O-su* had given him.

Unlike his father Sakichi, who enjoyed smoking and drinking, an indulgence which eventually led to his high blood pressure, Kiichiro was always much more moderate. In fact, he was not fond of alcohol and preferred a clear head for his ruminations about automobiles.

Seeing Kiichiro engrossed in his sketches, one of the *o-mame* approached him and asked, "*Kii-san*, what are you drawing? Stop drawing choo-choo trains all the time and play with us, pretty please."

"These aren't choo-choo trains. They're auto bodies."

"Oh, cars. Are you going to make cars at your company, *Kii-san*?"

"Yes, we are."

"Oh, great. Can we ride in them?"

"Sure you can."

"How many? One, or two?"

On hearing the word *car*, all the girls gathered around Kiichiro.

"No, not one or two. We're going to make thousands and tens of thousands, even hundreds of thousands. The roads of Japan eventually will be filled with Toyoda cars."

"Oh, that's great, *Kii-san*! Don't ever give up!"

The *maiko* and *o-mame* had clapped their hands and shouted with delight. But now Kiichiro was regretting his openness and enthusiasm that evening, for they had undoubtedly been his undoing. When Risaburo visited Yayoi, he must have heard of Kiichiro's boastful remarks from one of the *o-mame*.

"What about it, Kiichiro?" Risaburo interjected in a more mollified tone. "Unlike me, you're a top engineer from Tokyo University. Even though the automatic loom was Father's concept and his achievement in the eyes of the world, it was actually you who perfected it. The number one loom company in the world -- a company in Manchester that we used to glorify -- bought the patent for it. Until then, there was no example of a first-rank company in the West buying a Japanese patent. Both Father and I thought it was a credit to Japan. It was with great pride we agreed to turn over the patent. Father knew more clearly than anyone it was your achievement, which is why he allowed you to use the one million yen obtained from the patent for research.

"Supposing the value of the yen has increased a thousandfold since 1926, that one million yen would be worth one billion yen at present, and if the value has increased five thousandfold, it would be five billion yen."

Risaburo broke off speaking and drank the tea that had been brought in earlier. During the long interrogation, it had gotten completely cold.

"One million yen is a lot of money," continued Risaburo. "It's the same amount as the total capital of our company. Still, I've decided that you should use it for your independent research. I agree with Father. But Kiichiro, won't you just give up on automobiles? Of course, it's fine if you want to devote yourself to cars as a hobby. I wouldn't mind at all if you poured the entire million yen into scholarly research on the automobile, the way Father donated one million yen to the invention of the storage battery. But to launch into mass production of cars as a business is too complicated and large-scale, and it's impossible given the strength of Japanese industry today. Even Mitsui and Mitsubishi have been frightened away. As a matter of fact, in Tokyo a number of companies have been ruined by the automobile.

"No matter how proud we are of ourselves as a *zaibatsu* in Nagoya, compared to Mitsui and Mitsubishi, Toyoda is just a little *zaibatsu* that could be blown away by a puff of wind. If we get into something like manufacturing automobiles, we'll be through in no time."

It's for the very reason that Toyoda can be blown away that we should decide to do it! thought Kiichiro.

However, he kept his dissent to himself. He had absolutely no desire to argue with Risaburo or anyone else. A verbal clash would only be futile. All Kiichiro wanted was to be left alone to pursue his study of the automobile.

His intention was not to proceed with work on the automobile without informing Risaburo. He simply was not yet knowledgeable enough to set his plan in motion. When the time was right, he would consult Risaburo and win his approval. Once this occurred, there would be no turning back.

I am Sakichi Toyoda's son. Don't ever forget that! said Kiichiro to himself.

Though Kiichiro suffered from a slight inferiority complex as a result of being raised apart from his real mother, when it came to his brother-in-law, Kiichiro felt superior. He knew that his father would have approved of what he was doing, even if it meant the downfall of the company Sakichi had built by means of his inventions with the loom.

"I don't know. I haven't decided anything yet," Kiichiro finally said. He smiled, feigning ignorance as he spoke in the Nagoya dialect.

"Oh, well, if that's the case, it's all right."

Risaburo had just lighted a cigarette when Kokichiro ran in from the garden.

"Father, the car is ready."

"Well, I'll be leaving then."

Kiichiro did not see him off. He did not even stand up. As Risaburo's tall figure disappeared into the earthen-floored room, Kiichiro turned once again to his designs for the body of a passenger car.

At last the horn sounded. As soon as the hired car had left, Hatako, who had seen everyone off, came into the room.

"Won't you have some tea in the front room?" she asked.

Hatako was calm and tranquil. She smiled brightly as she made the invitation. It was as though she were totally unaware of the acrimonious atmosphere generated between the two brothers.

"Uh-huh," answered Kiichiro as he looked up at his wife.

The two went into the adjoining eight-mat room that faced south. The only other presence in the room was a scroll that hung in the alcove, looking on with a serene expression, as it had from the time the house was built. *A hundred ordeals, a thousand trials, and the matter is finally accomplished*, read the scroll.

The Chinese characters were written in a squarish, cursive style with bold strokes. In small characters on the left side was a signed dedication to Kiichiro's grandfather, Ikichi, proving this was the calligraphy of a famous priest of the Lotus Sutra sect to which Ikichi and Sakichi had belonged. The characters of the signature were so abbreviated that Kiichiro could hardly read them.

That saying befits my father better than my grandfather, thought Kiichiro.

To Kiichiro, however, the idea of success through blind perseverance represented a naive Japanese style of idealism appropriate only to a man of religion. According to his philosophy, in the process of enduring so many trials, those meant to be destroyed would be destroyed, and those meant to be ruined would be ruined. Also there could exist a road to success other than through suffering and tribulation.

While drinking the green tea and nibbling on the steamed cakes Hatako had brought him, Kiichiro thought of how ironic it was. The fact that Sakichi had never removed this scroll from the alcove indicated how much he cherished these words.

Sakichi had been born in 1867, the year before the Meiji era began. He was the eldest son of Ikichi Toyoda, who worked on the side as a carpenter in this farming village, and his wife, Ei. Sakichi had three brothers and sisters: Han, Heikichi, and Sasuke. Because he lived in a remote village, and also because it was customary at that time, he attended only elementary school. After that he helped his father and worked as a carpenter. At the age of seventeen or eighteen, Sakichi felt a new life's ambition growing deep inside him. From that point onward, he desired only to be an inventor of looms.

It was a destiny that would lead to endless trials and anguish. Early on he suffered ridicule from nearly everyone. He was labeled a lunatic and a good-for-nothing dreamer. At times he remained in his hometown, at other times he led a transient life, moving from Tokyo to Mikawa, often leaving his family behind. Eventually Tami, his first wife and Kiichiro's mother, could not endure the neglect and had to leave him.

As he began making inventions, Sakichi ran a small weaving factory in Nagoya and continued his research. Again and again his factory prospered and then failed. But even so, on both fronts -- invention and business -- Sakichi moved slowly forward.

What a difficult path he had walked: nothing but a hundred ordeals and a thousand trials, thought Kiichiro.

Balancing his teacup on his knee and gazing at the scroll, Kiichiro began to daydream about the past. He recalled being abandoned by his mother, who had no alternative but to relinquish her infant son and leave the Toyoda family. He recalled how Sakichi had become a total prisoner of his inventions and how little attention he paid to his family. Kiichiro had become virtually orphaned in his own home and received much of his upbringing from his aged grandparents.

From infancy to boyhood, Kiichiro longed for the mother whose face he did not know, all the while hating and resenting his father, Sakichi. The family had become wealthy during the time he studied at the Number Two Higher School in Sendai and the Engineering Department of Tokyo Imperial University. Sakichi had been hailed as the "King of Inventions" for his many developments and improvements of the loom, but Kiichiro bitterly denied his father's accomplishments. To him, Sakichi had done nothing more than any other engineer could have done with the right desire.

As Kiichiro grew older and his experience with technology and development deepened, his hatred and contempt gradually abated. During the year since his father's death the previous autumn, he'd had a complete change of heart about Sakichi's "technological" accomplishments.

What was the source of the power that led Sakichi to continue to walk along such a difficult path of developing the loom?

Kiichiro felt the question lodged deeply in his heart. As he looked up at the old scroll on which was written, *a hundred ordeals, a thousand trials*, he was no closer to an answer than he ever was.

Suddenly he felt stifled and stood up, saying, "I'm going out to walk for a little while."

"Don't catch cold," Hatako said. She called the maid for Kiichiro's sweater and then placed it over his shoulders. Standing at the gate to send him off, she handed him an umbrella. The sky was heavy with clouds and looking like rain.

As Kiichiro went out through the gate of the old house, he cut a strange figure indeed. Wearing a dark brown wool sweater over the vest and pants of his mourning dress, with traditional Japanese wooden clogs on his feet, he walked along the neatly-trimmed hedge swinging a western-style umbrella. Inside the hedge was the front garden with a luxuriant stand of cassia, arbutus, holly, and other mature trees. Behind them was a large, old-fashioned two-story house with a tile roof. Sakichi had built the new house adjoining it on the left for Aiko and her husband to live in after they married. The *tatami* rooms all faced south and were light and airy.

In back was a low hill, not even twice the height of the house, thickly covered with pines. It was difficult to imagine Sakichi having been born in this house, since he was said to have been raised in abject poverty. In its day, the residence could have been taken for the main house of a village headman or the wealthiest farmer in the area.

As Kiichiro turned to leave the old house he could see the village of Yamaguchi, which lay in a long, narrow valley running from north and south. The valley was lined with cultivated fields, looking much the same as the many other valleys scattered among the low hills lining the west end of Lake Hamana. In front of the Toyoda house flowed a brook with grassy banks. About a mile to the south, the blue cars of the Tokaido train wound through an opening in the hills. On quiet days, the faint whistle and clacking of the train could be heard. Though the railroad marked a change from the old days, the area remained the epitome of a tranquil rural landscape.

As Kiichiro walked along the road skirting the low hills, he wondered how many hundreds of years his ancestors had lived in this poor village. The land itself was unforgiving. Prolonged rains flooded the fields or drought burned them out. It was a fate shared by all the valleys in the low hills west of Lake Hamana. Adding to the hardship was the poor quality of the soil. Compared to the rice fields near Owari, fields in this area were considered to be doing well if their yields were 50 percent of a normal yield.

When he had walked approximately fifty yards, Kiichiro came to a path that curved to the right and climbed around a hill. Without thinking, Kiichiro followed the path and began the ascent. He passed a chicken house and a shed for farm implements. Then the path narrowed sharply, losing itself among the dry and drooping grasses. The hill rose up abruptly to the right of the path. A light rain began to fall. The dense trees on the steep slope of the hill cast a dark shadow on the path, adding to the gloom of the landscape.

Finally, the path came to an end in a very small, flat area surrounded on three sides by the hill. Directly in front was a dense bamboo grove which moaned in the wind and darkened in the twilight.

The house where I was born is in that bamboo thicket. Sakichi was born and raised there, too, thought Kiichiro.

He gazed into the bamboo thicket. He had not come here in more than twenty years -- not since his boyhood. During his long absence, the bamboo thicket had encircled a half-crumbled stone wall on the face of the hill, as if to hide all evidence of human occupation. The flat area was open now only on the west side, so the birthplace and childhood home of both Sakichi and Kiichiro received no sunlight, except when the summer sun moved to the west.

The one-story house still standing had a straw-thatched roof and was fairly large. In winter it was shaded and unbearably cold. During the rainy season, the dampness attempted to rot the house from the inside out. The stagnant heat of summer brought with it the plague of mosquitoes, gnats, fleas, and ants. There was no shelter from the sun in the western sky, which was said to drive one crazy. It was also said that poisonous pit vipers lived on the hill behind the house.

Clearly Sakichi's goal in life was to escape from this thicket. It is my goal, too! murmured Kiichiro to himself.

To understand the symbolic difference between the old place and the current Toyoda family residence, was to better know why this quest was so meaningful. The two were separated by a single, small hill. The side where the current house stood was open to the south and east, and was blessed with abundant sunshine and fresh air. The side where the old house stood was cold and sunless. It looked like the land on which one would expect the poorest farmer in the village to live.

Kiichiro remembered how happy he had been when the present house was built. The year was 1906, and Kiichiro was in the highest grade at the elementary school in Nagoya. Sakichi had attained a fair amount of success elsewhere in Japan, but had a strong desire to build his new house near his birth place.

During summer vacation, Kiichiro came to the village with his father to see how construction was proceeding. He heard the loud voices of the many carpenters talking when Sakichi was not around.

"Inventors are really something, aren't they? They say Master Sakichi used to be like us, a country carpenter. But he's made a big success of himself and now has the means to build this second house. He really is somebody important."

Though Kiichiro came to resent Sakichi's neglect and preoccupation with inventions, at the time, hearing his father praised in the country dialect of western Shizuoka filled his young heart with pride.

Someone like Risaburo just wouldn't understand! Kiichiro resolved to himself as he looked around. *The source of the passion that urged Sakichi on and drove him to continue walking single-mindedly along the thorny path of invention, was surely his desire to escape from this dark "thicket."*

Kiichiro was feeling the force of inheritance moving within him. Just as Sakichi had longed for blue sky and sun and fertile ground, Kiichiro felt the urge to find his place in the sun. He also realized that his father had started with nothing, in abject poverty, and had become a success. Undoubtedly this was why he had chosen the path of the inventor, for an inventor must make something from nothing.

Comparing Sakichi's humble beginnings to the empire he had built brought home to Kiichiro how fully his father had fulfilled his passion and dream. Today the Yamaguchi Village appeared affluent. Well-constructed houses were situated in sunny spots here and there, in sharp contrast to the remains of the old Toyoda house. Perhaps Sakichi's dream had been in part responsible for the progress of the entire village. One only needed a cursory understanding of the area's history to see how things had changed.

The Kosai area had been the poorest in Shizuoka Prefecture at the beginning of the Meiji era. Within Kosai, Yoshizu Village (the old name for a part of Washizu

Village) was cold and had no geographical advantages. The inhabitants remained somewhat backward and barely eked out a subsistence living.

It was in such an environment that Sakichi had grown up. Poor, starving peasants were scattered throughout Yamaguchi Village. In less than twenty years since the beginning of the Meiji era, its population had decreased by 20 percent.

Though illiteracy was common in the village, Sakichi had had the early good fortune of studying under an elementary school teacher named Mr. Sada. It was Mr. Sada who gave Sakichi newspapers and magazines and opened his eyes to a whole new world of ideas. Sakichi became an avid reader and soon learned that among the nations of the earth, Japan was very poor, just like Yamaguchi Village. It was also because of Sada that Sakichi was introduced to the subject of patents and patent regulations, which marked the beginning of his fascination with invention.

Though he didn't know it at the time, this was the birth of his escape from poverty and the "dark thicket," not only for himself but for his homeland. Japan lay like a backward village at the foot of a damp, dark mountain. Sakichi's inventive spirit would go down in history as helping to raise it up.

Sakichi chose the loom as the object of his inventions. At that time Enshu and Mikawa were the center of a small textile industry. It was probably inevitable for Sakichi, who had been born and raised in the area, that the loom was the most familiar "machine."

"That's why, no matter what hardship I encounter, I'm going to make cars!" Kiichiro muttered, making a sudden leap from his father's loom to his own passionate interest in automobiles. He looked upward with deep reverence.

The sky had become even darker, and the drizzle had turned into a fine, cold rain. Kiichiro made no move to open the umbrella Hatako had given him. He was too lost in thought. Even if he were to gamble on the establishment of an automobile manufacturing industry, as Sakichi had gambled on the perfection of the loom, he would undoubtedly confront innumerable social thickets.

Kiichiro could count on resistance from his family and the "elder statesmen" of the company, whom Sakichi had left behind. *Invention always dares to challenge the unknown*, Kiichiro thought. *It therefore brings immediate criticism from the pessimists, who point out that most inventions never come to fruition. And those inventions that do work are often insignificant and quickly forgotten. The odds against an invention making an impact are terribly great. Still, if Sakichi had given up, he would have remained in this dark thicket.*

The company that Sakichi left behind is very successful. If it does nothing to change, it will likely remain secure in its success and stay on high ground in the bright sunlight. On the other hand, if I drag the company down the unknown road in my quest to develop an automobile, I may plunge us right back into the dark thicket where this all began.

Even assuming everyone connected with Toyoda rallies around the project, on the roads of Japan the thicket of potent foreign economic competition is always waiting. With rivals like Ford and General Motors, Toyoda might be left by the wayside.

However, if Japan looks on passively while Ford and General Motors move to monopolize our automobile market, the thicket will become even more dense and foreboding. In the end, other Japanese industries will succumb to foreign domination and Japan will be reduced to an economic colony, its bones sucked to the very marrow.

No, I'll do it. Even if Risaburo and the others don't understand!

Kiichiro felt a rush of exhilaration that accompanies all momentous decisions. His die was cast. As he stared into the darkening bamboo thicket, he was oblivious to the cold autumn rain that was now falling harder.

Chapter
2

THE YOUNG CAMPANIONS

The next day, Kiichiro returned to his Nagoya residence and resumed his normal work routine, which involved frequent travel. One day he would be in Osaka, a day later, in Tokyo, and the following day he would be back at Toyoda Automatic Loom Works headquarters in Kariya. This was his primary place of business.

Though today Kariya has all the trappings of a modern metropolis, in 1932 it still maintained the look of a rural town. Historically, it had been a castle village by the sea. Toward the end of Japan's civil war era, the Mizuno clan had built a castle that eventually gave rise to the Tokugawa shogunate. From that point forward, ruling clans came and went, but the character of this castle town changed very little. It remained primarily a marketplace for local farmers. Even as times changed from the Meiji through the Taisho to the Showa eras, the character of Kariya remained constant.

By the early 1900s, only a small portion of the castle ruins and the castle gate remained, but they had long since been overgrown by tall grass and cherry blossom trees.

The first real factory, a Toshiba facility, was built in Kariya in 1918. In 1923, Toyoda Spinning and Weaving, Ltd. built a branch factory there. That was followed not long after by construction of the manufacturing plant, and in 1926 the Chuo Spinning and Weaving, Ltd. factory was built. All three operations were Toyoda concerns.

Toyoda Automatic Loom Works was the world's leading loom manufacturer until the Great Depression pulled the market out from underneath it. It was a time of crisis everywhere. Labor problems intensified as unions sought to protect the jobs and incomes of their members. Soon restrictions were placed on the employment of minors. July of 1929 saw the enactment of a law prohibiting youths from working late-night factory hours, and the resulting increase in labor costs made survival even more difficult for Japan's manufacturers.

Spurred by fierce price competition, the spinning industry launched major cost reduction measures to offset skyrocketing labor costs. Large companies that had amassed great fortunes during the immediate post-World War I economic boom now began to study new manufacturing techniques and used their resources to upgrade production equipment.

Toyoda Automatic Loom Works was busy perfecting a high-draft spinning machine that doubled the normal output of thread. Prior to this innovation, spinning machines could stretch unfinished cotton only six to twelve times its original length. With the new technology, the cotton could be stretched to twenty or thirty times its original length. The result was a 50 percent reduction in the number of spinning machines needed to produce any given quantity of thread, which amounted to enormous savings in materials and labor.

The Automatic Loom Works was also pouring money and research into the development of a cotton carding machine, a device which took fibers already stripped and cleaned by a cotton gin and prepared them for spinning.

Before Sakichi's death, Kiichiro had been responsible for overseeing development of much of this new technology. Sakichi had long since moved his home to Shanghai, having taken up residence there in 1920. Though often returning to Japan, Sakichi could not participate directly in the research and development areas of his Toyoda companies due to his age and chronic illness. Consequently, all technical decisions were made by Kiichiro, with the help of Iwataro Okabe, Toshizo Suzuki, and Risaburo Oshima. Okabe, Suzuki, and Oshima were all part of Sakichi's original engineering "brain trust" and had a great many years of experience.

Among the three engineers, only Oshima held a university degree. Suzuki, like Sakichi, had inventive talent, while Okabe was a highly organized and superb draftsman. Even though he was now seventy years old, Okabe had not given up drafting. A man of traditional ways, he would adorn his household Shinto altar on New Year's Day with his drawings, ruler, compass, and his other drafting tools and offer his prayers. Only then would he drink the traditional New Year's sake.

These three aging engineers were not the only ones Kiichiro had access to. There was plenty of new blood in the company. In 1927, Jiro Iwaoka, a mechanical engineering graduate from Tokyo University, joined the company, followed in 1931 by Hiro Shimachi, a Nagoya University graduate. Shortly after, Takeaki Shirai, a Shizuoka University graduate, and Ryuichi Suzuki joined Kiichiro's group. When the time was correct for moving into development of the automobile, it was young engineers such as these men who would carry the bulk of the weight of research.

The new spinning machines were given their trial runs in the research labs of the Toyoda Spinning and Weaving branch factory. When they delivered excellent results and proved trustworthy, they were installed in a number of the large Japanese spinning firms. The founder of Kureha Spinning Ltd., one of the more aggressive Japanese operations, encouraged Kiichiro and his staff to keep building innovative machines: "Since Kureha is a new company, it should taste everything that is new."

Whenever he was in the Kariya factory, Kiichiro could be found covered with grease by the end of each day. He valued hands-on experience over theory, often telling Iwaoka, "Those who have degrees always use logic, but you don't use logic to conduct your work. When we need to apply logic, we'll look to the scholars for assistance."

Seeing young employees glued to their desks in the drafting room, Kiichiro would warn: "If you want to become engineers, you can't be sitting in the office like this. You have to get out onto the factory floor and work with the machines until you're covered with grease! If nothing needs to be done, then take a seat in the middle of the factory floor. Engineers must be so covered with grease that they can't eat or hold a pen without first washing their hands."

Kiichiro normally did not spend his time in idle talk. When the topic of conversation involved technical matters, however, he would stand on the factory floor lost in discussion for hours. Otherwise, he had his hands on the machinery, instructing the young engineers: "One must work on-site more than three years to properly formulate a plan. You'll understand that in time."

Kiichiro rarely issued a reproach to his workers but he did rely frequently on parables and analogies to get his points across. His manner of instruction was open, friendly, and noncondescending. Most often his aim was to instill in his assistants the discipline to study a machine until they understood and mastered it completely. In return for that type of focus, he never became angry when they blundered:

"You may make mistakes. Try it again and give it your best effort. The important thing is that you must learn from your mistakes and apply that knowledge in the future."

These were exciting times at the Toyoda Automatic Loom Works. Not only was the factory new, but the work to develop the new machines was extensive and challenging. Convinced the workers exerted greater energy than their counterparts at other companies, Kiichiro rewarded their dedication by providing free nutritious meals at the company cafeteria.

The factory's workday began at seven in the morning with a hearty breakfast, which always included *miso* soup. For lunch, a curry sauce fortified with meat and vegetables was served with unlimited rice. Considering these were depression years, the company meals were welcomed feasts for all.

After the factory closed at five o'clock, it was Kiichiro's habit to continue working until late into the night. Shutting himself off in the factory drafting room, he devoted his time to drawing. At other times, he went next door to the "secret room" to work on small machinery. This room was actually a Toyoda Spinning and Weaving Ltd. research laboratory which had been outfitted with a bed. Kiichiro often worked so late that he simply slept at the company compound.

At that time, Kiichiro did not have a company car and the trains had usually stopped running for the night when he finally put his work aside. A company car would have been a great convenience, but Toyoda Automatic Loom Works and Toyoda Spinnina and Weaving did not provide one for any of its employees, including its president, Risaburo. The reason was not that there were no cars around.

Automobiles had first appeared in Nagoya as early as 1906. In 1912, the Nagoya branch manager of the Osaka-based Kitahama Bank began using an automobile called *Aichi Number One*. Close on the heels of the Kitahama Bank, the branch manager of Mitsui and Company purchased an automobile for company use. Soon the prefectural office, city hall, and the tax office, as well as large businesses, had purchased cars for business purposes.

Even car rental agencies had been in existence since 1912, and taxi service since 1917. By the year 1931, there were two hundred taxi and car rental companies in Nagoya and a total of more than one thousand automobiles in operation. A public bus system had been started and the number of trucks on Nagoya streets was increasing weekly. While a few of Nagoya's vehicles were European-made, the vast majority were made in America.

One of the reasons Toyoda Automatic Loom Works and its parent company, Toyoda Spinning and Weaving, Ltd. did not own company cars was the modest size of their operation. They also placed a high priority on economy. But the real, unspoken reason was that the company was suspicious about cars. The Kitahama Bank could be thanked for that. In 1914, Mr. Nakanishi, the bank's branch manager and owner of the *Aichi Number One* car, was arrested and charged with embezzling 1.1 million yen (the equivalent of several billion yen by today's monetary standards). Of course, the bank eventually went bankrupt, but not without rumors that the car was somehow responsible for its demise. Thus, a widespread superstition about owning company cars evolved among Nagoya businesses, and Toyoda Automatic Loom Works was a major subscriber.

To show what power this superstition held over the business community, the number of company cars in operation in Nagoya remained the lowest of all six metropolitan areas in Japan.

Without company transportation, Kiichiro and Risaburo commuted by train from their residences in Nagoya to the Kariya factory, or were chauffeured to the plant when winter or poor weather made it difficult to catch the train. Kiichiro usually left for work before dawn and ate his breakfast at the plant. He, in fact, looked forward to eating with his fellow factory workers and engineers and missed the pleasure whenever business took him away from the factory for extended periods of time.

During his absences, he would write each day to Oshima or Suzuki concerning business matters. The letters would carry postmarks from Kobe, Sendai, Tokyo, or Osaka. Almost always, when Kiichiro returned to the factory, a new machine or other piece of equipment would be waiting for him, at which point he would always say:

"It is imperative we increase the accuracy of the automatic loom and spinning machine components. To accomplish this task, we must utilize machine tools that provide the highest level of precision possible."

Because of Kiichiro's progressive philosophy, state-of-the-art machines from the United States and Germany were constantly arriving at the factory. He was also the one who had pushed for fully electrifying the foundry. Under Kiichiro's direction, there was constant upgrading. As a result, the factory's casting machine, the first of its kind in operation in Japan, made it possible to chrome plate the spinning machines. Furthermore, Kiichiro hired a skilled laboratory technician, Susumu Wainai, to work on chemical research. With an eye on changing the production line into a conveyor system, the firm also began exploring hydraulic engineering systems.

When the company began operations, it had five hundred employees. Now, despite the depression, the work force had expanded 20 percent. This philosophy of innovation, largely a product of Sakichi's and Kiichiro's inventive spirits, was steadily giving the company a strong competitive edge.

One clear November day, nearly a month after Sakichi's funeral, a telephone call came from a Nagoya importer of foreign machinery. The firm had received new machine tool catalogs from Germany and wanted to show them to Kiichiro.

"I will come by to look at them immediately," said Kiichiro, always anxious when it came to new machines, especially high-precision ones. He quickly called in Jiro Iwaoka, one of the newer, extremely talented engineers.

"You should go with me to see these new catalogs," Kiichiro told Iwaoka. "I'm sure you'll learn a lot."

Kiichiro and Iwaoka left the factory in the afternoon, catching the train at the Kariya station. Only third class seats were available, but that didn't bother Kiichiro. He was occupied the entire time with drawing machine tools in his notebook.

Sitting next to him and glancing over his shoulder, Iwaoka was puzzled. In the eyes of young Iwaoka, these machine tools seemed too sophisticated for the production of looms and spinning machines.

I wonder what kind of machine Mr. Toyoda is always thinking about, mused Iwaoka.

The firm's most advanced automatic loom and spinning machine products had already reached the finished goods stage. There were no other special development projects currently underway or, to his knowledge, even planned.

I wonder how much further we have to go to reach the level of precision that would satisfy Mr. Kiichiro?

Iwaoka had long wanted to ask Kiichiro that very question, but he had kept it to himself, thinking it disrespectful to put such a question to an executive director of the company. Iwaoka looked at Kiichiro several times during the train ride, each time feeling the temptation to pose his question. But Kiichiro was always hunched over his notebook of drawings.

At the train station, a chauffeur was waiting for them in a new Chevrolet. The Nagoya importer's office was located near the Nagoya Castle, which gave Iwaoka a little more time alone with Kiichiro. Seeing the notebook finally closed, Iwaoka braced himself and blurted out, "Well, I think it's really wasteful...."

"What is wasteful?" Kiichiro asked with a quizzical look.

"I think we have equipped our factory with high-precision, ultra-sophisticated machinery that can't be found in any other spinning machine factory. Yet you seem to be working on a piece of machinery which has even more precision. I think such a machine would be too good for us."

Oh, THAT's what he's talking about, thought Kiichiro. He hesitated to tell Iwaoka what he was thinking, but then decided to let this bright, hard-working, studious engineer in on his idea bit by bit.

"I want to show you something interesting," smiled Kiichiro. He then directed the driver to head for a bridge not far away.

Turning to Iwaoka, Kiichiro said, "Look carefully at both sides of the street as we travel along."

The car crossed the bridge and approached the Nagoya Chamber of Commerce and Industry.

"What do you see?" asked Kiichiro.

"Well, I see the Chamber of Commerce and Industry building and a shrine. Besides that there are ordinary company buildings, stores, and factories," replied Iwaoka.

"Now what do you see right in front of you?"

Sticking his head out the car window, Iwaoka answered, "On the left, to the south I see a company called Hinode Motors. Next to that is a noodle shop and in front of that is the Hinode Motors parts store. On the right, to the north there is a Toyo Construction Company and next to that is a bookstore and a doctor's office...."

"OK, let's go," Kiichiro said to the driver, directing him to return to the original route.

"Read out the names of the stores and offices as we drive by," Kiichiro instructed.

In the spirit of an anxious schoolboy, Iwaoka did as he was told: "Frank K. Miyazaki Company; Hosono Scrap Yard; Kawamoto Tire; Nagoya Branch Office of Japan Automobile Company; Nisshin Motors; Nagoya Branch Office of Safe Automobile Company; Showa Motors."

At the next corner was a liquor store and a coffee shop. These were the only two stores on the block.

Turning to the other side of the street, Iwaoka recited: "Nakagyo Motors; Van Motors; there's a doctor's office; Hosono and Company; Safe Automobile Warehouse; Kawamoto Pump Company; and there's a barbershop."

The driver made a right turn onto a broad thoroughfare that led to the Nagoya Castle. On that street there was a branch office of Mitsui Bank, Dai-ichi Motors, and Nakano Automobile Company. Kiichiro ordered the driver to stop the car in an empty lot by the Mitsui Bank.

"Would you please get me two packs of cigarettes? I'm in no hurry. Take your time and keep the change." Kiichiro gave the driver some money, and the driver got out of the car. Turning to Iwaoka, Kiichiro asked, "What kind of companies did you see?"

"A lot of automobile-related companies -- dealerships and repair shops."

"That's right. There are many other auto dealerships in town, but most of them can be found in this area. What do you think they sell at these dealerships?"

"Uh, well, vehicles of course, passenger cars and trucks," Iwaoka replied with a puzzled look on his face. What was Kiichiro getting at?

"Passenger cars and trucks -- that's obvious. What I'm asking is, what make of vehicles?"

"They're Fords and Chevrolets. I think Nisshin Motors is a distributor of the Willis-Knight automobiles used as taxis around here. Hinode Motors is a distributor for General Motors cars."

"That's exactly right. Kawamoto distributes Fords, Showa has General Motors cars, and other companies all distribute either American or European makes. Is there any operation that sells Japanese cars?"

"None that I know of. But maybe..." Iwaoka answered, his voice trailing off, still puzzled about where Kiichiro's questions were leading.

"You're right. There are none," replied Kiichiro.

"It is tragic that we have so many automobile distributors packed into this one city, yet if we were to search all of Japan with a magnifying glass, we wouldn't find a single company that sells domestically-built vehicles!

"According to the 1930 registry, there were 1,029 passenger cars, 261 trucks, and 200 busses operating in Nagoya. Of those, how many do you think were built domestically?"

"I really don't have the faintest idea," Iwaoka replied. "But, come to think of it, I've never seen a domestically-built vehicle."

"I haven't either. I don't know it for a fact, but the figure's probably near zero. Can you foresee a future for Japan in which there will be automobile factories located at the foot of Mount Fuji?"

Iwaoka's eyebrows shot up. He'd never thought of such a question. Now he suddenly realized what Kiichiro was talking about.

So, that's what Mr. Toyoda has been up to!

As soon as Iwaoka understood what Kiichiro was about, he felt as though a hopelessly tangled skein had suddenly unraveled into a single thread. With a flush on his face, Iwaoka stammered in a high pitched voice, "Then, Mr. Toyoda, you, uh, want to build a CAR?" Kiichiro smiled and nodded his head.

"So that's why you're always searching for newer, more advanced and higher-precision machine tools!"

"That's right. And I want everyone to become familiar with these machines," Kiichiro responded.

"Now I understand!" Iwaoka exclaimed, greatly moved.

Kiichiro wasn't exaggerating when he put the number of domestically-built vehicles at zero.

Of the more than ten automobile-related companies they had driven past, not a single one was a distributor for a domestic automobile maker. The only cars on Japanese roads were imported American and European models. That missing domestic automobile was what Kiichiro Toyoda was planning to build.

To impress upon Iwaoka the composition of the automobile industry in Japan -- and the pitiful state of domestic capabilities -- Kiichiro had decided to take the engineer along on this particular drive. Once Iwaoka realized Kiichiro's intentions, he was both profoundly impressed and unnerved by the daunting challenge Kiichiro so calmly faced.

"But, isn't it an awesome task to manufacture automobiles? It not only requires high precision but it's also very complex," Iwaoka ventured.

"Do you really think so?" Kiichiro chuckled. "You're not alone. Everyone in Japan thinks so. Nevertheless, Americans turn them out like jelly beans, and the Germans and the British are rapidly getting into the act. In England, even blacksmiths and the sons of repairmen are making cars in their backyards. In fact, they're called 'backyard builders.' "

"Then, would we build cars that way?" Iwaoka asked.

"No. The time will soon come when cars will be used by the Japanese public as an everyday means of transportation. Just as Ford and General Motors do, we must manufacture passenger cars for the general public. Also because they will be mass-produced, they will be inexpensive. But most important, they will be designed and built in Japan by Japanese hands. Ford and Chevrolet can go back where they came from."

"But," stammered Iwaoka, "aren't we some twenty or thirty years behind the Americans? Their annual production is in the tens of thousands, even millions. So far, as you point out, we produce none. The gap in technology is immense. Don't you think it's too large to bridge?"

"Yes and no. Actually we are not just twenty or thirty years behind. It's something more like fifty years," replied Kiichiro matter-of-factly.

"In 1885, a few creative efforts began to shape the history of technology. Germany's Daimler invented the gasoline engine; then a year later, he built a four-wheeled automobile around it. In that same time period, Benz built a three-wheeled automobile. Sakichi, you remember, was just getting started as an inventor. Within three years, the world's first automobile manufacturing company -- Panhard-Levasseur of France -- was established. By the time Sakichi completed his first wooden power loom in 1897, already the first Ford automobile had been introduced in the United States. And in 1900, the first self-propelled vehicle, a steam-powered automobile called a Locomobile, was imported."

"There is," replied Iwaoka, "an enormous difference."

"Yes, you're right," Kiichiro said with a smile. "But people exaggerate things by giving them such names as 'inventions.' A car is simply a carriage with a gasoline engine mounted on it. Only the engine can be called an 'invention.' By the way, do you know who invented the automobile?"

"The inventor of the automobile?" Iwaoka mused. "No, I don't."

"Of course not. No one invented the automobile! No single person dreamed up this useful thing that rolls on wheels! Incidentally, tell me who was the inventor of the loom?"

"Oh, now I see!" Iwaoka shrieked.

"Yes, now you understand. When we talk about the technical progress of the automobile, we are referring to the accumulation of knowledge, the process of putting together many tiny inventions made by many different people. If we were to compare that process to the length of time it took to develop human civilization, fifty years isn't even worth mentioning. On that scale, it doesn't even amount to a single day. We can also say that progress walks a thorny path, but one that is shared by the many people who have walked it before. In the case of Sakichi's loom, it can't be said that it was a true invention. It's clear its technology stemmed from the evolution of ideas and information. The same can be said of the automobile."

"But," said Iwaoka anxiously, "isn't automobile manufacturing a risky business, requiring enormous amounts of capital to fund a very large-scale operation?"

"Risky? Sure. But others are doing it. Even if the Toyoda companies go broke making the effort, if that establishes a Japanese automobile manufacturing industry, I'd be satisfied."

Kiichiro left off the conversation when he saw the uniformed chauffeur returning to the car with the two packs of cigarettes.

His final words to Iwaoka were, "I've told you this only because in the near future, you will be one of those put in charge of automobile production. But please keep this information strictly confidential. Until I make a formal announcement, you must let no one know what we discussed. In the meantime, you should thoroughly study such subjects as the fundamentals of automotive engineering."

"Of course," pledged Iwaoka, speaking with a new purpose in his voice.

We can build an automobile! Iwaoka said to himself.

His level of excitement still hadn't tapered off by the time he arrived home in Kariya later that day, but he continued to evaluate the meaning of Kiichiro's comments, just in case he had any doubts about the matter. After all, it required a mighty leap of faith to believe that those rough sketches of experimental gears, parts, machines, shapes, and gadgets which kept Kiichiro so engrossed really related to an automobile: *He's right: there are no historical records containing the names of individuals who invented things that contributed to the progress of human "civilization," things like the loom and the automobile. The only names that appear are the ones who accumulated tiny bits of technology to improve upon whatever existed previously.*

The prototype of the wheel and the loom are mentioned in ancient Japanese mythology. In the well-known Japanese narrative of the Sun Goddess, "loom," "shuttle," and "temple of priestly vestments" appear. Loom technology apparently has been known to various people of the world since the Stone Age. Yet it is said the loom was the first significant machine invented. Today, while the loom's impact has been tremendous, it would be difficult to trace all of the ways it has influenced mankind. As thousands and thousands of years passed, untold numbers of individuals added their thought and labor, bit by bit, piece by piece, to ultimately create today's fully-automated, high-tech mechanism. While the identities of past contributors may be lost in the mists of time, we do remember and honor as "inventors" those who created crucial elements or made major improvements. For the loom, one such major improvement was contributed by Sakichi, Iwaoka thought.

Iwaoka knew the history of this improvement very well. During his lifetime, Sakichi Toyoda earned eighty-four Japanese patents and thirteen foreign patents. Most were related to his loom, including, the 1902, 1903, and 1909 patents for the automatic shuttle-changing device. That mechanism -- the heart of the true "automatic loom" -- was globally accepted as a *bona fide "invention."* Its innovation was entirely unique.

A loom is a deceptively simple machine that weaves the weft into the warp to create cloth. Whereas the warp can be of any length, the length of the weft is limited by the size of the shuttle which carries it back and forth. In old-style textile factories, every time the shuttle of the weft ran out of yarn, the machine was stopped and a new shuttle added. This "down time" naturally cut into production and boosted operating costs. With the introduction of the automatic shuttle-changing device, "down time" was totally eliminated, and the weaving industry moved into the new age of the "automatic loom."

During the period when Sakichi was developing the automatic loom, he operated a small storefront business in Nagoya. The sale of looms funded his continuing research, an activity which would not have been possible without his second wife, Asako, whose energy and strong business sense really made the company run.

The eldest daughter of a farmer named Hayashi, Asako came from the same village as Sakichi's first wife, Tami. For whatever reason, Asako seemed better suited to endure the many eccentricities of a husband obsessed with invention. Tami had felt abandoned by her husband after their son Kiichiro was born on June 11, 1894. No sooner did Kiichiro come into the world than Sakichi was off to Tokyo pursuing his inventions. Rumors of his neglect and eccentricity spread quickly, and Tami's family, the Sahara's, prevailed upon her to leave Sakichi and return home. Though Tami loved Sakichi and understood him perhaps as well as anyone, eventually she succumbed to the unhappiness of her situation and did as her parents wished.

Three years later, in July of 1897, Sakichi married Asako. Asako jumped right into Sakichi's business working from dawn to dusk while Sakichi concentrated on making his improvements on the loom. The two complemented each other extremely well. While Sakichi modified the hand loom, then developed his power loom, and eventually created the automatic loom, Asako served as the consummate manager. She ordered materials, prepared meals for workers, supervised the factory, handled payroll, and dealt with all suppliers and wholesalers. She handled everything from negotiating bank loans to redeeming goods at the pawn shop to meet household expenses, giving Sakichi freedom to concentrate on his work.

When Kiichiro was taken from his grandparents to live with Asako and Sakichi, Asako was already engulfed in her responsibilities at the loom shop. She had very little time to spend with the new child, and Kiichiro genuinely suffered from this lack of nurturing and affection. Not long after his arrival, Asako gave birth to Kiichiro's half-sister, Aiko. Though one might have expected that Aiko would have received the lion's share of attention from her natural mother, Asako played no favorites. She scolded her two children equally when they misbehaved, and did not pamper either of them.

As a youth, Kiichiro had a weak constitution, perhaps due to malnourishment and being uprooted at such a tender age. His performance in elementary school was disappointing, for which he was constantly scolded by his stepmother. When he entered Meirin Middle School, his grades remained erratic, and his tuition often went unpaid to cover the expense of Sakichi's research. Kiichiro trembled when report cards were posted, fearful of the repercussions of his stepmother's anger.

It's little wonder that Kiichiro grew up as a quiet, melancholic boy. His only source of joy was his good-natured, gentle half-sister, Aiko, who adored her half-brother above anything else. Because their father was consumed with his research, and their mother with maintaining a business, the Toyoda household was like a desert island where a shipwrecked brother and sister grew up consoling each other.

It was not that Asako lacked love for her children. She was so busy and had to work so hard to manage both her business and the household that she had little time for them. To keep them amused, Asako had a game of hiding their after school snacks. It was a way of sharpening their wits. But for Aiko and Kiichiro, this game seemed little more than just another of life's many torments.

In one respect, Kiichiro was developing into a mirror image of his father. Whenever he had a spare moment, he passed the time drawing simple pictures of machinery in the corner of the room, pretending he was designing something. This idle fascination soon evolved into a full-scale obsession, just as it had in Sakichi.

If only Sakichi had been a normal father, thought Kiichiro, *my mother would not have left this house.* This quandary of his youth and even early maturity burned deeply in his heart, and for a long time he despised his father for being self-absorbed with his inventions. This anger usually manifested itself in attacks upon his father's legitimacy as an inventor:

Whenever we discuss machines, Sakichi's thoughts seem clumsy and simple. Even if he is called the inventor-king, he's had no education and doesn't understand how to systematize anything. Anyone could have done what he did.

It didn't help matters any that Sakichi's philosophy as a "self-made man" continued to deny Kiichiro the support he needed. When it came to high school and college, Sakichi insisted that schooling was useless and refused to give Kiichiro a college education. Appalled by this "irresponsibility," Sakichi's brother, Heikichi, assumed the sponsorship of Kiichiro's advanced education, telling Sakichi, "if you're going to act that way, then I'll pay his tuition."

Kiichiro's lack of respect for Sakichi's achievements was reinforced by many such instances of neglect, but it also became a force that drove Kiichiro to improve himself and actually better his father.

When Kiichiro was ready to graduate from the university in 1920, Sakichi was president of Toyoda Spinning and Weaving. Enjoying the prosperity made possible by the post-World War I economic boom, Sakichi had built a flourishing company in a northwestern suburb of Nagoya. Kiichiro joined his father's firm soon after his trip abroad with Aiko and Risaburo and quickly began making improvements on Sakichi's automatic loom. Because of Kiichiro's keen insight into mechanics, he was able to bring full automation to the loom, allowing it to live up to its reputation of being "automatic."

As his innovations gained wider and wider respect, Kiichiro's determination not to be outdone by his father became that much more intense. The final reward came in 1925 when Patent Number 65156 was awarded Kiichiro's invention. This marked the birth of the fully "automatic loom" for which Sakichi had become famous.

It was in this context that Kiichiro made an offhand comment one day to Iwaoka. "Sakichi's invention is nothing to get excited about. Any engineer or any school could have done it."

Puzzled by the strange "heresy" of this opinion, Iwaoka resolved that he must have misinterpreted. Given Kiichiro's unique attitude toward the evolution of invention, he must have meant something quite different. Iwaoka thought to himself:

Sakichi accumulated past technical knowledge to build his loom. We must do the same by accumulating the knowledge needed to build a car. The dawn of Japan's automobile age is coming. In that dawn, Mr. Toyoda will come face-to-face with a great challenge. And since it is Mr. Toyoda who will face that challenge, there is no doubt but that he will definitely prevail!

Iwaoka had worked under Kiichiro for almost five years, and respected him from the bottom of his heart, pledging to himself: *Regardless of how many problems he encounters -- and there will be many -- I'll risk my career to face the challenge with Mr. Toyoda.*

Now, more than just Kiichiro's die was cast.

Chapter
3

SECRET START

Just as Kiichiro's quest began to gain an early momentum, global events set up a series of roadblocks to test the strength of its purpose. The world had felt the grip of the "Great Depression" for some time, but now war clouds were gathering over the Chinese mainland.

Although the Sino-Japanese War didn't officially start until 1936, the first shots were fired in September of 1931 in what came to be known as "The Manchurian Incident."

Tensions had existed between Japan and China since the late 1920s. An ever-increasing competition to gain a dominant foothold in Manchuria simply brought the matter to the boiling point. Although Manchuria had been a part of China since the early seventeenth century, Chinese control of the area had begun to erode at the end of the nineteenth century as Russian political and economic influence increased in the region. Tsarist Russia's influence was especially strong in southern Manchuria where major commercial developments, including a railway system, had been built. Furthermore, Russia had acquired a leasehold on the Liaotung Peninsula or the Guandong Leased Territory from China. As a result of the Treaty of Portsmouth, which concluded the Russo-Japanese War in 1905, these interests and concessions were ceded to Japan.

Within the next twenty years, Japanese presence in southern Manchuria grew commercially and militarily as the Japanese colonists urged their government to assert a more visible role in Manchurian affairs. By 1920, Chinese authority in the area had deteriorated continually as political factionalism continued in southern Manchuria. As a result, various Japanese-controlled agencies sought to expand their interests and jurisdiction. One such agency was the South Manchuria Railway Company, which operated the major railway line in Manchuria. It not only came to control "attached lands" -- land on either side of the railway -- but also adjacent towns and villages, causing much antagonism between the Japanese and the local Chinese officials.

The continuing friction and bitterness was caused by the Guandong Army, the Imperial Japanese Army's field command in southern Manchuria. It was this military garrison that was most determined to consolidate Japanese control over the area to the point where southern Manchuria could be separated from China proper. In particular, it was the middle-echelon staff officers of the Guandong Army who insisted on bringing about a violent, rather than a negotiated, solution to the Manchurian issue. They believed that the takeover of Manchuria was the key to providing Japan with strategic security and economic self-sufficiency.

The stage was set then for a violent confrontation. On September 18, 1931, officers from the Guandong Army garrison at Mukden dynamited a few feet of the South Manchurian Railway near the city. Claiming that Chinese saboteurs were responsible, the Guandong Army declared a state of emergency. Japanese troops seized control of Manchuria and within a few weeks, the Guandong Army had occupied most of southern Manchuria as a "defensive measure." This was all done despite the efforts of the Japanese civilian government and the military high command in Tokyo to suppress the completely unauthorized operations of the Guandong Army staff.

The inability of Premier Wakatsuki's government to control the aggression of the Guandong Army led to his resignation, and exposed the dangerous uncertainties within the military chain of command, as well as throughout Japan's entire political structure. Furthermore, it demonstrated the degree to which civilian leaders and the Japanese public had lost confidence in the government's ability to solve foreign problems through international cooperation and negotiation.

The usurpation of power by the military signaled by the Manchurian Incident paralleled the economic distress that characterized the Japanese economy during the 1920s. Japan had prospered during World War I, shifting from a debtor to a creditor nation and building up its industry, shipping, and foreign trade, while the major western industrial powers were concentrating on military build-up. However, this all came to an end in 1920, when the Japanese economy fell into a severe depression. Two more setbacks followed: the great Tokyo Earthquake of 1923 resulted in the loss of billions of dollars' worth of facilities and property, followed by the unprecedented financial crisis of 1927, which resulted in widespread bank failures. The economic depression took a turn for the worse with the world-wide Great Depression of 1931. In spite of the Depression, productivity continued to increase as a result of technological improvements and rationalization of industry. Mining and manufacturing production increased significantly, but because of a drop in prices, the value of total production decreased substantially.

During this period, various disparities began to appear in the economic sector. The first to feel the squeeze were small and mid-sized enterprises, as the rate of bankruptcies began to rise. This was followed by a concentration of capital and resources in the *zaibatsu* (large financial cartels). Ignoring the plight of the small business entrepreneur, the government encouraged the growth of even larger cartels. This period was also characterized by much labor unrest as unemployment mounted. The scene in the countryside was not much better. The fall in the price of agricultural products created social unrest, especially among tenant farmers.

It was the Manchurian Incident that embarked the government on a program of increasing military expenditures, which led to an economic turnaround. Swamped with orders for military equipment and supplies, the armament industry led off a gradual but accelerated economic recovery. Other developments also helped; earlier, Japan had halted gold exports, and suspended them again in December of 1931. With that, the value of the yen plummeted in currency exchange markets, sending prices of imported goods in Japan soaring. The steep rise in the price of foreign equipment had much the same effect as a protective tariff, suddenly conferring a strong pricing advantage on domestic manufacturers with suitable products, as Toyoda Automatic Loom Works did. Before the devaluation, the spinning and weaving industry had largely used imported looms. For Toyoda, the intensive research and design paid off as orders for its automatic looms poured in, in wake of devaluation.

Essentially, this is the backdrop against which the drama of Kiichiro's ambitions would unfold.

As the New Year came and went and the winter months wore on, Kiichiro was busy with his customary routine. It would appear from every outward sign that he'd forgotten about building automobiles. If there was anyone at the factory who knew this not to be true, it was Iwaoka.

When the appropriate time comes, Kiichiro will issue the orders. Until then, I must prepare myself accordingly, thought Iwaoka.

Iwaoka had taken Kiichiro's instructions to heart. Each night after putting a full day's work in at the factory, he'd scour books and journals on automotive engineering, never getting to bed until after midnight. With only a few hours sleep, he'd be right back at it the next day.

This was a busy but happy spring for Jiro Iwaoka and his fellow engineers at Toyoda Automatic Loom Works. Iwaoka had received a promotion and was now in charge of the production area. The design area was buzzing with new life, including Takeaki Shirai, a recent graduate from Shizuoka University.

To accommodate the surge in orders, the engineering staff expanded to keep pace. There were many new fresh and eager faces, young engineers happy to be working at the frantic pace of a flourishing factory. No sooner did they meet one shipping deadline than another rapidly approached. No one had a chance to stop and think about how hard he was working. The close teamwork, pride in quality and workmanship, and the company's economic success generated a strong sense of accomplishment and camaraderie.

As the days flew by, Iwaoka continued to add to his growing knowledge of automobiles. His research confirmed the accuracy of all but one of Kiichiro's observations. True, the number of domestically produced cars was small, but it wasn't "zero," as Kiichiro had maintained. As Iwaoka learned from his study of history, Japan had been involved with automobiles from nearly the outset of the industry.

In 1900 the first automobile, a steam-powered "Locomobile," was imported by Japan. Only two years later, working under the aegis of the two-wheeled society of Tokyo and using a gasoline engine and parts imported from the United States, an engineer named Kunosuke Uchiyama "assembled" the first "domestically built" automobile, a four-passenger sedan. By 1904, Torasuke Yamaba had built a four-wheel, two-cylinder, steam-powered bus.

Catching the "automotive fever," the Two-Wheeled Society of Tokyo built a larger passenger car boasting a twelve horsepower, two-cylinder gasoline engine. It was completed in April of 1907, and the society dedicated it to the family of Prince Arisugawa. Relying more on domestic technology, materials, and parts, this vehicle could be considered as Japan's first "homemade" automobile.

While there is further evidence of Japan's early interest in the automobile, attempts at manufacturing remained sporadic and lacked continuity. As a result, they fell far behind the United States, whose car industry was steaming forward at full throttle.

In 1908, Henry Ford had cranked up his revolutionary mass production system to produce the famous Model T. General Motors had also begun operation with its Buick and Oldsmobile divisions. The advantage the Americans enjoyed in the skill, technology, and ability to produce at competitive prices over the nascent Japanese automobile industry was uncontestable, but various Japanese firms continued their research and manufacturing efforts.

By the end of the Meiji era in 1911, the Two-Wheeled Society of Tokyo publicized the seriousness of its intentions by changing its name to Tokyo Automobile Manufacturing Company. Also entering the fray were such established firms and would-be auto makers as Yamada Ironworks, Shiba Automobile Manufacturing Company, Miyada Manufacturing Company, Japan Automobile Trading Company, and Kaishinsha. With the exception of Kaishinsha, however, all of these ventures failed before getting off the ground.

In 1912, Junhiro Toyogawa's Hakuyosha was established. Though it later failed, this firm can rightfully lay claim to being Japan's first bonafide auto maker.

The story is an interesting one. Junhiro Toyoawa was the eldest son of Ryohei Toyogawa, the top director of the Mitsubishi conglomerate during the early 1900s. When Junhiro first proposed the manufacturing venture, his father and other Mitsubishi executives vehemently vetoed it. But Junhiro never faltered in his belief that Japan needed a viable automotive industry to secure a position among the rapidly industrializing nations of the world. Despite his father's opposition and without his consent, Junhiro used Mitsubishi assets to found Hakuyosha. The purpose of the company was to build a truly domestic automobile, not to imitate an American or European model as other Japanese companies had done. From machine tools and production line equipment to the design of the car, Junhiro attempted to build everything in-house.

After ten years of research and prototype development, in 1921 Hakuyosha introduced a passenger car called Aresu-go. The Automo-go followed in 1924. On the surface, there seemed to be success, but the high cost of production and low profit continued to undermine the enterprise. Junhiro was forced to approach Mitsubishi for a bailout. Because Mitsubishi had never supported the project from the outset, it refused any financial assistance, and Junhiro's company went bankrupt soon thereafter in 1928.

In many respects, Hakuyosha anticipated and epitomized Kiichiro Toyoda's vision of a totally domestic automobile industry. They also cast a dark shadow over that vision, serving as a warning to Kiichiro of the dangers which lay ahead and providing ammunition for the nay-sayers and Risaburos of the world. But then again, national and global events would have something to say about the fate of the Japanese automobile industry.

The Japanese military was quick to grasp the significance of self-propelled vehicles for transporting and supplying armies in the field. Very early on, they encouraged domestic firms to develop vehicles the armed services could use. Among the firms patronized by the military were Tokyo Gas and Electric, which started automobile production in 1916, and Mitsubishi Shipyard of Kobe, Kawasaki Shipyard, Okumura Electric of Tokyo, Train Manufacturing Company of Osaka, and Osaka Ironworks, all of which entered manufacturing in 1918.

Impressed by the role automobiles, trucks, and tanks played in Europe during World War I, the military began in May of 1918 to subsidize domestic firms willing to work on such vehicles. To their credit, they could see that private firms couldn't afford to spend the money necessary to develop vehicles solely for military use.

In 1920, Ishikawajima Shipyard undertook automobile production, followed three years later by Toyo Automobile Company of Osaka and Utility Automobile Company. All three took part in the military subsidy program.

Japan was not alone in this approach. In the early years of the automotive industry, most western nations directly or indirectly subsidized domestic producers in return for building suitable military vehicles. The rationale was simple. From a cost standpoint, it would have been difficult for any nation's armed forces to be certain it could reserve a sufficient number of vehicles for war time use from the stock of those produced during peace time. Moreover, given the speed and progress of technology at the time, whatever was produced and stockpiled for military purposes would soon be rendered obsolete. Subsidy programs were a prudent move. Every aspect of the automobile industry was closely scrutinized by the military, from research and development, to the practical elements of durability, load-carrying capacity, and ease of maintenance in the field. In return for the financial boost, manufacturers were expected to stand ready whenever military emergencies arose.

During World War I, the system worked as well as could be expected, given the immaturity of the industry. But after the war, many vehicle producers in Japan returned to manufacturing their principal products, letting the automotive industry dwindle to only a few concerns. What finally put an end to these ventures was the Great Depression. Only Tokyo Gas and Electric was able to survive.

Throughout the many ups and downs of the industry, Japan continued to have more than a passing fascination with cars, domestic-made or otherwise. Then in 1923, the Tokyo Earthquake brought home the true utility of automobile and truck transportation. With total disruption of the rail system, the country lay paralyzed but for its small "mobile fleet." After that point, the automobile changed from just a neat contraption and a toy for the rich to an essential link in the country's welfare. Because the burgeoning need for automobiles could not be met by financially troubled domestic manufacturers, the country turned its eyes to the United States market, particularly to Ford and General Motors.

By 1932, Ford and General Motors had turned this advantage into a virtual strangle hold on the Japanese automobile market by means of their efficient knock-down assembly plants. At a combined annual production of 23,206 units in 1931, they manufactured more cars in a week than all three car companies in Japan produced in a year. In the same year Tokyo Gas and Electric, Ishikawajima Automobile Company, and what was later to become Datsun Motor Company, then Kaishinsha, produced a total of 437 units. This was the sad state of affairs in the domestic automobile industry at the time of the Manchurian Incident.

Once the powder keg had been ignited by the "railroad bombing," the Japanese army swiftly occupied Manchuria and joined the fighting with its Guandong Army unit in and around Shanghai from January 28 to March 3, 1932. However, under heavy censure from the world community, Japan agreed to a cease-fire to avoid a full-scale war. The cease-fire, however, did little to deter Japan from her primary goal of securing a firm hold in China.

In September of 1932, a puppet government called Manchukuo was established and unilaterally declared an independent state. It was headed by P'u Yi, the ex-emperor of the Manchu dynasty who had taken refuge in the Japanese concession at Tientsin six years earlier after being driven out of Peking. He was immediately coronated as Emperor K'ang Te, Emperor of Manchukuo. When the world court refused to recognize the puppet state of Manchukuo, Japan withdrew from the League of Nations and global tensions began to mount.

Japan itself was in turmoil. In October of 1931, right-wing radicals had staged an unsuccessful coup d'etat against the military-dominated cabinet. Then on February 9, 1932, young naval officers joined members of a civilian right-wing group -- the Blood Pledge Corps -- hatching a plot to assassinate the nation's top financial and political leaders, including a high-ranking Mitsui official on March 5. The scheme culminated in the assassination of Premier Tsuyoshi Inukai on May 15, 1932.

The era was marked by strident militarism and, increasingly, by authoritarian rule that edged ever closer to fascism. Angry voices called for Japan to liberate Asia from the grasping western imperialists and create a Greater East Asia Co-Prosperity Sphere. Buffeted by harsh economic times and manipulated by a tightly controlled and highly propagandistic media, the average Japanese citizen had little power to avoid being sucked into Japan's militaristic frame of mind. Those who did avoid it were still swept up by the winds of change and progress. One who was most excited by the times and ready to answer the clarion call for progress was Iwaoka. As Kiichiro had disappeared again on one of his periodic odysseys, Iwaoka read vociferously to gear up for the challenge ahead:

The war will spread further. And on the continent's battleground, great quantities of cars will be needed. It seems the need is urgent, and I'm sure that Mr. Toyoda is well aware of that fact.

Kiichiro was indeed "gearing up," as Iwaoka had suspected. He had gone to Tokyo and Osaka to examine factories producing motorcycles and three-wheeled automobiles. Four or five days had been spent visiting parts manufacturers. In Tokyo, Kiichiro had also gotten together with three close friends from his Tokyo University days: Kazuo Kumabe, an assistant professor of mechanical engineering at Tokyo University, who was the first one in Japan to lecture on automotive engineering; Hideo Kobayashi, now responsible for promoting government use of automobiles at the Ministry of Railways; and Kaoru Ban, in charge of promoting the development of the domestic automobile industry at the Ministry of Trade and Commerce.

The topic of conversation never strayed from the domestic automobile industry and related events. That year, 1932, had seen a number of interesting developments in the automotive arena. The Ministry of Trade and Commerce had ordered the three existing domestic auto producers and the Ministry of Railways to build an automobile prototype to specifications issued by the Ministry. As a result, a triumvirate of Nagoya companies pooled their resources and developed the Atsuta-Go. Including the prototype, twelve cars were built before the financial strain halted production. As the story of the Asuta-Go unfolded, Kiichiro listened intently to see precisely where his plans might fit in. His major worry, however, continued to be the precariousness of national and global affairs.

On January 15, 1933, the United States announced its decision not to recognize Manchukuo, in effect denouncing Japan's move as an act of imperialist aggression. Understandably, relations between the United States and Japan rapidly deteriorated.

Then, a half a month later on January 30, Adolf Hitler drove a solid wedge into his country's leadership by virtue of the popular mandate given the Democratic Socialist Party in the general election. President Hindenburg was forced to appoint Hitler Chancellor, but found the situation highly objectionable. Offering Hitler one slight after another, Hindenburg scoffed at his new cabinet, neither delivering a welcoming speech nor giving it the customary charge for the upcoming administration. Instead Hitler startled everyone with a speech of his own in which he solemnly pledged to observe the Weimar constitution. Those opposed to Hitler recognized the pledge for the farce that it was, given the fact that he was already on record as wanting to crush "that cancer, democracy," and to repudiate the Treaty of Versailles.

Soon after taking office, Hitler disclosed a plan that was of great interest to would-be Japanese car manufacturers like Kiichiro. He used the occasion of the 1933 Berlin Motor Show to announce his intention to produce the Volkswagen, or German People's Car. Surprisingly, its specifications were very similar to those Kiichiro had in mind for the mass-produced car for the Japanese common man. The Volkswagen was to (1) have a maximum speed of 100 kilometers per hour, (2) get 14.3 kilometers per liter of gas, (3) have a capacity of 4 to 5 passengers, (4) have an air-cooled engine, and (5) be priced at no more than 1,000 marks. Since Germany was located in a cool climate, an air-cooled engine would be practical and simpler than a water-cooled one. The lowest-priced car then available in Germany cost about 2,200 marks. It was Hitler's feeling that "the people's car" could and should be produced for less than half of that.

Hitler quickly assigned the job of building the prototype to the talented automobile designer and fellow Austrian, Ferdinand Porsche. Porsche's design ultimately became the famous Volkswagen "Beetle" after World War II.

As developments unfolded rapidly in Germany, a revolution of a different sort was in its infancy at the Toyoda Automatic Loom Works. It was at the end of March, 1933. Takeaki Shirai, an engineer who'd been with the company barely a year, had just received two small packages mailed from Osaka. To his great puzzlement, the address label had Shirai as not only the receiver but the sender as well.

"I wonder what this is," Shirai said, turning to Iwaoka. "I don't have the faintest idea what it could be."

"Open it," Iwaoka replied. Eyeing the box, he took out a knife from a lab coat pocket and cut the twine. Inside were a number of shiny metal objects.

"What do you think they are?" Iwaoka asked, grinning broadly.

"Hmm...they appear to be small engine parts."

"You don't say," said Iwaoka.

"Why were they sent to me?" asked Shirai.

"Look carefully at the handwriting on the mailing label," Iwaoka replied, laughing as he pointed to the label.

"It's Mr. Toyoda's handwriting, can't you see? Look, there in the corner, there's a 'K.' You'd better study the contents before he comes back or he'll be upset," Iwaoka said and then quickly left.

Now I see! This might be something that Mr. Toyoda would do. Mr. Iwaoka has been working under Mr. Toyoda for much longer than I, so he is used to such things. But this is a first for me. I'm still a little baffled, thought Shirai.

He untied another piece of twine and removed the wrapping to find silver-colored engines the size of thimbles.

Ah, the metal parts in the first package are components of these engines.

Shirai carried the parcels back to his desk and took notes as he examined and measured the contents. The miniatures appeared to be motorcycle engines with cylinder blocks made of cast metal.

OK, I'll be ready to make a report to Mr. Kiichiro whenever he gets back.

Shirai didn't have long to wait. The very next day Kiichiro returned and called both Iwaoka and Shirai into his office. Instead of asking Shirai about the engine and parts, he simply instructed: "I want you to build ten engines just like the one I'm holding. Shirai's task is to take apart the finished product, make a sketch of the parts, and copy the designs. Iwaoka should try to duplicate the parts in our factory. Please tell Wainai to thoroughly evaluate the quality of the material. You should build these as quickly as possible." And then he left the room.

Wasting no time, Shirai and Iwaoka went to the chemistry lab and informed Wainai of the assignment. Wainai took one of the duplicate parts sent by Kiichiro, broke off a piece, and scraped off shavings for analysis.

Everyone was excited to get started and worked on nothing else. Yet the spinning machine factory was operating at full capacity, which meant "the special project" would be relegated to work after hours.

During the time Iwaoka and his staff were working with these small engines until late into the night, Kiichiro was in a frenzy mustering his resources. Early April found him in Osaka. No sooner did he return than he boarded the night train to Tokyo to see Kumabe. When the train arrived early the next morning, Kiichiro headed for the Mechanical Engineering Department at Tokyo University, arriving just as the building opened. He briskly entered Kumabe's office, uttered an abbreviated greeting, and jumped right into the business at hand.

"I have finally made up my mind to earnestly start making automobiles this fall. I have some idea of what kind of car I want to build, so I came to discuss my findings with you."

If Kiichiro seemed presumptive or blunt, it was simply his way, and Kumabe was not offended by it. Turning his chair around and facing Kiichiro, he replied, "I see. So the time has finally come. Tell me about your plan."

"My goal is to produce inexpensive passenger cars for the general public, much like Germany's Volkswagen. The vehicle called for by the Ministry of Commerce and Industry is a truck, not a passenger car. Therefore, it does not compete directly with Ford and Chevrolet models. My plan is different. The car I intend to produce will go head-to-head with Chevrolet and Ford. For that reason, I want its size to be comparable to theirs. I'm not aiming simply to close the gap; in the future I want to challenge American car manufacturers and eventually replace imported cars with domestically made models throughout Japan. Consequently, annual production figures should be at least 10,000."

"I'm really impressed," Kumabe said exuberantly. "If we can do it that way, interchangeable parts can be used. How do you actually plan to go about this?"

"That's what I came here to discuss with you," said Kiichiro. "Regrettably, our company possesses virtually no expertise in automotive technology. First, I would like to make a complete imitation of a Ford or a Chevrolet, mostly using their parts. It is my intention to mimic American models as a form of rehearsal. Through this training, we will differentiate the strengths from the weaknesses."

"That's fine," agreed Kumabe.

"Then gradually," Kiichiro continued, "we'll develop domestic production of parts. Once we have a few years experience, we'll be able to develop our own designs. Since the goal is to build a passenger car for the general public, rather than one with unique technical capabilities, I plan to build an automobile that's both reliable and by virtue of mass production, low-priced. That's why I'll use either a Ford or a Chevrolet as the model. My personal interest runs more to vintage cars, but that is of no value to us in this project."

"I approve of that, too," Kumabe said, nodding his head.

The "vintage" cars referred to by Kiichiro were made by now defunct foreign manufacturers. Following the end of World War I, in 1919, the world's automobile makers consisted of those who predated the war and several munitions manufacturers who switched over to automobile manufacturing. Many talented and creative engineers worked for these firms and produced superb, often unique, automobiles. In the aftermath of the 1929 United States stock market crash, the bulk of these automobile makers fell by the wayside and with them the quality cars they designed and produced. The only survivors were large, capital-intensive manufacturers using mass production techniques.

"You may already know what I'm going to say," said Kumabe with a very serious expression. "If you take a close look at the American market, you might discover things you never expected. Currently in the United States, Ford's lead in the automobile industry is gradually being eroded by Chevrolet's aggressive manufacturing program. On the basis of total production quotas, General Motors stole the lead from Ford back in 1929. But Ford still holds the lead for the most cars sold for a single model type. It is only a matter of time before that situation changes too. Why will Chevrolet eventually surpass Ford? One reason is that it's more stylish and in some areas of engineering far superior.

"Without question, Chevrolet has a better engine," Kumabe continued. "Until last year, Ford's engine was the Type A -- reliable but, by today's standards, technologically obsolete. So last year, they changed to a Type B, a V-8 suitable for a luxury car. As Ford's philosophy has always been to mass-produce low-priced cars, the Type B moved them into a market they're not entirely comfortable with. That's one problem. But they have also had difficulties casting the larger, more complicated engine block. For that reason, they're giving up on a trial production. We should take our clues from this and look to the Chevrolet engine as our model.

"What the Chevrolet lacks in power and efficiency is sufficiently compensated for by its low cost. It is dependable and technologically fairly simple. Chevrolet is also currently working on a model with independent front wheel suspension. The aim is to produce a smoother, more stable ride. Other advantages are its lighter weight and easy method of mounting the engine. But the big difference is that Chevrolet is trying to make changes, while Ford is stuck in one way of doing things, which makes the Ford highly idiosyncratic and difficult to duplicate. It is truly an odd duck when it comes to design and engineering.

"We have to keep an open mind and think very carefully about these points. What appears to be a car's weaknesses can be very deceptive. In a very strange way, these weaknesses can be the very sources of the car's strengths. For example, Fords are built with solid parts and what I've described as idiosyncratic may be very unique to another engineer," concluded Kumabe.

"I see," said Kiichiro, nodding thoughtfully. "Thank you very much, you've been a big help. But another problem I see is the nature of materials used in making the cars -- particularly steel. It's said that the Model T's success is due to the ready availability of vanadium steel in the United States. Is it possible to produce steel of equal quality in Japan?"

Kumabe was amazed. *This man continues to foresee one obstacle after another without showing any sign of weariness. I wonder if there is any limit to his toughness?*

Then Kumabe responded, "I really can't say for sure. It's not my expertise. You should ask Professor Honda."

"You're right," Kiichiro replied. "Why didn't I think of him myself?" Kotaro Honda was the president of Tohoku University in Sendai and widely known as an authority on metallurgy.

Kiichiro had been visiting with Kumabe for hours, yet had not even taken a sip of his tea. This didn't surprise Kumabe. Their long friendship dated back to their university days, and Kumabe was familiar with Kiichiro's intensity and self-absorption, as well as other quirks and little oddities. At the same time, Kumabe knew that Kiichiro would willingly do anything asked of him, and once he accepted a task, he would always see it through. Kumabe understood Kiichiro was not one to engage in idle talk, but he also knew his old school chum was truly a warm-hearted man. Still, he was a little surprised to see Kiichiro rise from his chair to leave without giving any warning.

"Why don't you relax a little," Kumabe asked with a wry smile. As he spoke he cupped his left hand, raised it to his mouth, and tossed off an imaginary shot of *sake*, adding: "Why don't we go out drinking tonight?"

Kiichiro appeared pressed for time, but his visit provided Kumabe with a good excuse to relax and go out for a few drinks with a dear friend.

"No thanks," Kiichiro answered with just a hint of regret. "As you suggested, I have to meet with Professor Honda; then I'll meet with Ban and Kobayashi. After that I'll catch the night train to Sendai."

"What a spoil-sport," blurted Kumabe, throwing up his hands in an exaggerated show of disgust.

The dramatic gesture completely missed Kiichiro as he grabbed his briefcase and then suddenly stopped, "Could you give me some of your people? I need them right away."

"People? Oh, you mean engineers. I can't provide you with people on a moment's notice."

"I know that, but I definitely need to hire some people this fall. Please look into it for me."

Nodding his goodbyes, Kiichiro left.

Kumabe smiled grimly, uncharacteristically irritated by Kiichiro's presumptuousness. He then attributed this rudeness to Kiichiro's abnormal preoccupation with the difficult road that lay ahead.

The next person Kiichiro had scheduled himself to see was Hideo Kobayashi, who worked at the Ministry of Railways. Upon learning Kobayashi was out of the city on a business trip, Kiichiro headed directly to the Ministry of Commerce to see Kaoru Ban.

"So, what's new?" Kiichiro asked as he breezed into Ban's office and walked up to his desk. "How's the truck? You know, the one being built to the Ministry's specifications?"

"I see you're your usual self. It's okay to act this way here, but be a little more courteous with Kobayashi, or you'll get another *rumble, rumble*," laughed Ban.

Kiichiro smiled broadly, then broke into a rare laugh.

Rumble, rumble was a long-standing, private joke relating back to their post-university days. It grew out of an incident that happened on September 1, 1923. Kiichiro had come to Tokyo to visit Kobayashi, then already on the staff of the Ministry of Railways. Kiichiro couldn't recall whether Kobayashi was ill or had merely taken a personal holiday, but he was at home that day.

In the course of their conversation, Kiichiro told Kobayashi about the large number of automobiles he'd seen during his trip to the United States and Europe a year earlier. Kobayashi nodded knowingly, telling Kiichiro that railroads had lost a lot of their ground to over-the-road transportation in the United States and Europe, following World War I. Increased use of automobiles was causing the railroad companies to fall behind in construction of new lines and maintenance of old ones. While that situation was not expected to occur as quickly in Japan, the Ministry of Railways was already studying the feasibility of government-owned buses and short-haul trucks.

As Kobayashi pounded his fist on the table to underscore his point, the Tokyo Earthquake hit full force. Scared out of their wits, the pair dashed out of the house and quickly became separated in the hysteria. Kiichiro ended up walking for miles through chaos and rubble until he reached a train station that was in operation. It was this experience which impressed upon him the vulnerability of railways in times of crisis and the necessity of mobile transportation. It also marked the genesis of a joke that never failed to evoke a grin from those who knew it -- the fist that made the earth quake, otherwise known as the inimitable *rumble, rumble.*

"Since Kobayashi isn't in, I guess there will be no *rumble, rumble* today," Kiichiro grinned. "I wanted to ask him what's happening with the legislation on automobile manufacturing. Do you happen to know how it's coming along?"

"It's moving fairly well," said Ban. "However, the plan to build a domestic automobile industry by consolidating some of the major *zaibatsu* like Sumitomo, Mitsubishi and Mitsui, will likely do little to capture the market from Ford and General Motors.

"For one thing, Japan is woefully deficient in basic manufacturing skills essential for the development of an efficient and competitive industry. Without these it's almost impossible to manufacture the great number of complex parts that go into an automobile. Moreover, it's such a risky, capital-intensive business that most companies approached by the military have opted for minimal participation. So far, the idea hasn't really gotten off the ground.

"If you make guns and warships, you are guaranteed complete government cooperation and financial assistance. Cars are a different story. Your success as a company is completely at the mercy of the free market. Profits are a lot harder to come by. To most businessmen, national welfare runs a distant second to making money. It's more important for them to pocket the profits from selling imported cars than to settle for less and help establish a domestic industry that'll benefit the country."

"I see you're as cynical as ever," Kiichiro interjected.

Ban smiled. "The military feels the way you do and is really upset with the present situation. General Motors and Ford are keeping close eye on our efforts to develop a domestic automobile industry. Already they're buying land, planning new factories, and signing up the top domestic parts and auto makers. In short, they're working hard to maintain their "across-the-sea" monopoly on the Japanese car market and make no pretenses about it. As you can imagine, this makes the nationalistic military establishment furious. I think you can count on passage of the law mandating domestic manufacturing of motor vehicles a lot sooner than anyone expected."

Looking intently at Ban, Kiichiro pondered a moment, then said, "Let me see if I've got it straight. The gist of the law is this: the government will neither subsidize nor tax domestic manufacturers. In return for this tax exempt status, it will, however, dictate the specifications manufacturers must follow in making their vehicles. Is that correct?"

"That isn't exactly the way I would put it," Ban replied. "The legislation is much more comprehensive than you're suggesting. True, it is designed to protect Japanese auto makers, but it also protects the legitimate interests of foreign companies like Ford and General Motors. They won't be permitted further expansion, but whatever they have already invested will be recognized.

"That's okay. I'm not afraid of competition. And I really don't want government protection and the control that always comes with it. But if the goal is to have us immediately shoot ahead of GM and Ford, we can't do it without government help. Even with help, it will be an onerous undertaking. So for this one time only, we'll go along with the plan." As he spoke, Kiichiro had a mischievous smile on his face.

"Then you are finally going to start?" Ban asked eagerly.

"Yes, I've made up my mind. I'm planning to get started by August or September. I just discussed this with Kumabe. My idea is to mass-produce a passenger car for the public, just like Ford and GM. I don't want to build a standardized vehicle to your ministry's specifications. If you don't mind, I'll let the other domestic auto manufacturers handle that one."

Ban sat motionless for a few minutes, deep in thought. Then he said, "I mentioned earlier that the joint business venture by the three domestic manufacturers didn't pan out. Well, there's a little more to the story. You're probably aware that two of those firms, Ishikwajima and Dat Motors, merged in March of 1933 and became Automobile Manufacturing Company. The director of the new company, incidentally, happens to be Yoshisuke Ayukawa of Nissan Industries."

"Yes, I've heard something to that effect," nodded Kiichiro.

"Well, Ayukawa is not your ordinary industrialist. He graduated from the Mechanical Engineering Department of Tokyo University in 1903, so he's about twenty years older than you. He worked at Shibaura as an engineer for awhile before it became Toshiba, and he then went to the United States and worked on the factory floor of a top-notch foundry for more than a year. After he returned to Japan in 1910, he established a company called Tobata Casting in the northern part of Kyushu.

"Ayukawa's achievements are indeed impressive. In 1918, coincidental to his move into the directorship of Kuhara Mining Company, he became either a director or president of a number of companies, including Tobata Casting, Tokai Steel, and Teikoku Casting. From there he branched out into a number of different industries and was successful in all of them.

"He's a classic entrepreneur, and his leadership skills are second to none." Ban went on to flesh out Ayukawa's background.

In 1927, the once-prosperous Kuhara Mining Company teetered on bankruptcy after incurring heavy damages during the Tokyo Earthquake. Already strapped for funds because of reconstruction, it suffered further setbacks at the hands of the post-World War I depression. Out of desperation, Ayukawa's sister, wife of the owner of Kuhara Mining, petitioned her brother to take the reins and revive the company.

Ayukawa developed a daring revitalization plan totally innovative for the time. Reacting to fears and reluctance of the banks to cooperate in a bailout, he reasoned: *we don't need the banks. We now have 15,000 shareholders. I propose that we make a public stock offering. We'll increase the number of shareholders ten- or maybe a hundredfold. Forget the bankers -- we'll let the public become owners of Kuhara.*

It was this reasoning that gave birth to public ownership of companies in Japan. When Ayukawa announced the dramatic decision to go public, he changed the name of the firm to Nihon Sangyo (Nissan) and brought a number of existing subsidiaries under the Nissan umbrella. Adding another unique business twist, Ayukawa mandated that the parent company would not have direct control of its subsidiaries, thus allowing them to remain competitors to spur mutual growth. The issuance of stock, matters of capitalization, sales quotas -- all aspects of the subsidiary's management remained independent of the parent company. Even more revolutionary, a subsidiary was allowed to establish and acquire new companies, in essence acting as its own parent company.

For the first few years, Ayukawa's company traveled a rocky road. Because it didn't have an established track record, a lot of people took a wait-and-see attitude. With resourcefulness and vision, however, Ayukawa gradually turned the company around.

At the time, the price of gold in yen had been fixed at a relatively low level for a long time. Ayukawa wrote a thesis stating that the quantity of gold mined should be directly proportionate to the price of gold. A copy was given to the Finance Minister, who was swayed by its argument and moved to raise the price of gold. Shortly thereafter, the stock price of Nissan's gold-mining subsidiary, the Nikko Company (Nihon Kogyo), posted a steady series of increases. Nikko profited and Ayukawa earned a huge premium on the sale of Nissan's stock holdings. Furthermore, the stock of the parent company, Nissan, which had been issued at fifty yen and had at one point dropped to twelve, now soared to more than one hundred.

This accounts for why Nissan was able to launch Nihon Kogyo and become a major conglomerate, controlling such companies as Hitachi Electric and Hitachi Works, a total of one hundred subsidiaries in all. Eschewing any and all bank loans, Nissan carried itself by buying up nearly bankrupt companies, nursing them back to health, and fattening its financial base with profits made from sale of their stock.

This was essentially the story Ban told Kiichiro, before he continued:

"As Mr. Ayukawa became director of the Automobile Company, that company then became part of Nissan. It's not official, but I hear that a contract has already been signed that transfers the Datsun manufacturing rights to Tobata Casting, one of Mr. Ayukawa's holdings."

"I see," Kiichiro said pensively.

"Ayukawa is a businessman of great instinct and vision," Ban continued. "Judging by some of the types of companies he's brought under the Nissan umbrella, it's apparent that automobile manufacturing was part of his plan all along. Today he controls several well-established paint companies, including Automobile Paint, and several electrical engineering and component manufacturing firms like Far East Electric. He's been making what adds up to extensive preparations, including directing Yasugi Steel Works to develop special types of high-strength steel.

"You can bet now that Mr. Ayukawa has decided to build automobiles, Nissan will adopt the American mass production approach, not the highly manual, small-shop methods of existing domestic manufacturers. Nissan is already negotiating for property to build a large factory in Yokohama."

"Hmm...I see. That's very interesting," Kiichiro murmured.

"Of course," Ban went on, "the government and the military will be all for it. If you plan to do it, you'll have to hurry, or else you'll get left behind."

"I would guess we're entering the race a little late already," Kiichiro said softly, his arms crossed and forehead furrowed in thought.

"You're absolutely right. And, as long as you're here old friend, I have to tell you something that is difficult for one to say, but it's very important. So I'll just come out with it," Ban said solemnly, looking directly into Kiichiro's eyes.

"If you really have finally made up your mind to go ahead with this, you'll have to act like a refined national industrialist. You may be well-known in Nagoya, but everywhere else you're just another stranger. You'll have to watch your manners. You don't offend us because we know you. We're used to your brusque manner and habit of showing up like you've just gotten out of bed. But it'll be a big problem if you dress and behave around others the way you do when you're with us. You just need to be a little more attentive and polite to people. And remember, a little flattery goes a long way."

"Hmm...." Kiichiro uttered, stroking his chin.

It was true that he never spent time in idle talk and was totally indifferent to his appearance. When he traveled, Kiichiro might wear the same soiled shirt for days and not even notice his trousers were worn and shiny at the knees. Nor did he mind that his beard had grown shaggy and he hadn't bathed for a week. He'd always been like that.

"Hey," said Ban, interrupting Kiichiro's ruminations, "do you still live by that commandment: *small talk is useless*?"

"Of course I still live by it, and I intend to keep right on living by it," Kiichiro replied emphatically. The words were uncompromising, but he smiled broadly and his voice lacked the slightest hint of anger.

What Kiichiro valued in himself ran completely counter to what Ban was advising him to do.

I knew I shouldn't have told Ban about such trivial things. That's why he's putting me on the spot. That just goes to prove once again that one shouldn't engage in idle conversation.

This thought took Kiichiro back to a former time when he had violated his pledge to avoid all small talk. One night in the late 1920s, Kiichiro was having a drink with Ban in a restaurant on one of his trips to Tokyo. He was so quiet and unresponsive that Ban asked him what was wrong. When Kiichiro didn't answer, Ban asked him if he was ill. Kiichiro then opened up and discussed what was on his mind. He began with a brief history of his father.

Sakichi had been enamored of China ever since making his first visit there in October of 1918. The following year, now leaning towards permanently settling in China, he went to Shanghai. Unfortunately it was an unsettled time in China. There were widespread and sometimes violent demonstrations against foreigners, calls for canceling concessions, and movements to bar foreign investment, including that by Japanese businessmen. Despite the turmoil, after much hard work, Sakichi managed to build a China spinning and weaving factory on a sixteen-acre plot and installed his most modern spinning machines and automatic looms. At first, the company was privately owned, but in November of 1921, Sakichi renamed it the Toyoda Spinning and Weaving Works and went public with it. Then he sent for his family, and Kiichiro and his wife, Hatako, accompanied Asako when she moved to Shanghai.

Hatako was pregnant at the time. As she neared the end of her term a few months after they arrived, she and Kiichiro returned to Japan. It was then that Kiichiro embarked on intense study of the automatic loom. Seeing a number of things he thought could be improved, he decided to stay in Nagoya until the job was finished.

As Kiichiro worked on the automatic loom, Sakichi revived his pet project with the circular loom, devoting all of his time to that and the management of the Toyoda Spinning and Weaving Works. From his earliest years, Sakichi had dreamt of perfecting this unique machine. Now with increased enthusiasm, whenever he finished a major component, he would immediately go back to Japan to patent it.

In the spring of 1927, during one of these trips, Sakichi suffered a stroke at his residence in Nagoya. It was a trying time for the whole Toyoda family. To get his father's estate in order, Kiichiro began organizing all of Sakichi's personal effects. While going through the papers in Sakichi's travel bag, Kiichiro found a thick notebook entitled, "Diary of an Inventor," dated in 1926. It was obviously written while Sakichi was in Shanghai.

At first, Kiichiro browsed through the writings, turning pages inattentively. Then he realized that the journal was a complete record of his father's quest as an inventor and he turned back to the first page to begin reading carefully.

Written in a reflective, yet enthusiastic style, the manuscript included negative comments about "commercial" inventors who couldn't see past the bottom line. Virtually every page bore testimony to the suffering inflicted on inventors by cunning, money-hungry businessmen and bankers who scorned inventors while exploiting them.

Sakichi wrote about this passionately, with an honesty and genuineness Japanese literati refer to as a "true stroke of the brush." Everything Kiichiro read made a very lasting impression on him, but one passage in particular moved him more deeply than the rest:

When one aspires to invent something, one must acknowledge that one will have time for little else, including the normal distractions of youth. When young, one is usually self-absorbed and fearless of failure. It is this optimism, however, that can lead to many mistakes, which could have been avoided had more disciplined and open-minded approaches been used. This is why it is necessary to repress the innocent optimism of youth and go against one's own natural inclination and cultivate a serious and brooding nature. This attitude takes time, dedication, and constant practice. One must let the environment mold one's natural talents and aptitudes until through mature deliberation one arrives at a state of serene self-reliance.

Many have written about the difficulty of doing this. Once when ill, I thought my sickness was caused by repression of my own natural instincts. So, for a good year and a half, I stopped thinking. I must say in all candor that I have never had such a joyful time as during that period. To this day, I don't know why that was the case; it was delightful -- as though I had gone to heaven. For the first time, I understood how one's natural abilities relate to enjoyment of life's pleasures. Yet controlling one's natural inclinations breeds a strength only suffering can bring. We who would create must suffer denial of one's natural inclinations -- for pleasure is not our goal. Rather, we must make every effort and willingly endure pain to repress our subjective dreams and open ourselves to the real environment, learning not to look at what lies only on the surface, but to see a thing for what it really is.

Every person is endowed with the ability to create, but unless this creativity is nurtured it withers away. As for those stupid people -- stodgy, unimaginative businessmen -- unless we resolutely compel ourselves to act against our normal disposition, we'll find it difficult to conceal what we're really thinking in connection with our creations. Unless we make the effort to derive our inclinations from the environment, we lose the fundamentals of inventing. When the inventiveness becomes habit, all obstacles will be pushed aside and it becomes the natural order of things.

Kiichiro read this passage several times, and then breathed a deep sigh, looking tenderly in the direction of his father's room. Until now, he had discounted and at times disdainfully belittled his father's achievements and inventions. He had assumed that his rural, uneducated father just happened to be at the right place at the right time and made a few minor improvements in the design of a loom, improvements anyone could have made under the same circumstances. After reading the passage and reflecting on it, he had a complete change of heart. Sakichi hadn't been born taciturn and indifferent to the "good life," he'd thoroughly resisted the easy path and had transformed his very personality in order to be an inventor. Bit by bit, he'd ferreted out each tiny improvement or revelation related to the loom. In the process, he had developed the discipline and mental toughness it takes to be a nonconformist and to realize a personal dream.

It must have been a very lonely path. At the time Sakichi was going through his rite of passage as a youth, in 1885, the winds of Westernization were beginning to blow over Japan. The youth movement for democratization of the country carried with it a strong conformist spirit, a code of conduct that emphasized extroversion and social interaction.

It's not difficult to see why Sakichi's entire path of solitary discipline was in total opposition to the times, as were his goals of fostering a "serious, brooding" nature. But the real test of his resolve was yet to come. Not until he immersed himself in his work on weaving looms did he learn how insensitive society can be. As he became more obsessed with his quest to be an inventor, the villagers in his home town ridiculed him severely, labeling him a lunatic and a fool. Fortunately Sakichi's stoicism was tempered enough to withstand these barbs of cruelty and he remained committed to his vision.

As he read of Sakichi's resolve and at last understood the high price paid by those who would be inventors, Kiichiro made a vow to himself:

I will stop all chitchat!

He had always been taciturn and as a student had no intention of standing out in the crowd; he never raised his hand just to be seen.

Small talk is not only useless -- it's downright harmful, Kiichiro thought to himself. At times when attending high school and college, he would chitchat with school chums. But even then, idle talk made him uneasy. Talking just for the sake of talking seemed a useless indulgence.

Kiichiro had already meditated at length upon his quest to mass-produce quality domestic automobiles. To develop the kind of self-contained, state-of-the-art industry needed to accomplish that mission meant doing what few other Japanese had done before. It dawned on him that were he to engage in social small talk, it could distract him from his goal and even complicate business relationships, which must remain clear and simple if they were not to create mischief in the future. As he saw it, idle conversation could also confuse employees about his role as a manager and lead to false expectations and hurt feelings.

How he arrived at this vow to end all chitchat is what Kiichiro had made the mistake of communicating to Ban once before. *Now it has come to haunt me,* thought Kiichiro. He quickly ended his business with Ban and took his leave.

That evening, Kiichiro headed toward Sendai to visit Shiro Nukiyama, an engineering professor at Tohoku University and an old friend from his high school days.

As Kiichiro campaigned around the country to lay the groundwork for his project, Iwaoka and Shirai grew more and more impatient. They wanted to finish work on the engine Kiichiro had ordered, but daily demands of the spinning business left them no time for working on anything else.

Sensitive to Kiichiro's real purpose, Iwaoka was especially anxious to finish the task and often would quietly approach Shirai and ask, "Hey, why don't you stay and work late tonight?"

Whenever they did work late, they had to be extremely cautious. To be seen by Oshima was okay, he actually knew more about what was going on than they did. But to be seen by others might mean there would be hell to pay, especially if they were caught by Iwataro Okabe assembling engine parts. Okabe was a director and he took his responsibilities seriously.

Whenever he did catch them, Okabe would chew them out royally, saying, "What on earth are you guys doing? You should be doing your job, not playing around with this silly junk."

Iwaoka and Shirai were stuck: they couldn't disclose what they were doing nor could they reveal they were working under the auspices of Kiichiro Toyoda.

At his level of authority, Iwaoka was able to enlist two or three experienced workers at a time to help with the late night work. When he was available, Kiichiro would also pitch in. It was his habit to work late in the drafting room and not uncommon for him to come out and get his arms greasy to the elbows helping the men with the engines.

It took roughly six months to complete the cylinder heads and assemble the engine parts, but at least now in the shop were ten shiny engines, all in a row per Kiichiro's instructions. August had already arrived. The cherry blossoms at Kariya Castle had blossomed and fallen, the long rainy season had ended, and the hot summer sun now was burning the black tiled roof of the factory.

"So, let's see if they'll run," said Iwaoka to Shirai.

Shirai connected the spark plug wires, used a spout to funnel gasoline into the tank, and then spun the flywheel. The engine sputtered a few times, and roared loudly to life, belching black smoke and emitting a thunderous noise disproportionate to its size. It still was a sweet sound to the two engineers.

When all of the engines were tested one by one, some of them performed more poorly than others, a few of them "seizing up" after a short run. Whenever that or anything else happened, the engine would be pulled apart and repaired, until finally all ten were in perfect running order. The total process took one week.

When Shirai asked what was to be done next, Iwaoka said, "Let's put engines on a couple of bicycles."

The engines were indeed installed over a lunch hour and the bikes rolled out into the large courtyard next to the factory. White smoke belched out of the exhausts as the engines began to purr. Iwaoka and Shirai hopped on their bikes and released the lever they'd rigged to lower the engine's flywheel onto the bike's rear wheel. Instantaneous locomotion! The courtyard quickly filled with curious factory workers, who roared with laughter at "the boys on their bicycles."

You don't know it yet, but soon this factory, this very courtyard, will be filled with cars built by us! This is our first automobile! Many factories will be built -- here, and over there -- and tens, hundreds, even thousands of cars will be rolling off the assembly line every single day. Bursting with pride, Iwaoka continued to ride his bike amidst the wild applause and cheering, face covered with dust and perspiration and tears flowing down his cheeks.

Completely in the dark about the broader significance of this "modern voyage," Shirai laughed gleefully as he rode his bike behind Iwaoka's.

On the afternoon of September 1, two weeks later, Iwaoka and Shirai were called in to a quiet corner of the factory to meet with Director Risaburo Oshima.

"Mr. Toyoda will start automobile production. I have just received top-secret orders. I will be in charge and you two will be the first two employees of the Automobile Department," Oshima intoned solemnly.

"I am scheduled to travel to the United States and Europe this month. The official reason for the trip is to oversee the transfer of patent rights to the Platt Brothers and to discuss problems relating to spinning machines and looms. The actual purpose of the trip is to study the automobile business. The order was issued by Mr. Kiichiro Toyoda, and President Risaburo Toyoda is not aware of it," said Oshima in a low voice.

"Your tasks will remain the same. Shirai will concentrate on design and Iwaoka on parts production. If Mr. Toyoda makes the official announcement while I'm gone and we're faced with an emergency, please do all you can to assist Mr. Toyoda. I'm counting on you."

As Iwaoka acknowledged this arrangement, he felt his heart tremble. He could see his own name and those of his compatriots being among the first to go down in the history of Japan's automobile industry. His life was truly in the hands of the automotive gods.

Since this was the first Shirai knew of the automobile project, he simply stood in stunned amazement. As soon as he realized that the "toy engine" he and Iwaoka had spent more than six months constructing was a dress rehearsal for a monumental manufacturing adventure, his legs nearly gave out beneath him.

Oshima then changed the subject: "Mr. Sakichi gave me his instructions before he passed away. When he had returned from his trip overseas on New Year's Day in 1911, he told me how there were nearly one hundred automobile manufacturing companies in the United States and how coach makers and bicycle makers were competing with each other to build automobiles. He talked specifically about Ford, who had built a large factory in Highland Park and was mass-producing the Model T car. He also said that in the United States the automobile is the preferred means of public transportation, and that some day, the same would be true for Japan. Unless we're able to build a respectable automobile domestically, Japan can't boast of being a world-class industrial nation. Mr. Sakichi kept saying over and over how much he wanted to find a way to build an automobile factory."

Oshima fell silent for a moment as he remembered the expression on Sakichi's face when this conversation took place. Oshima had been close to Sakichi from the very beginning, and the respect he held for his employer had become an almost religious reverence. *Now it's up to Sakichi's son,* he thought, and then he continued:

"When the Tokyo Earthquake hit in 1923, I knew Mr. Kiichiro was in Tokyo. Mr. Sakichi was living in Shanghai at the time, so I felt responsible for keeping an eye on Kiichiro for Mr. Sakichi. Afraid something might have happened to him, I immediately went there to look for him. I spent hours searching among the ruins before I finally realized it was a waste of time. I came home in utter despair. My nerves were shot and I was on the verge of tears. Then I heard that Mr. Kiichiro had returned to Nagoya by train, covered with mud, but safe. At that moment, all the energy seemed to drain from my body. When Mr. Sakichi returned from

Shanghai the following year, I told him this story with Mr. Kiichiro present. Mr. Sakichi thanked me, and after thinking it over for awhile, said that in such extreme circumstances, an automobile could be a godsend. Turning to Mr. Kiichiro, he said, 'Kiichiro, why don't we go into the car business?' Mr. Kiichiro smiled and didn't say anything.''

Iwaoka and Shirai listened attentively as Oshima went on.

"In November, 1927, Mr. Sakichi was awarded the Imperial Merit of Honor for his many achievements over the years, and on the fifteenth of that month, he was invited to the Nagoya Palace where he was decorated by the Emperor. On that honorable day, he returned to his home to host a small celebration party. In his speech, he said to Mr. Kiichiro, 'I invented the loom and was able to earn money from it, but I have also worked hard for my country. For that reason, today, I was showered with honors. Yet it's foolish to assume that taking over a father's business should prevent the son from exploring new ventures. Why don't you think of something else to do, Kiichiro? How about automobiles?' Mr. Kiichiro just listened and smiled.

"And another thing...." Oshima said, pausing as he reminisced.

It could not rightly be said he was getting too old, but Oshima cherished the memory of Sakichi so genuinely that it brought his heart to his throat. Young men such as Iwaoka and Shirai could not fully understand this pathos, but they were moved nevertheless. Wide-eyed, they waited for Oshima to complete his thought.

"Although Mr. Sakichi said it," continued Oshima, "I'm sure there are directors in this company that have never heard of such things. So until the official announcement is made, you are unofficially Mr. Kiichiro's personal staff. Difficulties may arise that I won't be here to handle, so please keep this to yourselves. Also, for the time being, please don't even mention it to your families."

"We understand," the two men answered in chorus.

After Oshima left, the pair clasped each other's hands with solemn determination. Iwaoka was twenty-eight years old and Shirai had just turned twenty-one.

Chapter
4

AN INDIVIDUAL CALLING

When Risaburo Oshima left for the United States, summer was nearly over. Business at the Toyoda Automatic Loom Works had been moving at a breakneck pace and there was no let up in sight. The busy plant was an odd contrast to the surrounding farming villages, where life flowed like a meadow stream, calm and uneventful. Most villages in Mikawa, around Kariya and Chiryu, did not even observe the custom of the lively late-summer festival-dances of the *obon* season. In all likelihood, if nature hadn't planted a few reminders, most of the villagers would not have known that autumn was approaching.

One afternoon in early October, for the first time in a long while, Kiichiro called Iwaoka and Shirai into his office. "Would you mind staying after work tonight?" he asked. " We'll start in the evening and work all through the night. First, however, there's something I'd like you to do by way of preparation."

Kiichiro also asked several other trusted employees to stay late to help in the construction of a wooden wall to partition off an area in one corner of the warehouse connected to the machine factory. The area would be constructed to prohibit people outside the automobile team from observing the activities of the group. That would ensure total privacy.

When Kiichiro was ready to move on a project such as the production of an automobile, he had two methods of relaying instructions. In some cases, he would simply state the objectives and turn everything else over to his staff. Typically, he'd come around with a scrap of paper containing a few hastily scrawled instructions and indicate the deadline for completion of the assignment, whether it involved the manufacture of a simple part or a complex machine. If he didn't list the raw materials or parts to be used, he usually wouldn't set a budget for the project or specify the method of construction either. This was his most common way.

Less frequently, Kiichiro would plan a project down to the last detail, particularly when he had a special design in mind. No matter how large or small the objective was, he would specify the dimensions to the exact number of centimeters and even millimeters (dimensions that amount to as little as one-twenty-fifth of an inch). As preparations for the work proceeded, he would then stipulate every tool and material to be used, even indicating where items were to be placed before the work began. Whether it was a hammer or a box of nails, nothing escaped his attention.

Kiichiro's instructions for the present task were of the second type. He specified precisely where the electrical wiring and sockets were to be put in the ceiling, also pointing out the number of lightbulbs and various wattages. Kiichiro's orders to Iwaoka and Shirai were very detailed and lengthy. How various machines were to be mounted and exactly what types of mounts were to be utilized were all covered. The list of instructions was in fact so exhaustive that both men got the strange feeling that work on the automobile was to begin *that very night*.

The primary objective, however, was to build the wooden wall. Iwaoka and Shirai were already one step ahead of Kiichiro. Anticipating the work to come, they very shrewdly enlisted the help of carpenters, two machinists, a pair of metal workers, and two electricians. These composed the "late hours team."

After their regular work, the men went to a restaurant in town and had supper together. When they were sure that both the factory and the office had been vacated, they returned and set to their task. As he pounded nails into the wooden partition, Iwaoka noticed that there was enough room within the special area for about four full-sized passenger cars. Around midnight, when the partition was nearly finished, a wary honk of a car horn sounded at the front entrance. When Iwaoka and Shirai went running out, they found Kiichiro behind the wheel of a car. They opened the front gate, and Kiichiro drove in, got out of the car in front of the warehouse, and walked inside to inspect the walled enclosure.

Iwaoka and Shirai were having a hard time trying to contain their excitement about the car Kiichiro had brought. Sensing their anxiousness, Kiichiro approached them and said, "It's a '33 Chevrolet. We're going to take it apart, so have a good, long look at it now."

The two sprinted out into the courtyard and carefully examined the car inside and out. Kiichiro had included the installation of outdoor lights in his instructions, and when they were turned on, the grounds were brightly lit. Since he had been put in charge of design, Shirai took out a sketch book and began making detailed notes of the vehicle's exterior features and appearance.

As Iwaoka and Shirai were doing that, Kiichiro gave the workmen further instructions for building shelves and tables. All in all, their work was excellent, which hardly came as a surprise to Kiichiro. Kiichiro spent all of his time at the factory and was well-acquainted with each employee. He spoke to everyone, asking questions and giving instructions. When employees told him about some of their own ideas, Kiichiro not only listened to them, but if he thought the idea was good, he acted upon it immediately. That was his way. He never drew attention to himself as "the owner of the factory," and he treated everyone equally, from foremen and engineers to trainees. It is little wonder that all his employees liked and trusted him thoroughly.

It was almost dawn before the arrangements inside the warehouse were completed. The men had constructed the framework of a small, but completely-outfitted pilot factory. Writing and sketching furiously, Iwaoka and Shirai were finishing their annotated sketches of the exterior and interior features of the automobile. As they closed their sketch pads, Kiichiro climbed into the car, drove it into the warehouse and parked it inside the wooden enclosure. Then he signaled for everyone to wrap up whatever they were doing and gather around him.

"Tonight, I have established my Automobile Club," Kiichiro announced. "From now on we'll tinker with this car every night. But keep in mind that this is my hobby. It's not, I emphasize, *not* company work."

The workers looked at each other silently, then all spoke at once:

"Looks like a pretty interesting hobby, doesn't it?"

"I hope they let me be a member of the Club from now on...."

Their oil-smeared faces were smiling as they bantered light-heartedly. Only Kiichiro remained serious:

"The area is pretty well set. The next thing you men will do is take this Chevrolet apart. We'll have fun disassembling it and putting it back together. Remember, this is *recreation* for me. If one doesn't take his recreation on the sly, it's no fun. So we'll enjoy this recreation only at night."

"Sure," "Yes," "Of course," came the responses.

"All of you, including Iwaoka and Shirai, are the only members of my Automobile Club. Because it's just recreation, there won't be official appointments, and you won't get overtime pay from the company. But I'd like you to enjoy yourselves with me as much as you can," Kiichiro told them, assuming, as usual, that everyone present would go along with him.

Looking around at the tired but eager faces, a senior machinist responded, "We understand, Mr. Toyoda. Right everyone? We'll do it. Whether it's work or play, we'll come in every night. It might be a good idea, however, to alternate evenings among ourselves so that we can get a little sleep. Otherwise our work during the day might suffer or we might get injured."

Speaking in what, for him, was a playful manner, Kiichiro replied, "Right. Iwaoka will make out a work schedule. I repeat, this is for fun, so I want you to do your best not to attract the attention of other people in the company. "It's a secret, remember...a secret."

For the first time that evening he spoke with a genuine smile. Reaching into his back pocket, he casually pulled out some money and handed it to the senior machinist.

"Have a nap and then buy everyone some breakfast with this. Thanks for helping."

"It would be rude to take this," answered the machinist. "But then again, it would be rude to turn it down. Thanks."

The machinist flashed the bills around for everyone to see, and then stuffed them into his overalls.

The next night -- which was hardly the next night, in view of the fact that they had worked until daybreak -- the team began taking the Chevrolet apart.

Two master mechanics were part of the unofficial new "Automobile Club." They took a unique interest in the project, and so the work progressed very well. After the body and engine were removed from the chassis, the '33 Chevrolet was disassembled piece by piece. Extreme care was taken to note the position and order of each part. That was where Kiichiro's tables and shelves came into play. All the parts were lined up meticulously in the order in which they had been removed. Now the bare chassis was all that remained. So far they had expended three night's work.

Next the engine was completely dismantled. Because this was a critical and complicated process, Kiichiro told Yoshio Yamamoto to help Shirai take copious notes, and for foreman Jirokichi Chikusa and foreman Sasuke Ikeda to keep good mental records. By now, membership in the "Automobile Club" -- Kiichiro's private army -- had increased to more than ten.

Not long after, Kiichiro called for a blackboard and began lecturing to his "Club" on the structure of the automobile. He taught them the name of each of the parts and carefully explained their interrelated functions. The lectures began with the engine, which had, among other components, a number of complicated cast metal segments connected to the cylinder block. These ran between the cylinder head and the manifold and looked like tentacles of an octopus.

The foundry workers quickly grasped the metaphor and laughed, high-spirited and amused by Kiichiro's witty comparison. "So it's because you want to make something like an octopus that you brought in all that confounded equipment, like the electric furnace and the molding machine, and made us spend hours and hours learning how to use them!"

The interjection brought a round of laughter, even from the electricians, who were only involved peripherally at this point.

Disassembly of the engine complete, there was a lull in the action. Iwaoka, Shirai, and Yamamoto took the opportunity to make precise sketches of all of the parts, while the other members of the private army took a break for several days. Kiichiro went to Osaka.

A "recreational activity" on the scale of Kiichiro's Automobile Club could not go unnoticed forever, and the first crisis arose while he was on that trip. One evening, as Iwaoka and the others were absorbed in sketching parts, the big sliding door of the "hidden fortress" clattered open, and the elderly company director, Iwataro Okabe, stood squarely at the entrance.

"What the devil are you guys doing?" Okabe asked, glaring fiercely at Iwaoka and then, one by one, scrutinizing the others.

"Uh, we're working overtime. Making sketches."

"Sketches!" Okabe thundered. "Sketches of what?"

Okabe stepped inside and began to look around. First he eyed the dismantled parts lined up neatly on the shelves and worktables. Then he turned his gaze to the bare chassis standing in the middle of the room. The engine, body, seats, and steering wheel had been removed, but the frame was intact with wheels still attached. There it sat, clearly betraying the essence of an automobile.

"It's an auto...." Iwaoka said, choking on the word.

"An auto what? An automatic loom? I've never seen a loom shaped like that before," Okabe hissed, striding over to the chassis and staring intently at the stripped down skeleton.

"No, it's an automobile," Iwaoka said. "These are the engine parts and that's the chassis."

"An automobile?" Okabe spit out incredulously, glaring first at Iwaoka and then at each of the others one by one. "What do you intend to do with those sketches? This company doesn't make anything like that. That's a disgusting foreigners' vehicle, and you'll cause trouble bringing it in here on your own and using company equipment and electricity."

"It's Kiichiro Toyoda's project," Iwaoka explained, reasoning that after they had been discovered by a company director, a half-baked cover-up would probably only lead to further complications. Certainly, Kiichiro had not intended to sneak around and work in secret forever. At some point, they clearly would have to make a proper disclosure to company officials or abandon their work altogether. Kiichiro had simply wanted to get things underway before objections could stop the project before it even got started. It was a case of acting first and asking questions later. Given the fact Okabe had caught them red-handed, there was nothing to do but confess.

"Kiichiro's order?" Okabe hesitated a moment and then drew himself up to his full height. "Even if it's Kiichiro, the company has its rules. Sneaking around at night working on these sorts of things without even mentioning it to the directors will cause problems. What if you injured yourselves or started a fire? Until we get to the bottom of this, please stop what you're doing," Okabe said firmly.

"Well, all right," Iwaoka replied, reluctantly turning to the others and adding, "let's wrap it up."

Iwaoka did not know whether Okabe had been tipped off by someone or had simply happened on them by accident. At first, Iwaoka cursed at Okabe's intrusion, but the more he thought about it, the more he realized it might work to their advantage. After all, more could be done in the open than behind closed doors.

The next day, a number of large packages addressed to Iwaoka arrived by freight train from Osaka. They had been sent by an entity calling itself Toyoda Motor Company, and the contents were all parts for a '33 Chevrolet sedan. When Iwaoka and the others brought these to the warehouse, they had to make their way through a crowd of people. Apparently word had gotten around, and office workers and employees on break had come to peer into the warehouse. No more could their workplace be referred to as a "hidden fortress." If he was reprimanded by Okabe upon returning from Osaka, Kiichiro did not show it.

Perhaps, thought Iwaoka, *Okabe did not feel free to openly criticize Kiichiro.*

In any event, Iwaoka felt he should report to Kiichiro at the first opportunity and relate the details. Kiichiro listened, then, without smiling, said simply, "Well, do a good job with that." Iwaoka left without being told a thing.

He's keeping everything bound up inside himself, Iwaoka thought. *Kiichiro will move ahead with dogged determination and push the plan through without consulting with anyone.*

Iwaoka was convinced that because Kiichiro had his mind set, he was sure to succeed. By being rash and creating hard feelings, those who opposed him would fall behind and soon not have a leg to stand on. No doubt Kiichiro intended to let people say whatever they wanted to say and, feigning indifference, would inexorably propel his "recreation" to the status of a "great enterprise." And, in fact, everything proceeded pretty much as Iwaoka conjectured.

One morning in early November, in a corner of the factory, Kiichiro introduced Iwaoka and other members of the Automobile Club to a muscular, sturdily built man:

"This is Kan. He's starting with the company today, and along with Oshima will be in charge of the Automobile Club. But I've only told Risaburo that he's come here as my general technical adviser. As yet I haven't touched on the subject of automobiles, so please keep it that way for now."

In not addressing Risaburo by his official title as "president," Kiichiro wasn't being disrespectful. Between themselves and also in public they were simply Kiichiro and Risaburo. It was the Toyoda family way and applied to all of its members.

Turning to Iwaoka with a big grin and offering his hand, the newcomer said, "Hello, I'm Kan. I'm looking forward to working with you."

The handshake was firm and strong, reinforcing Iwaoka's impression that here stood a solid, responsible man. Kan appeared to be in his mid-forties, perhaps seven or eight years older than Kiichiro. While not very tall, he was powerfully built, with broad shoulders and a muscular chest. His large, thick lips and prominent jaw made Iwaoka feel even further that here was a man of great tenacity and will. He was not handsome, but the clear, sparkling eyes behind the thin, gold-rimmed glasses implied a formidable intelligence.

In a deep, rich voice, Kan added, "You're Iwaoka, right? You were at Kuramae, weren't you?"

"Yes," Iwaoka answered. "The Mechanics Department, class of 1927."

"I thought so," Kan replied. "I was in the same department, class of 1914."

"Oh, you're THAT Kan -- the one who pioneered the Atsuta and the Kiso Coach!" Iwaoka exclaimed, raising his voice in mingled surprise and admiration.

The Atsuta, a passenger car modeled after the deluxe American Nash, was the one built cooperatively by three Nagoya companies -- Okuma Ironworks, Nippon Sharyo, and the Okamoto Bicycle and Auto Manufacturing Plant. The Kiso Coach, Japan's first coach-style, low-floored bus, was designed and was being produced by Toyoda Loom Works. It was said that Toyoda Loom Works had been asked by the Atsuta group to take part in production of the passenger car but had declined, choosing to focus their efforts on the coach. Kan, as head engineer at Toyoda Loom Works, had been in charge of both its design and manufacture.

What a formidable person Kiichiro is to be able to entice the top brain away from an opposition company, Iwaoka thought in amazement.

Although originally founded by Sakichi, Toyoda Loom Works was now completely independent and had no connection with Toyoda Spinning and Weaving and Toyoda Automatic Loom Works. Classic business betrayal led to this state of affairs, constituting a major chapter in the Toyoda history. Around 1902 or 1903, Sakichi had been operating a private company in Nagoya called Toyoda Shokai. He had set up a textile factory in Takedaira-cho, and two or three years later established a loom manufacturing factory in Shimazaki-cho, both of which were successful. During that time, Sakichi's originally all-wood power loom had evolved into a half-wood, half-metal model using the very first automatic shuttle-changing device. Eying the success of Toyoda Shokai, the Mitsui Trading Company approached Sakichi with the suggestion that he expand the firm's working capital by bringing in top Tokyo, Osaka, and Nagoya financiers and incorporating the company. That, Mitsui argued, would permit enlarging the factory and developing additional facilities, thereby accelerating expansion of his growing business.

Sakichi hesitated at first. He'd joined forces with Mitsui once before and failed. In their favor, however, it was Mitsui who had given Sakichi encouragement early in his career and they had promoted the sales of the wooden power loom and later the half-wood, half-metal models. After much soul-searching and vacillation, Sakichi followed Mitsui's recommendations, and Toyoda Loom Works, Inc., was established in December of 1906.

Sakichi turned everything over to the new company -- his own funds, factory, equipment, employees, the loom he had developed, all of the technology, and even his patents. Then came the Russo-Japanese War in 1905 and after it, a severe depression. Sales plummeted and the firm's financial backers laid the blame on Sakichi for what they saw as inept management, citing his preoccupation with invention. Sakichi was driven from his own company, a company he had founded to produce the machine he himself had invented and refined. The ousting of Sakichi was nothing short of criminal. Having put all he had into the company, he was left stripped of everything.

With the prosperity that accompanied World War I, Toyoda Loom Works became enormously profitable, and a long legal battle over Sakichi's patents ensued. Sakichi was extremely embittered. His life's work lay in rubble and he hated the avaricious men who had done that to him. Never again would he trust financiers or banks, an attitude that would govern the philosophy of Toyoda Automatic Loom Works and later, of Toyota Motor Company for decades to come.

When Sakichi got back on his feet, Toyoda Automatic Loom Works came to be seen as the arch enemy of Toyoda Loom Works. Now Kiichiro had pulled a major coup by enticing away its top engineer.

How, Iwaoka asked himself, *did Kiichiro manage to pull that off?*

"I need you to help establish a domestic automobile industry in Japan!" was what Iwaoka imagined Kiichiro saying to Kan. No doubt, Kiichiro had met Kan somewhere and, in his usual straight-forward manner, had gone straight to the point and persuaded Kan to join his team.

Iwaoka was in fact correct. Kiichiro had bluntly outlined for Kan the full dimensions of his daunting enterprise, complete with the terrible risks involved:

"I'm going to make a mass-produced automobile based entirely on Japanese technology. I won't have any outside help and the car will not be subsidized by

Ford or GM. I want to build a Japanese car industry strong enough to drive GM and Ford out of our domestic market. If the family fortune and all of the Toyoda companies created by Sakichi are destroyed in the process, I'll have no regrets. I must have you in our company!''

Though Kiichiro had spoken with great feeling of his ambition, he had also presented a reasonable defense of his ideas. In the end, however, it was the passion of Kiichiro's vision that won Kan over, that and his selfless desire to see Japan free at last of the bondage and influence of foreign investment and manufacturing.

When Iwaoka learned of this exchange, his awe of Kiichiro was increased a thousandfold. He recalled Kiichiro's axiom: ''the right person does not just come asking to be hired; one must go to the right person with the right appeal.''

True, Iwaoka nodded to himself, comforted by Kiichiro's keen insight into business and human nature.

Kan, whose full name was Takatoshi Kan, originally hailed from Kagawa Prefecture on the island of Shikoku. His family had not been well off, so he received government assistance throughout his education at Kagawa Normal School. Next he entered Tokyo Higher School of Engineering in preparation for a college education, continuing under the same government assistance program. Because Kan could not pay his own tuition, when he finally did enroll in the mechanical engineering department of the college at Kurame, he was a ''special status'' student, which meant that he was obliged to serve a term teaching once he received his degree. For all practical purposes, he attended the same classes and received the same education as everyone else.

Being very bright, extremely studious and determined, Kan graduated with the highest grades ever achieved in the special status program. Upon graduating, he taught at a school for Sumitomo employees and then joined Toyoda Loom Works.

On the very first day after accepting Kiichiro's offer and joining his company, Kan put on dark work clothes and came to the small pilot plant in the warehouse. Until then, the private Automobile Club had been just feeling its way along. But now that the operation had acquired an outstanding leader, it took an immediate and positive direction. During his time at Toyoda Loom Works, Kan had single-handedly planned and brought about the construction of the Shinkawa Plant. In the automobile division, he had been in charge of casting engine blocks and other components. With that background, he was naturally much more at home with automotive engineering than were Iwaoka, Shirai, and Yamamoto. In truth, everyone in the new Toyoda *Automobile Department* received a valuable education from him.

The dismantling of the Chevrolet had proceeded as far as the chassis, and the crew already was putting one section back together. At the end of the month, it was taken apart once more, but this time during reassembly newly-purchased parts were used in place of the originals. To locate these parts, Kiichiro and Kan had to spend time away from the Kariya factory.

Kiichiro had taken Kan with him repeatedly to Tokyo and Osaka. After each trip, large parcels were delivered to the Automobile Department, a department that was non-existent in that it had no official recognition within the company.

This created interesting problems. The person most often put in a difficult position by the department's "persona non grata" status was Jiro Iwaoka. Whenever parcels arrived, it was Iwaoka who took the heat. But parcels weren't his only problem. Now that work was proceeding faster than in the early days of the project, more specialized machine tools were needed. Whenever Iwaoka filled out a purchase order and took it to Okabe, Okabe would flatly refuse to approve it, saying, "I don't know anything about this sort of thing." Each time, Okabe would glare fiercely at Iwaoka as if to say, "Our company has nothing to do with automobiles, so I can't give this my approval. If you have so much free time, why don't you spend a little more of it in the factory, where they're really busy? After all, it's the factory and its spinning work that are paying your salaries. If you want to work all night, work all night there."

I suppose the automobile will never register on his gauge, thought Iwaoka, musing that each person has his own unique gauge. Okabe was honest and sincere, but he was an engineer with the old-fashioned temperament of a craftsman and had spent his entire career focused on Sakichi's loom. *His* gauge was obviously attuned to textile machines, which he regarded as sacred, producing as they did one of the basic necessities of life -- clothing. They were as important as food and shelter. *For Okabe,* thought Iwaoka, *the automobile probably stands for little more than a foreign contrivance further paving the way for the vice of luxury among the wealthy Japanese.*

By now, Kiichiro's plan should be evident to everyone, and the staff ought to concede that the Automobile Department actually exists, thought Iwaoka. *Unfortunately, Okabe does not possess a gauge attuned to automobile production, even if it is Kiichiro's project.*

But then, how many people do have the kind of gauge on which Kiichiro's vision would register? When Iwaoka thought about it that way, Okabe's inability to grasp Kiichiro's ambition made him wonder how many others would have an equally narrow outlook and would stubbornly oppose Kiichiro's plans in the future.

At the end of November, Kiichiro and Kan began engaging a hired car and riding out to the suburbs every day. Although the two never mentioned where they went or what they did, when Iwaoka asked the driver, he learned that their destinations included various locations in Kariya City; the nearby suburbs of Otaka and Higashiura; the area along the port of Nagoya; Taketoyo, some distance down the Chita Peninsula; the plain of Ronchigahara in Koromo, within the hills of Nishikamo County; and they even went as far as the area around Kameyama in Mie Prefecture.

"The two of them get out of the car and stand in the empty lot, talking very seriously about something," said the driver.

Ah hah! They're looking for land to build an automobile factory on, thought Iwaoka. *Of course, if they're going to take on the mass production of cars in earnest, the land on which the Toyoda Spinning and Weaving and Automatic Loom Works factories stand is definitely too small.*

For some time now, Kiichiro had stayed away from the corporate offices, going directly to the manufacturing area in the morning and leaving there in the evening, as though hoping not to meet Risaburo any more than necessary. One afternoon toward the end of November, however, Kiichiro was summoned to the President's office. He was in the middle of questioning Iwaoka and Shirai at their proper work stations in the spinning machine area, when a messenger interrupted with the message from Risaburo.

"He called for you to come right away. He's like this," said the young messenger from General Affairs, gesturing with a frown and laying his index fingers across his forehead to imitate veins popping out on Risaburo's forehead. Understanding the situation, he gave Kiichiro a knowing smile.

Without a word, Kiichiro left the machine room with the young man, his slightly angry walk and silent shrug of his shoulders intimating that Risaburo was being an annoyance.

I wonder if a storm's brewing, Iwaoka and Shirai both thought to themselves as they watched Kiichiro walking away.

Given the strain between Kiichiro and Risaburo over the issue of automobile manufacturing, Iwaoka's and Shirai's fear of an impending storm was well warranted.

When Kiichiro entered the President's office, Risaburo was standing stiffly with his arms crossed. Blue veins stood out on his forehead, just as the messenger had gestured.

"What is it? Did you want something," Kiichiro mumbled in a low, indifferent voice. Without asking if he could sit, he simply sat down on the sofa.

"Yes. It has come to my attention that you submitted a requisition for the purchase of four hundred to eight hundred acres of land in Koromo. Is that true?"

"Not exactly," Kiichiro responded calmly. "I simply asked if the company would approve the purchase of the land if I decide to buy it."

"What do you intend to do with that land?" Risaburo demanded.

Lighting a cigarette, Kiichiro remained silent as he exhaled the smoke.

"Are you going to buy it with the company's money or your own? Are you thinking of building a big second house?" Risaburo asked insistently.

Again, Kiichiro did not reply. "Or do you want to build a factory? If that's the case, shouldn't you get my consent as President?"

"To the President...," Kiichiro mumbled, so softly Risaburo couldn't hear what he said. Then, looking Risaburo directly in the eyes, he said, "If and when I've settled on a specific plan, I'll talk with you about it. It's not my nature to indulge in vague chitchat before I've done my homework."

"If you say you haven't decided on a plan, then you haven't decided. But that doesn't mean you don't want to do something, does it? So what do you want? I'm not saying I won't discuss it with you," Risaburo said in a conciliatory voice.

Kiichiro did not reply. Silently, he thought about an incident a year earlier involving the manufacture of spinning machines.

It's just like that all over again. It simply doesn't do any good to discuss something with him, thought Kiichiro to himself.

The incident Kiichiro was thinking of occurred at a time when the sales of spinning machines had dropped and business was poor. To break out of the slump,

Kiichiro had suggested again and again that they embark on the manufacture of a new-style spinning machine he had been developing. There was every indication there would be a large market for the new machine, but Risaburo refused to listen, insisting, "This company was established to manufacture the automatic loom Sakichi invented. If we branch out into anything else, we'll dishonor him. I absolutely won't allow it."

The mention of Sakichi was obviously meant to be an emotional argument, but the real reason for Risaburo's objection was his fear of taking risks. Kiichiro persuaded Risaburo Oshima and Rizo Suzuki to help him and went ahead with the project anyway. When it proved successful and yielded the company high profits, Risaburo didn't have the strength of character to even acknowledge the venture.

The bitterness Kiichiro had felt at the time still lay heavy on his heart. *That's what discussing something with Risaburo gets you,* he thought.

"I'm still waiting for an answer," Risaburo said hotly.

"I said I don't indulge in chitchat, didn't I," Kiichiro replied curtly.

"You call this chitchat," Risaburo fumed, the blue veins on his forehead throbbing. "This isn't chitchat. The President is officially asking the managing director what it is that he wants to do. Make up your mind and tell me."

In a rare use of the word "Dad," Kiichiro replied, "Dad said there's no point in two brothers doing the same thing and a child shouldn't just imitate his father. Dad always said that one should do something new."

Kiichiro seldom brought up his father on his own accord, but even on those rare occasions when he did talk about him, he always called him "Sakichi." That may have stemmed from his objectivity as an engineer, but if so, it was reinforced by the fact that from early childhood he had hated his father and intentionally ignored him. But on this occasion Kiichiro repeated the word "Dad," and the effect was not lost on his brother-in-law.

"I know that," Risaburo responded. "So tell me what you want to do."

With just the hint of a sparkle in his eyes, Kiichiro said, "What I'd most like to do is make airplanes, I guess. I have a general idea for a new plan for an autogiro, too. Among the smaller things I've been toying around with and have just about finished a design for is a new sewing machine."

Startled, Risaburo asked, "So are you saying you want to make airplanes at Koromo?"

Trying not to laugh out loud, Kiichiro answered, "I can't build an airplane, at least not now. And it looks like the autogiro is also out of the question at this point."

A sly smile tinged the corners of Risaburo's mouth and the blue veins calmed down, as if to say he recognized the absurdity of Kiichiro's comments. "Well, then, it is the automobile after all. I've heard that recently you brought a car into the factory and have been taking it apart and putting it back together. So you do intend to make cars, don't you?"

"Didn't I say I haven't decided anything. But if it is a car, wasn't it you who once said at the old house in Washizu that you didn't mind if I got involved with automobiles, whether for pleasure or research?" Kiichiro asked innocently.

"That was, that was...." Risaburo was choking on his words. Yes, he'd said that on the day Sakichi's ashes were interred more than two years before. But he'd seized upon it as a convenient response to Kiichiro's feelings as he attempted to make his brother-in-law abandon the notion of manufacturing automobiles. The phrase, "for pleasure or research," had been nothing more to Risaburo than a figure of speech.

Having turned the tables on Risaburo, Kiichiro pressed his advantage. "The land at Koromo is really cheap. Besides, it's certain that in the future the automobile age will come to Japan and high speed highways will crisscross the country from one end to the other. And when they do, no matter how you look at it, roads located anywhere near Nagoya are bound to go through that area. It'll be useful land. Even if we build some type of factory on it in the future, it'll be beneficial all around. That area is deserted and unsuitable for cultivating rice or most other staples. Just like Dad always said, if we can get by without using agricultural land for industry, it's good for the country. If we buy it up and do nothing more than grow potatoes, it'll pay for itself and the farmers will be happy. So when I come to you and say the deal has been finalized, please approve the payment for it."

With that, Kiichiro stood up and quietly left.

Sandbagged by his own words and disarmed by Kiichiro's keen persuasion, Risaburo had been unable to come up with any suitable counterarguments. Kiichiro's two references to Sakichi as "Dad" -- who was like a god in this company -- also had Risaburo stumped. All he could do was stand there in amazement, watching Kiichiro disappear.

Risaburo had called Kiichiro in with the intention of putting an end to his foolish notion about building automobiles, but as it turned out he gained nothing from the confrontation. Kiichiro, on the other hand, had gained a great deal. First, he'd gotten Risaburo to recognize the existence of the Automobile Department, which meant that it would now be all right for him to build any number of experimental cars in the name of "research." Then he had won for himself the right to "consult" with Risaburo on major decisions, not "ask" for his permission to do it. As for the hundreds of acres of land at Koromo, they were as good as bought.

After Kiichiro left, Risaburo must have buried his head in his hands and lamented his misfortune in having such a formidable brother-in-law.

In addition to gaining recognition of the Automobile Department's existence, Kiichiro inferred he'd also won Risaburo's approval for the construction of a pilot production plant. With that resolved to his satisfaction, he moved the very same day to put his inference into action. When returning to the planning room from the President's office, Kiichiro immediately called in Takatoshi Kan and ordered him to start right away on the design for the new plant. Next, he called in Jiro Iwaoka and ordered him to determine what machine tools would be necessary and to place orders for them.

Kiichiro's original idea was to construct a fairly large-scale pilot plant with a machine shop and a sheet metal assembly line, each with an area of four thousand square yards. A third structure of eight hundred square yards would house a materials laboratory, and a two-thousand-square-yard area would serve as a warehouse -- hardly the sort of thing one could classify as a private "recreational" Automobile Department.

However absurd this plan might look to others, without the slightest hesitation, Kan immediately set about planning the facility. Iwaoka, too, was beginning to see what an enormous undertaking lay ahead. Tipped off by the machine tool orders he was in charge of, Iwaoka was filled with admiration for Kiichiro and Kan, these fearless men who dared to think big.

Kan threw all of his considerable energies into the project, burying himself in detailed drawings and floor plans. He was taking obvious pleasure in supervising the design of the new facility: "This materials laboratory represents a plan thought up by Dr. Ryonosuke Yamada, a close friend of Mr. Toyoda and a professor at their old school, the Tokyo University of Engineering. It features a mechanical properties lab, a physical properties measurement room, a microscopic lab, a chemical analysis room, a paints lab, plus a combustible materials lab and an electro-metallurgy room. It's outfitted with every kind of specialized equipment and is more sophisticated than many materials labs in mediocre universities and research centers. Both the assembly plant and the machine shop will have complete assembly line systems with conveyer belts. It's going to be wonderful."

Kan worked quickly. He was physically sturdy and, despite his age, didn't appear to be bothered by working all night for two or three nights straight. By the end of December, his calculations were nearly finished. Soon Iwaoka could be told to begin ordering the machine tools.

Kiichiro seemed to be enjoying the fact that he had acquired this faithful steed named Kan, and Kan also seemed delighted at his good fortune in being put through his paces by this rough, taciturn but talented horseman named Kiichiro, who allowed him to gallop about to his heart's content. The two were perfectly matched. Kiichiro had grand ideas and an inexplicable talent for developing them by sheer tenacity and will. And Kan had the technological expertise to translate Kiichiro's ideas into action, though he could not match Kiichiro's vision and outright flashes of genius. Above all, Kan was methodical, honest, and unsparing of himself, endowed with a robust constitution that was the fountainhead of his apparently endless stamina. In the race to develop a domestic automobile, he proved himself valuable countless times over.

Thus the two men paced and kept pace with each other. Kiichiro would check Kan's layouts as soon as they were finished and make a decision about them. If they met his approval, he would then determine the types of machines needed and where to install them, at which point, he would turn an itemized list over to Iwaoka for ordering. Iwaoka would check the items against his catalogues and choose the best supplier. To minimize lead times and to give himself back-up, he first tried to find a domestic supplier. But he often found that Japanese machine tool companies either did not make the items needed or had fallen far behind modern technology.

When Iwaoka encountered this situation, he'd ask Kiichiro, "I want to order some things from abroad. Is that okay?" But Kiichiro usually instructed him to "wait a little while on the foreign orders. Just let them accumulate." Apparently Kiichiro had something in mind that he was not disclosing.

As Kiichiro's automobile manufacturing plan progressed, the rest of the world was also moving ahead. In the automobile industry, the graceful, flowing lines of the Pierce Silver Arrow attracted great attention at the Chicago World's Fair held in May of that year, presaging the end of the square, carriage-like shape that had until then characterized the automobile. In the international arena, Hitler's Germany, like Japan before it, withdrew from the League of Nations on October 14, 1933, and subsequently withdrew from the International Disarmament Conference. Then on November 16, as if trying to throw a curve into world politics, the United States and the Soviet Union abandoned the hostile stance they had long maintained against each other and formally renewed diplomatic relations.

With 1933 drawing to a close, a long distance telephone call came for Kiichiro from Tokyo on the afternoon of December 26. The call lasted a long time, but for the most part Kiichiro just listened, occasionally responding with "Uh-huh," and "Hmm." His face, however, clearly reflected tension and excitement, and one could see he was making an effort not to miss a single word.

The call from Kaoru Ban at the Ministry of Commerce and Industry conveyed the urgent information. Earlier that day Nissan's Yoshisuke Ayukawa had established a company named Jidosha Seizo, a move that indicated Nissan was going forward with full-scale mass production of automobiles. Ban wanted to warn Kiichiro that the domestic automobile industry would sooner or later seek a strong government protection policy and that unless he was prepared to move quickly, he might miss the boat.

After hanging up the phone, Kiichiro went to Risaburo's office and requested that a meeting of the board of directors be held before the end of the year.

"For what -- what's the urgent business?" asked Risaburo.

Grimacing slightly, Kiichiro replied, "Well, I don't know if we have any business or not. If I don't have any business, I'll fill in by presenting next year's plans, or something."

"I'm not going to schedule a meeting on such vague grounds," Risaburo said emphatically, the irritation clearly evident in his tone.

"It won't be vague on that day. Please schedule the meeting," Kiichiro responded in a steely voice, a fierce expression on his face and his feet planted wide apart.

As he entered his forties, Kiichiro had grown heavier and had gradually come to resemble Sakichi. Having never seen Kiichiro assume such an imperious posture before, Risaburo was startled by the feeling that he was being addressed by Sakichi himself. It was such a strange departure from Kiichiro's normal demeanor that it nearly startled Kiichiro himself.

"What a problem you are," Risaburo muttered under his breath. With a frown of consternation, he grudgingly agreed to call for a meeting on December 30.

"Thanks," Kiichiro said with an innocent smile.

Kiichiro left straight for Tokyo, returning just as the board of directors was to meet in the President's office at 2:00 P.M. On this particular day, the term "board of directors" was something of a humorous overstatement. Normally the directors of Toyoda Automatic Loom Works consisted of Rizo Suzuki, Risaburo Oshima, Iwataro Okabe, Sakichi's younger brother Sasuke, who was President of Toyoda Spinning and Weaving, and Murata and Nishikawa. The last three served as the company's auditors. As director at Toyoda Spinning in Shanghai, Nishikawa could not very well attend on such short notice, and the auditors normally were not present at board meetings anyway. Because Oshima was abroad on business, "the board" presently consisted of four people -- Risaburo, Kiichiro, Suzuki, and Okabe.

According to holdover feudal customs, Suzuki and Okabe could not lift their heads in front of their masters, the Toyoda brothers. So this particular board of directors meeting was, for all intents and purposes, a discussion between Risaburo and Kiichiro.

One could not have guessed from this meeting that the Toyoda companies were considered to be very progressive by Nagoya standards. In most other "family" companies, the board of directors were all relatives of the President. No matter how many contributions an employee had made to the success of the company, he almost never became a director. This was particularly true of companies managed by second and third generation members. Having founded the company himself, Sakichi was in a position to make a different imprint. It was his belief that family relationships were no sign of ability or achievement and therefore instituted a promotion system based on accomplishment, not blood ties. This philosophy generally carried over to all of his companies.

When all four of today's directors were present, Risaburo announced the start of the meeting and said, "Today, Kiichiro has something to say." Nodding to Suzuki to begin taking the minutes, Risaburo turned to his brother-in-law and said, "Kiichiro, stand up and make your speech."

"I'm fine this way," Kiichiro replied.

With a lift of his chin, Risaburo signaled Kiichiro to stand up.

Kiichiro forced a smile, stood up and announced, "Today I want to discuss with you the establishment of a new Automobile Department in our company."

When he said this in his usual low voice, a tense look flitted across the faces of Risaburo and Okabe. In contrast, Suzuki kept his head down and wrote furiously, showing no expression as Kiichiro continued his presentation.

"It goes without saying that this company was built on looms. But a company is a living thing. It shouldn't always stick to one product. May I remind you that Sakichi felt the same way. Products must progress with the times. Looking at the current state of affairs, our company, for the term ending in September, had actual sales of 846,000 yen for looms and 1,176,000 yen for spinning machines -- a total of 2,022,000 yen. Even if we subtract the cost of raw materials and other expenses, we still have recorded a net profit of over 100,000 yen for the first time in our history."

Today a 100,000-yen net profit would be nothing to brag about. But in the early 1930s, it represented a significant accomplishment. By conservative estimates, if the value of the yen is assumed to have increased about three thousandfold since that time, 100,000 yen for a half year's profit translates into an annual profit of 600 million yen today. By more liberal estimates, assuming the yen has increased five-thousandfold, 100,000 yen translates into a whopping one billion yen in today's money market. For the early years of the Showa period that began in the latter part of the 1920s, with Japan mired in the depths of depression and saddled with an economy so small it couldn't begin to compare with today's, to record that kind of profit put Toyoda Spinning and Weaving and Toyoda Automatic Loom Works into a special class of "high profit companies."

"Since I'm not an accountant and have no knowledge of that end of the business, I have to confirm these figures with Risaburo. My guess is that I've been conservative in my profit estimates. At any rate, I think the business is going along extremely well. Yet we must never get secure in our success and forget the necessity for change.

"Even though this company at first only produced looms, from 1930 on, loom sales have dropped by half. Now we're sustained by our newer product, the spinning machine. Moreover, when we look at overseas exports, at one point they exceeded 600,000 yen for half a year. Unfortunately, the international situation has steadily worsened since the Manchurian Incident and in the first half of this fiscal year, we posted a disappointing export total of barely 18,000 yen."

Risaburo had been listening somewhat inattentively to this point. As the subject turned to profit, however, his ears quickly perked up. He found himself nodding in total agreement with Kiichiro. Yes, these figures were indeed correct.

"Now we must carefully assess the current mainstay of our business -- spinning machines meant for domestic use. According to the experts, the domestic market will saturate at around ten million spindles. Already this year we've surpassed the 8.6 million spindle mark. It should be clear to us that we are nearing our limit in sales. That is why I think the time is right to develop a new product. We are a machine manufacturing company, not a cosmetics or clothing company. And so I'm asking you to consider the automobile. If nothing else, we can revise our articles of incorporation to make research and trial manufacture of automobiles a possibility."

Then Kiichiro sat down. For a while, silence hung heavy in the air. The first to speak was Risaburo:

"But, Kiichiro, isn't there some other work that's more suitable? I know that we have to develop a new product, but a lot of companies have gone under trying to break into the automobile industry. Isn't it too great a challenge and hopelessly dangerous?"

"Yes," replied Kiichiro. "It's a great challenge, but no, it's not hopeless. You probably read in the newspaper that on the twenty-sixth, Nissan's Yoshisuke Ayukawa founded Jidosha Seizo, capitalized at ten million yen. He's going to build a large plant in Yokohama and start American-style mass production. So, if we're going to do it, we can't afford to wait."

"But..."

Risaburo started to say something, but Kiichiro ignored the interruption and went on speaking. "Even supposing Ayukawa doesn't do it, and no one else does either, I would want to do it all the same. If it's work that anybody can do, it doesn't appeal to me. This is so difficult that no one else will try their hand at it, which leaves me resolved to do it no matter what. Father...."

Upon saying "Father," Kiichiro grimaced. "I really don't like saying Father, because when I was young, I felt contempt for him. Looms were simple machines that anyone could have made. Had any university mechanics class seriously applied itself to the project, it could easily have created the sort of things that Sakichi struggled so hard to invent. Yes, he lacked a formal education, but that did not soften my derision for his accomplishments, despite the obvious glory our country accorded him."

Okabe stiffened, with dissatisfaction written all over his face. Clearly he felt Kiichiro was speaking rashly and offensively.

"But recently I've come to see my mistake. Perhaps the academics could have done it if they had tried. But they didn't do it and Sakichi did. And he did it while putting his life on the line and suffering from a pathetic lack of fundamental knowledge and research funds. After all, he began in total poverty."

Kiichiro's words betrayed a rare agitation: "I remember very well the time Sakichi built the factory in Yoneda-cho, around 1911 or 1912. He had no money. Even when an important customer would come in from Osaka, Sakichi would serve him cheap noodles for lunch. When we were better off, Sakichi would send me to buy inexpensive box lunches from Nagoya Station. Yet Sakichi never gave up on his inventions, even after he had been driven out of Toyoda Loom Works and went abroad out of desperation. The new factory and our house were built with loans he managed to scrape together. This was his last stronghold.

"Shortly after we moved to Yoneda-cho, there was a terrible typhoon. Had the factory collapsed in that typhoon, Sakichi would have been done for. I remember very well what happened then. Mom ran around putting up supports, and I was holding Aiko, who was trembling with fear. Right next to us, Father had his arms around a pillar with his face pressed against it. Though I thought at the time he was praying for our safety, he later told me that he had been thinking about something completely different. He had been wondering how a strong wind would act on wooden products and had pressed his ear to the pillar to hear its vibrations. I hated Father in those days, yet I was impressed by his inventor's spirit.

"I've gotten way off the subject, but not without good reason. Sakichi's courage and spirit have something to say to all of us about the development of automobiles. At present, the United States and Europe are going great guns making cars. Wherever you look in the industrialized western world, cars are being made by human hands. Mitsui and Mitsubishi say we can't do it in Japan, but that's only because they're conservative aristocrats whose power lies in their money. And that's their shortcoming: they won't do anything risky. If someone does take the risk and succeeds, people will say anyone could have done it, just as I said that anyone could have invented what Sakichi invented. What I'm saying is this: it's not a matter of whether or not it can be done, but of who will do it. You understand that, don't you?"

He paused. For the usually reticent Kiichiro, it had been a rare speech.

"But is there sufficient demand?" Risaburo asked, his resolute stance against building cars apparently softened by Kiichiro's words. The expression on his face as he asked the question was serious.

"There's nothing to worry about on that score. Last year in the United States, Ford manufactured 342,000 cars and General Motors produced 500,000. The total number of automobiles produced in the U.S. per year is 2,332,000, and that figure is growing daily. Even England and the countries of Europe are making automobiles. As long as there is a demand, someone will manufacture them. Looking at it conservatively, even Japan ought to be able to make and sell 10 percent of the U.S. production, or around 200,000 units."

"Ten percent of the U.S. output?" asked Okabe in amazement.

"You needn't worry," Kiichiro replied. "Our naval production is 53 percent of theirs. Japan has 60 percent of the number of warships the U.S. has. So 10 percent or thereabouts in automobiles is..."

Seeing Okabe frown, Kiichiro paused.

"But," Okabe muttered darkly, "do we have the money, the funds to devote to such risky business? It must take a tremendous amount of money."

"Is it so risky?" Kiichiro asked, beaming uncharacteristically as he answered Okabe in the Nagoya dialect.

"This is only for your ears," he continued, "but soon the government will provide assistance. I went to Tokyo for that reason. I can't give you any names, but I met with important military leaders and high officials in the Ministry of Commerce and Industry.

"I don't like asking people for help, but in this case it can't be avoided. Because a businessman like Ayukawa, who has the latest information, has already started, if we don't hurry, we'll lose out. In any event, we'll decide to proceed only with research at this point. If the research goes well, we can make up our minds later."

After mulling it over briefly, Risaburo stood up and announced his decision. "The purpose of today's meeting was to officially add research and trial manufacture of automobiles to our articles of incorporation and to increase our working capital for that purpose. Assuming you have approved the motion, I'll propose the idea to a general meeting of the stockholders."

Turning to Kiichiro, he asked, "How much of an increase in capital will we need?"

Speaking now in his more accustomed diffident manner, Kiichiro calmly replied, "About two million yen at first."

Risaburo gulped. The total capital of the automatic loom division was only one million yen, and Kiichiro was asking for double that in a voice he might use to order a cup of *sake*.

"Will that be enough?" Risaburo asked, obviously thinking hard. He already saw that this enterprise would turn into an extraordinarily large investment.

Kiichiro did not reply. He simply smiled and nodded slightly. It was obvious the amount of money would not be sufficient, but Risaburo's blood pressure had begun to go down and Kiichiro didn't want to send it soaring again.

"When will you start the Automobile Department?" asked Suzuki, looking up from the minutes he was taking and opening his mouth for the first time.

"September 1," Kiichiro promptly responded.

"What?" asked a befuddled Suzuki. "September of next year?"

"No, this year. Our start has to be earlier than that of Ayukawa's company," Kiichiro said sternly. "Actually my Automobile Department was unofficially started on September 1, with a directive from Oshima to the department members. With your approval, we'll make that day the official start of Toyoda automobiles. This will be an important point later on, so please don't fail to record it that way."

"I understand," Suzuki replied.

With everything now settled, the meeting of the board was adjourned.

Kiichiro shifted into high gear from then on.

First he sent a telegram to Risaburo Oshima in England, informing him that automobile manufacturing had been formally approved. He was to leave off his talks with Platt Brothers and go immediately to Germany, where he was to buy certain machines and send them to Japan. Included was the long list of machines to be ordered from abroad that Iwaoka had been keeping.

Before long, a reply came from Oshima. His telegram began, "AUTO MANUFACTURE SURPRISE LIKE BOLT FROM BLUE." He was obviously playing dumb out of deference to Risaburo and the others. Kiichiro smiled wryly, thinking Oshima was quite a performer. The message continued, "WILL DO MY BEST TO CARRY OUT INSTRUCTIONS."

Next on Kiichiro's list was Takatoshi Kan. Kan had finished the plans for the pilot plant and was finally ready to start construction. That was turned over to Iwaoka, and Kan was assigned the task of drawing up a parts timetable, making use of his experience on the Atsuta and the Kiso Coach.

Kan's knowledge of automobile manufacturing technology, however, was limited to the largely manual industry of Japan at that time. It was not adequate for an understanding of the mass production methods Kiichiro was aiming for. To re-educate Kan and prepare him for construction of the factory, as well as for layout and automobile manufacturing methods of the future, Kiichiro decided to send him to the United States, the home of the mass production system.

On January 18, 1934, Kiichiro and a group from the department bid Kan *Bon Voyage* as he set sail for San Francisco from Yokohama on the *Asanma Maru*.

Chapter
5

THE FIRST PROTOTYPE

On January 29, 1934, ten days after Kan left on his trip to the United States, the shareholders' meeting of Toyoda Automatic Loom Works was held. On the agenda were Kiichiro's proposals to expand the firm's working capital and to revise one section of the articles of incorporation. Capitalization would be increased from one million to three million yen, and two clauses would be added to the articles under corporate objectives: "purchase and sale of manufactured motors as well as automatic transport machines; and steel manufacturing and other metal refining businesses."

Risaburo had already done the legwork to obtain support, so the measures were approved without any obstacles.

With formal preparation out of the way, the time had finally come to start production of the first prototype. Kiichiro marked the occasion with a brief presentation to the engineers and workers of the Automobile Department, now expanded well beyond his original team of volunteers:

"Within this year, we will complete work on the first prototype. Please work together and give us your best effort."

As it was already the end of January, there were only eleven months left. Eleven months to complete an automobile for which not a single part had yet been manufactured! It would be fair to say that Kiichiro's timetable hovered between optimism and downright foolhardiness.

The factory itself was still an empty plot of ground. The floor plan hadn't even been finished. Iwaoka was to use whatever blueprints Kan had completed to date so that construction could move forward. But building the plant would take time. Next, many more machine tools were needed beyond the handful already acquired for research. The plan had been to send Kan to the United States to catch up with Oshima, who was already there. The two were to research, select, and purchase the necessary machine tools and then ship them to Kariya. The only problem was that no one, including Kan and Oshima, had any idea of the various types and quantities of parts required to build a car. More importantly, they had no steel to build the car and the workers had no technical training or experience whatsoever in making automobile parts, let alone building a complete car.

If any of the growing Automobile Department team was daunted by the immensity of the task ahead, they didn't show it. Everyone in each of the respective areas hit the ground running. There were false starts, mistakes, disappointments, and regressions, and they sometimes got in each other's way as they bulldozed ahead in fits and starts, a frantic tangle of buzzing, chaotic activity. But somehow they moved on.

That frenzied transition from "non-existence" to full-blown operation resembled nothing so much as the state of confusion and chaos created by a giant earthquake. Perhaps the only thing keeping the entire project from being buried in the rubble was the fact that everyone had an assigned task.

In preparing parts designs, Shirai and Yamamoto were to work closely with Iwaoka, who was now deeply immersed in laying out the factory layout. In some respects, their labor turned out to be less of a learning experience than it could, and likely should, have been. As various parts were assigned by Kiichiro, Shirai and Yamamoto drew entirely upon Ford and Chevrolet parts as their models. They were engaging in copying exercises at the expense of a critical understanding of the physical and structural principles involved.

Kiichiro would carefully check the design of each part. If it passed muster, he handed over the blueprint to Iwao Tatematsu, whose job was to actually procure the part. The guidelines Kiichiro gave Tatematsu were direct and straightforward: "Find an existing domestically-made part, if possible. If you can't find one already in production somewhere, then we'll try to have a domestic parts maker create it for us from scratch."

That was consistent with Kiichiro's goal of developing a completely domestic industry, and he was determined to move in that direction from the very beginning.

When Tatematsu received Kiichiro's instructions, he thought, "This is a piece of cake." But the situation quickly proved otherwise, and Tatematsu returned to Kiichiro with an unhappy report: "What do you mean by 'existing domestic parts makers!' There aren't any. Or if there are, they're impossible to find!"

Kiichiro simply responded, "You must look for them."

"I will try to find them. But what Mr. Shirai has said boggles the mind. One cannot look for just one part. An automobile component consists of many parts…thousands of parts…minute parts. If we're talking about parts the size of a rivet, then we're dealing with a scale of tens of thousands. It's impossible to find everything."

"No," Kiichiro answered firmly, "you must look further. If we don't find every last one of them, then we can't build an automobile. It's as simple as that."

Tatematsu started his search in Nagoya, then went to Osaka, Kobe, and Tokyo, stopping at every shop or outfit that billed itself as a job shop or parts manufacturer and buying whatever they had that matched the parts on his shopping list.

No one knew better than Kiichiro how difficult the parts search would be, but he kept his concerns to himself so as not to turn the others' discouragement into despair. His stomach, however, was in constant knots over parts: *At this stage, we shouldn't be buying these things in such large quantities. We should first thoroughly research what's available, determine what we can make or have made, and then gather and test all the samples. And we need to decide on the type of automobile to build, then move ahead with the design. Unless these decisions are made, it will be impossible to purchase parts in large quantities. Maybe we're putting the cart before the horse by first searching for parts. Yet if we don't do it this way, we'll never meet our production deadline. It's probably a moot point anyway. What will likely happen is that we'll end up being forced to use Ford and Chevrolet parts.*

Kiichiro spent much of his time shuttling back and forth from Nagoya to Tokyo and Sendai. In Tokyo, he relied on Kumabe as his consultant, anxious to complete all of the prototype specifications. For the parts search, he not only relied on Tatematsu, but also sought advice from Kazuo Kawasanada. In addition to being a friend, Kawasanada was an authority on automotive parts who often took Kiichiro on tours of machine and job shops and parts factories. Kiichiro depended heavily on Professor Honda of Tohoku University for advice on how to proceed most efficiently. At first, playing the devil's advocate, Professor Honda argued that the only way the project could succeed was to build a steel mill. First of all, no domestic steel maker would be willing to invest in manufacturing the very specialized types of steel needed for automobiles. And secondly, whatever steel Japan was currently producing was being snatched up by the military for production of warships and armaments, or it was used for civilian purposes in building railroads and shipyards. For the time being at least, steel for automobiles had to come out of whatever was left over from shipbuilding. No, to be on the safe side, advised Professor Honda, Kiichiro had better include a steel mill in his plan.

Because Kiichiro's reasoning was very different from Professor Honda's, the notion of having to build a steel mill came as a shock. By his way of thinking, only limited amounts of steel would be needed in this early prototype-production phase. After all, they weren't planning on moving into full-scale manufacturing right away. Monthly quotas were anticipated to run about two units and even at full production they likely wouldn't exceed a thousand units. Was a steel mill needed for this? Apparently Professor Honda's advice was very persuasive, because Kiichiro's plan for an automobile factory now included a steel mill.

To build this mill, Kiichiro recruited Benzo Fukada, former chief engineer for Daido Steel, and an expert in steel-making. The facility would be equipped with a four-ton and a two-ton electric furnace, a small rolling mill, eight stamping machines, and for research, 300-, 150-, and 35-kilowatt Ajax electric furnaces.

The next item on Kiichiro's agenda was machine tools. Risaburo Oshima had just arrived in London from the United States when he received Kiichiro's telegram concerning start-up of automobile manufacturing. Oshima immediately left for Germany.

Unlike Suzuki Okabe, Oshima had graduated from technical school and spoke and read English. Following Kiichiro's directions, he concentrated on metal-cutting and metal-forming machine tools, but soon discovered that German-made boring and honing machines used to bore out and finish the engine block cylinders were especially well-suited for the type of testing Kiichiro had in mind. So Oshima bought several and shipped them off to Japan. Upon returning to London, Oshima found a message waiting. He was to go to the United States, where he would team up with Kan. Oshima departed at once and arrived in New York considerably ahead of Kan. Kan's ship had been delayed by bad weather and Kan himself had suffered a bout of sea-sickness. He arrived in San Francisco via Honolulu on January 31 and then took the train cross-country, arriving in New York on the afternoon of February 6. He had sent a telegram ahead, and Oshima was there to meet him at the station.

Kan kept a detailed record of events during his trip to the United States, filling a notebook with page after page of neat, intricate script. At various places, he made rough sketches of machinery and kept lengthy records of the day's happenings. The opening paragraph of this journal reveals the complexity of Kan's and Oshima's task:

> *The objectives of this trip are, first of all, to study the various aspects of manufacturing methods needed for automotive production. Second, to research the various kinds of machine tools required for automobile manufacturing. Third, to look into materials. And fourth, to study the sales and service networks. There are a great many other things to be studied. Lumping them all together under the phrase, 'the objectives are to study manufacturing methods,' would not present an accurate picture of the complexity of the task at hand. In other words, we must study every detail of how to heat, cast, machine, brake-press and otherwise shape and form metal; how to mount glass, produce seats, dashboards, and other interior fittings; how to assemble, align, and paint and chrome-plate the components; and how to monitor the process for efficiency and for quality. Given the state of technological development in our country, to fully grasp the fundamentals of these methods would call for an immense amount of effort and study -- and a lot more time than we have at our disposal. As it is we can only observe and make notes on the operations we see right in front of us. Unfortunately, we have no time to learn the basics; we have, in fact, only a few months to get the job done. Moreover, the evaluation and purchase of machine tools and equipment needed to at least get the start-up stage off the ground is a high priority of the trip, putting yet another demand upon our already severely constrained time. Because of the great time pressure, we have to tightly focus our efforts on areas where we'll find the greatest concentrations of advanced technology, so we've decided to travel around the United States. For all of these reasons, we frequently have to skip meals and are so absorbed in our work throughout the entire trip that weekends are forgotten.*

Elsewhere in the journal it is apparent that Kan and Oshima traveled from dawn to dusk throughout New England, visiting two or three factories a day in cities and towns whose names were totally unknown to most Japanese. On Sundays, when factories were closed, they'd either spend their time studying methods, technical manuals, spec sheets, and catalogues, or visiting automobile shows whenever possible. There obviously was little time to sleep.

Another theme that emerges from this journal is the ambivalence shared by Kan and Oshima over the selection of machine tools and other equipment. If their criteria were efficiency and productivity, they'd be shipping nothing but dedicated or "special-purpose" machines back to Japan. These were eminently appropriate for mass production, but Kan and Oshima could not easily proceed in that direction. Part of the problem was that no one knew what the automobile's final design would be nor what level of production would be chosen.

Since "general-purpose" machine tools, such as basic milling machines, engine and turret lathes, shapers and planers, and drilling and boring tools, are highly adaptable, they can be used in the manufacture of many different designs. Dedicated equipment, on the other hand, can be applied to only one specific design, which allows more readily for mass production and lower unit costs, but does not allow for future modification of the design.

Oshima summed up the quandary they were in: "We are just starting in this business and very likely we'll be forced to change our plans every year. If we go with dedicated, special-purpose machines, we end up being forced to throw some or all of them away every time our designs have to be changed. In that case, we'll never be able to earn a profit."

Following this line of reasoning, Kan and Oshima concentrated on the more versatile and adjustable general-purpose machine tools and accessories, and reluctantly passed up the special purpose machines with their high-productivity, low-cost potential. Among the general-purpose machine tools they purchased were a press for stamping out auto bodies, as well as a six-axis cylinder boring machine and some deep-hole honing machines that together would eventually produce the six-cylinder engine used in Toyota automobiles.

In some instances, Kan and Oshima had no choice but to go with a specialized piece of equipment, such as the Gleason Gear Works gear-cutting machine, used for making the type of gear used in rear-axle drive automobiles. Whenever this happened, they reasoned that "the necessity of the part" and the high level of productivity afforded by the particular machine would allow it to pay for itself before becoming obsolete. These were always difficult decisions, but Kan and Oshima would never make a purchase unless they were in total agreement. When a purchase was made, delivery was firmly set for no later than the end of March, and that meant off the ship and in Kariya.

After working with Kan for ten days, Oshima left New York on February 16. He drove cross country in a slick new Chrysler DeSoto "Airflow" to catch his ship home from San Francisco. The "Airflow" was both an education and an exhilaration for him. Traveling at speeds up to eighty miles per hour, Oshima learned what driving in America was all about. And he learned something about current trends in American design. Introduced only a short time before his trek across the United States, the sleek, shapely DeSoto "Airflow" represented a dramatic departure from the prevailing earlier blunt-nosed, box-like models. Ironically, though Oshima didn't know it at the time, the first Toyoda Automobile, the Model Al, would later be patterned after the very car that he was driving.

Everything considered, Kan's and Oshima's sojourn in America was a key step forward for the Automobile Department. Machines they had ordered were already arriving in Kariya, where the automobile plant was nearing completion. Iwaoka made sure they were installed and conformed with the layouts Kan had prepared before leaving. This kept him so busy that he got very little sleep.

By the time the various machines had been specially positioned and mounted in the factory, Kumabe and Kiichiro had made several more coups in enrolling topnotch engineers for the project. Kiichiro had learned, for example, that one of his high school and university classmates, Seigo Ito, was in charge of production of Japan Air Brake Company's three-wheeled motor vehicle and had persuaded him to come and work at Kariya. About the same time, he had persuaded Higuma Ikenaga to join his operation. Ikenaga was another former university classmate and the man who had designed the small passenger car for Hakuyosha -- the famous Automo-Go. After Hakuyosha collapsed, Ikenaga learned that Tokyo Gas and Electric was working on a special automobile design and had gone to work for that firm before joining the Toyoda team.

With Kumabe at the administrative helm, the new automobile operation began implementing the basic plan of attack outlined by Kiichiro, Oshima, Kan, Ikenaga and Ito:

(1) We will utilize the strengths of both automobiles (Ford and Chevrolet) by mass producing a new Japanese automobile for the public that will rival imports in price and performance.
(2) Production methods will be patterned after the mass-production methods used in the United States but will not be direct imitations; rather, we will utilize research and creativity to come up with production methods best suited for Japan.
(3) The potential weak link in an industrial operation is its internal manufacturing. Whether a company can stay in business or not is primarily determined by its efficiency and productivity. For that reason, specialized steels and machine tools must eventually be manufactured in-house.

Based on these guidelines, the features and design characteristics of the first prototype, the "Model A1 Passenger Automobile," were determined in May, just about the time of Oshima's return. They read as follows:

(1) Parts relating to the body, frame, and engine should be such that genuine Chevrolet parts can be readily used.
(2) Parts relating to the chassis, steering mechanism, and drive-train of the automobile should be such that genuine Ford parts can readily be used.
(3) The 1934 DeSoto "Airflow" sedan will serve as the model for the body style.

For now, the prototype would be a blend of Chevrolet and Ford components and DeSoto styling. All critical parts were to be built as exact, interchangeable imitations. Gradually, as technology would allow, more and more domestically-produced components would be phased in, and eventually dependency upon foreign parts would be done away with completely.

Kiichiro's rationale for eschewing the Ford and Chevrolet body styles in favor of the DeSoto "Airflow" was shrewd and pragmatic. He first took into account the fact that doors, hood, trunk, fenders, and body panels could be less exact without hurting appearance or hampering assembly. Also, they could be easily and inexpensively modified at any time to update the car's appearance without affecting performance. Gears and other high precision parts, however, were less forgiving. If not manufactured to precise tolerances, they would inevitably fail and thus jeopardize the entire effort.

The body style Kiichiro had in mind derived from the DeSoto "Airflow." This choice was very progressive for the time, as many American manufacturers continued to use the square design carried over from the horse-and-carriage days. The first real departure from this square design came in the form of the aerodynamic 1933 Pierce Silver Arrow. At first, the sleek, rounded look of the Pierce Silver Arrow caused mixed reactions. But the car's high performance and speed quickly brought it into favor among the elite American automobile devotees and planted the seeds of a new styling trend. The DeSoto "Airflow" incorporated the jaunty lines of the Silver Arrow and helped to reinforce this trend. By borrowing the DeSoto's styling concepts, the Toyoda A1 prototype positioned itself at the forefront of "the new look." The only feature adapted from the old "horse-and-carriage" appearance was the step-like running boards under the doors.

Though Kiichiro and Oshima were excited about the new design, they didn't neglect the fundamentals. As Kiichiro said, "The heart of the automobile is its engine. So first, let's build that."

In May, the automobile group purchased a 1934 Chevrolet sedan. Using its engine as their model, they were able to start trial castings for the cylinder block, cylinder head, and pistons by June. Both staff and engineers at Toyoda Automatic Loom Works were confident of their expertise in casting quality metal parts. After all, they'd casted thousands of metal components for looms and spinning machines, and felt that producing engine parts would present no real great challenge. It was a sore lesson to learn that automobile engine parts are in a league very different from loom parts.

In a typical foundry operation, molten iron is tapped from the furnace into a ladle, hoisted up by a crane, and then poured into a mold made out of sand. Various materials must be inserted into the sand to create the shape the cast part will take on when the molten metal is poured. These ingredients must then vaporize as the hot metal enters, thus permitting the metal to take their place and acquire the intended shape.

All of these steps were properly followed by the Toyoda foundry engineers. The molds seemed sound. Metals were tested meticulously for content and poured at the correct temperature. Yet one after the other, the castings failed. After an entire day's production, perhaps only one casting was salvageable. And even this would be of such poor quality it wouldn't be useable and eventually would have to be scrapped.

"It's all right to fail in the beginning," Kiichiro reassured his struggling staff, adding, "but it's no good if we can't find ways of improving. To be able to market our product, we need to maintain about a 95 percent success rate. To date, we have more than a 95 percent rate of failure. Where are the defects?"

No one had an answer, and even Kiichiro was dumbfounded when the only response he could get from his foundry engineer was, "Well," followed by a frustrated shake of the head.

Although Kiichiro stressed the necessity of a 95 percent success, even Ford was able to achieve only a 90 percent rate in casting cylinder blocks for its Model T. This provided little solace in light of the present failure rate for Kiichiro's group, but it did underscore the difficulty of making metal casts for automobile engines.

The problem seemed to be with the materials and method used for making the core. Because the mold was so complex, there was not sufficient time for the core to set before it broke apart and crumbled. Even Kahei Seko, the expert on core making at the Toyoda Automatic Loom Works, could not prevent this from happening.

One reason for the difficulty lay in the fact that the cylinder block, the largest component of a car engine, presented a three-dimensional shape that had no approximate counterpart in castings made for looms. Its hollow, highly irregular structure contained a large number of different-sized holes. Since the A1 engine had six cylinders, six holes had to be bored and honed to accept the pistons. Other holes and passageways constituted air and gas intakes and exhausts, making the final product a foundry engineer's nightmare.

Once the problem was ascribed to the core, the foundry experimented with solutions. For instance, flecks of gold were added to the core's basic component of sand in an attempt to increase the core's strength. Next the core was dried to a specific temperature and painted with a clay-like mixture consisting of charcoal and graphite. Other methods known at the time were applied, but nothing seemed to work. The task was proving a thankless one indeed, but in all fairness to Kiichiro's team, it must be pointed out that technology at the time had simply not removed all of the mysteries of casting complex cylinder blocks and heads. Finally, it was decided to elicit the expertise of Kazuo Ohara, another of the foundry's talented engineers.

With Kiichiro and staff immersed in the mysteries of core casting, the month of June flew by and the long rainy season came and went. On July 20, a hot summer day, Kan returned from America and was met by Kiichiro at the port of Yokohama. On July 22, the two of them boarded the return train to Nagoya. The entire trip was an extended progress report, as Kiichiro attempted to bring Kan up-to-speed. Problems with casting the cylinder block were a major topic of conversation, and Kiichiro ended by saying: "We're not getting anywhere with it. Please discuss it with Oshima, put your heads together and figure out how they are doing it in America."

"Hmm..." Kan mused, "let's first try the oil core method being used by Ford."

Without taking a rest after his long trip, Kan arrived at the factory early the next morning and started to work with Ohara. Their goal was to experiment with the oil core approach. According to this approach, the core mold for the hollow interior of the engine utilized natural silverdust mixed with linseed oil, soybean oil, and China wood oil. The theory was that the resiliency of these materials allowed the core mold to better hold its shape as it was moved around and fitted into the casting mold.

"That seems like a good idea. Let's try casting it right away," Kazuo Ohara said cheerfully. Collecting the new ingredients, Ohara started the casting process. Kan joined Ohara to watch the test pour, as did Kiichiro, whose concern was growing daily.

"Okay...since this is the first time, I don't know what to expect. Be careful and please stay back," instructed Ohara.

After making sure Kiichiro and the others were standing far enough away, Ohara poured the molten iron into the casting mold. Immediately it popped and sprayed up to the ceiling.

"Watch out!" Ohara screamed, as white-hot metal droplets showered the factory floor, lighting up the factory like a fireworks display.

Kiichiro observed the cascading molten metal and, without flinching or showing any sign of an expression, told Ohara, "This must be related to the distribution of the oil. If Ford is also using this, then in principle, there shouldn't be any problems. You should earnestly experiment with this." He turned and hurried back to the drafting room.

Ohara had a formidable task ahead of him. Most of his time was spent experimenting with different proportions of oil. But day after day, molten iron sprayed up to the ceiling every time it was poured into the cast.

The hot foundry job dragged on through the dog days of July and August, and the workers were forever drenched with sweat. Determined to solve the mystery, Ohara worked day in and day out, from dawn until nine or ten at night.

Kan, too, devoted all of his time to the foundry, so much so that the salt from his perspiration permeated his clothes and dried, turning the color of his black uniform white. The female workers who prepared the cores in the upstairs section of the foundry were as anxious as Ohara and Kan to see progress. Every time a new batch of molds was lowered by the elevator, they would go to the stairway and peer down when the casting was poured. On good days they'd gleefully tell Ohara, "Today, the molten iron poured in quietly," and on bad days, they'd glumly report, "Today, it spouted ... maybe something is wrong again with the core."

On one such day in August, upon returning from a trip to Tokyo, Kiichiro sent instructions to have Risaburo Oshima meet with him at a hotel in the resort town of Karuizawa. As soon as he saw Oshima, Kiichiro said, "Conditions in China are changing rapidly, so I'm thinking of also building trucks."

"What do you mean by conditions in China?" Oshima asked in a startled tone.

"Ever since the Manchurian Incident, relations with England and the United States have been gradually deteriorating. Many trucks will be needed to transport troops and supplies for the war in China, but at this rate, we can't depend upon imports of American trucks. The demand for domestically-made vehicles will increase.''

"I see," Oshima mumbled, as Kiichiro continued: "At Mr. Yoshisuke Ayukawa's Nihon Sangyo, the plan is to change the name of the automobile subsidiary to Nissan Motor Company on June 1 and manufacturing will begin for Datsun trucks. If we're also going to do it, we can't be sitting still.''

" And?" Oshima asked.

"I want to make myself clear," Kiichiro said, " I do not plan to give up on passenger cars. Until the bitter end, my goal is to mass-produce an automobile for the public. Although I've had only a little experience, I've discovered how difficult it is to make a passenger car. When it comes, for example, to producing just the body, Japan has none of the required technology whatsoever.''

"That's right," nodded Oshima. The troubles the group was having with designing and constructing the body, patterned after the 1934 DeSoto, was an all too familiar subject.

Discouragement was beginning to show in the faces of the others, but Kiichiro remained steadfast in his commitment, as a diary entry for July of 1937 indicates:

Because it is difficult, we must do it. Since nobody else is willing to do it, I have decided to do it. I might be called a fool for doing this, but unless there is such a fool, nothing new will come about in the world. Therein lies the curiosity of mankind and the result of my lifetime efforts. If I fail, it won't be due to my lack of effort; therefore I'm going to bet my life on it.

Kiichiro characteristically thought and acted as though every obstacle was simply another challenge. But that didn't change the fact that his people faced a slough of difficulties. Development of the car's body was proving a beast of a problem that no one had anticipated. Because Japan's underdeveloped domestic automobile industry could not support heavy investments for high-speed forming presses used by United States producers, Japanese automobile manufacturers were forced to rely primarily upon "hand-built" methods. This situation would have to change in order for Kiichiro's group to gear up for mass production. For the time being, however, they would use manual construction to supplement limited use of the forming presses they had acquired.

When the forming presses proved too "general purpose" for Kiichiro's needs, and given the total lack of experience with them among his engineers, Kiichiro sought the help of Kawasanda. Kawasanada introduced Kiichiro to engineers at the factory of Sugiyama Steel Works in Tokyo, where Kiichiro witnessed firsthand how forming presses were used to produce fenders. Kiichiro was so impressed that he contracted with the factory for production of the body panels he needed. Manufacture of the specialized dies used by the presses was begun at once. Considering the United States had an entire mechanized industry devoted to tool and die production, making the dies by hand was yet another poignant reminder of how far Japan had to go to become competitive.

Even the technology involved with producing metal alloys for the dies was primitive. The alloys had to be hard and resilient enough to withstand the high stress of the manufacturing process. Kiichiro asked the venerable Professor Tokushichi Mishima of Tokyo University to research this aspect for him.

In regards to Professor Mishima's research, Kiichiro remarked to Oshima one day: "It is progressing in such a fashion that technology flows, so to speak, from the branch to the trunk and vice versa. Viewed that way, it seems as though we are condemned to play an endless game of catch-up."

"But," he continued, "unless we do it, we won't be able to build a car. The Sugiyama factory is manually constructing forming press dies to produce the body parts for our Model A1, but this will take about a year and a half to complete. Meanwhile, they are also building the body of the A1 prototype by hand. We can't just sit around and not build a body, and yet automobiles cannot be mass-produced 'by hand.' "

It was during the same conversation that Kiichiro introduced to Oshima the notion of building trucks: "If we build trucks, we can gain some time. We've gotten the engine casting process into shape, and I've decided to use this time to start this other venture.

"We'll continue building the automobile by hand, and we'll use the car engine we're now building as the engine for the truck. The truck body should be much easier to build than the car body. Your job will be to design and build that truck."

"I see. And?" Oshima said quizzically.

"It must have a payload some four to eight times greater compared to a passenger car," continued Kiichiro. "You also must take the poor roads of Japan into consideration. Design-wise, you must pay close attention to how fast the wheels turn and other matters that relate to the axles."

"Yes, I understand," Oshima nodded.

"Remember, we don't have a lot of time," said Kiichiro. "Based on our progress on the engine, I see it taking about six months to complete the first truck prototype."

"Six months!" exclaimed Oshima, taken aback, yet already making mental calculations.

Starting with the basics, Oshima thought to himself, *if everything has to be designed from scratch, there is no way a prototype can be completed that soon. But if we utilize Chevrolet and Ford designs and parts wherever possible, we can minimize the amount of time required. Still it will be close to impossible. With a little luck we might just pull it off, but to be on the safe side....*

"I'm not so sure about six months, but if you can give us three additional months, then somehow...."

"All right," Kiichiro replied, "I'm counting on you."

Kiichiro opened his notebook and started working on his drawings again. Oshima knew this was a signal that the conversation had ended. He took his leave and headed back to Nagoya, where he called in his two assistants and told them about the new assignment. For the next few weeks, the trio shut themselves up in the drafting room and worked on "Model G1" -- the new truck design.

By September, Ohara and his engineers started making real progress in casting the cylinder blocks. The amount and distribution of the oil in the sand and binder used for the core had been stabilized, and fiery iron particles no longer spewed out when the molten metal was poured into the mold.

"I think we'll be okay from now on," Ohara said to his assistants. Their clothing was saturated and their faces black with the oil they mixed with the sand day after day.

Somehow a "respectable" casting began to emerge.

"Put it on the boring mill," Ohara exulted. "There shouldn't be any further problems."

Unfortunately, when the casting had been mounted and boring of the cylinders was begun, it was evident that all of the problems hadn't been solved. The casting was flawed with "nests" or "blow holes" -- cavities where there should have been solid metal. These nests were caused by the premature cooling and hardening of the molten iron thus allowing gases emitted from the core to create unwanted hollow pockets. While the cause was easily apparent, the remedy was not.

With Kan heading the group, Ohara and his assistants spent days trying to eliminate the "nesting" problem. Many solutions were proposed and tested, each one failing as miserably as the last. Then it was decided the rim of the core should be made thicker, an idea which turned out to be the correct answer to the problem. It was by such fits and starts that usable castings for the cylinder blocks, heads, and pistons were produced, until the day finally arrived when the engine of the first prototype automobile could be assembled.

It was already September 25. Kiichiro and the entire staff stood anxiously by as gasoline was poured in, the throttle set, and the engine cranked over. To everyone's amazement, there was a sputter as eyes widened, and then a loud roar as the engine began to run.

"It's running! Look, it's running!" screamed the factory workers. Some began shouting, "Banzai! Banzai!" -- the cry traditionally uttered to celebrate a triumph or to signal the beginning of a new era.

Kiichiro and the engineers knew it was too early to yell "Banzai." The engine was running, but a big question remained as to its power and efficiency. To test this, the team removed and replaced the original engine in the Chevrolet with the engine they'd spent months building. The results were very disappointing. The Toyoda engine developed a meager thirty horsepower, only half of what the Chevrolet engine generated while running at the same RPM's. So much for all of their effort and painstaking care.

Kan, Oshima, and Iwaoka were visibly shaken up. Ohara and his workers, who had toiled so hard amidst the dirt and oil, were heartbroken. The only one apparently not discouraged was Kiichiro, whose expression remained calm and dispassionate.

"Okay. We'll replace each part with a Chevrolet part, one by one, and test the engine after each change. That way we can immediately see which ones are at fault," he said as he walked over to the engine and started to take it apart, getting his hands dirty and oil-splattered in the process.

One by one the parts were replaced with Chevrolet parts, the engine reassembled and placed back into the automobile, and horsepower measured. One by one the Chevrolet parts were then replaced with the originals, the engine reassembled and the entire process gone through again. By patiently doing this over and over, the engineers could determine from the change in horsepower which part was defective. There was only one hitch. The assumption was that the power loss was caused by only one faulty part, when in fact a number of faulty parts working in conjunction could be the cause.

Day after day the tedious task dragged on until everyone was thoroughly sick of it. No one wanted to look at another engine part, yet they felt relatively certain this process of elimination was moving them closer to their answer. By sheer undaunted perseverance, the crew finally pinpointed the intake manifold as the source of the problem.

"So this was it," Kiichiro said. "Break it apart quickly and check out what's inside."

The long struggle had greatly expanded everyone's understanding of the inner workings of the combustion engine.

Internal combustion engines have a pair of manifolds: the intake manifold -- to conduct gas and air mixed in the carburetor to the cylinder where it's ignited; and the exhaust manifold -- to conduct the by-products of combustion out through the exhaust system. As this was a six-cylinder engine, it had twelve passageways, two each connected to one of the cylinders. For the engine to run smoothly and develop full power, each passageway had to bring an equal amount of gas to the cylinder. When the engineers checked the interior of the intake manifold, they discovered "flashes," or pieces of metal that intruded into, and were partially blocking, some of the passageways, thereby "starving" the engine of fuel. The extent of such "flashes" depends on the quality of the core, so while it's possible to file or chisel them off, the real answer is to improve the core.

With more attention paid to the intake manifold portion of the cores, the engine now produced forty-five to fifty horsepower. For everyone else the improvement was considerable, but Kiichiro wanted more:

"There is still something wrong here. Although it has been improved greatly, it's still lower than the Chevrolet."

Testing continued and other defective parts were improved. Yet the prototype engine failed to match the output of the Chevrolet engine. Perhaps the problem was bigger than just the engine. As it turned out, this was indeed the case.

The parts of an automobile most directly responsible for power and efficiency are, in order of importance, the engine, the transmission and drive shaft, and the differential gears, which translate power from the engine through the drive shaft, to the rear wheels. At any one of these junctures, a power loss can occur.

Because it had been decided from the outset that, with the exception of the engine, all elements of the drive train would be patterned after Ford parts, it was assumed that quality would never be a question. Kumabe had pointed out to Kiichiro during their early discussions that Ford gears were solidly built. It was now becoming apparent, however, that the design of the Ford gears was so idiosyncratic that duplication was nearly impossible. When Iwaoka repeated this to Kiichiro, Kiichiro had a quick come back:

"How about the Chevrolet?"

"Comparatively speaking, I don't think Chevrolets have any specific peculiarities, and its parts are easier to utilize," Iwaoka answered.

"Okay then, let's make do by using the Chevrolet. After we complete the first prototype, then we'll deal with the finer points," Kiichiro said. As usual, his solution was pragmatic and efficient. Kiichiro wasn't in the habit of fogging "the big picture" for the sake of a few details, a trait greatly admired by Iwaoka.

Iwaoka lost no time substituting Chevrolet gears for Ford gears, but found the problem still wasn't fixed. He consulted again with Kiichiro, explaining that the Chevrolet gears were a puzzling anomaly. They didn't conform to any known configuration for the number and size of the gear teeth and were very different from the "standard beveled gear."

"That's an important point," Kiichiro said, closing his eyes as he thought. The only solution was to go back to the drawing board. "Unless we come to a thorough understanding of gears before we move forward, we'll continue to make costly mistakes and only lose time in the long-run. No, we must stop now to study gear technology. Please let me handle this one, and wait for my instructions before proceeding further."

Kiichiro took out a pencil stub and wrote a letter to Professor Shiro Nukiyama, his friend at Tohoku University. As soon as he received a reply from Nukiyama, Kiichiro called Iwaoka into his office.

"Mr. Nukiyama asked Mr. Naruse to help us. As you know, Mr. Naruse is still an assistant professor, but he's the foremost expert in Japan on gears and is admired in engineering circles around the world. I want you to go and study with him."

Though Iwaoka could not really be spared at this point, Kiichiro still sent him off to Tohoku University to study for forty days. The decision to make short-run sacrifices for making long-term gains demonstrated Kiichiro's sharp instinct and sureness about his priorities.

Iwaoka took the Chevrolet differential gear with him and left for Sendai in early November. Naruse was ready and waiting. After examining the gear, he told Iwaoka, "You won't be able to understand this by applying normal bevel-gear theory."

Naruse took Iwaoka into a classroom and had him sit down for his first class in gear technology. Going to the blackboard, Naruse drew some figures and then launched into a lecture. He was extremely thorough and patient, asking Iwaoka at every turn whether he was understanding what was being said. Not a point was to be missed.

Naruse's considerateness toward Iwaoka stemmed from his own great admiration for Kiichiro. A month or two before Iwaoka's visit, Kiichiro had come to Sendai to call on Nukiyama. At the time, Nukiyama had said:

"I have a student here named Masao Naruse. He's from Chiba Prefecture. Because of family circumstances, he had to study under adverse conditions, and therefore received his education later than normal for his age group. Consequently, he's still an assistant professor, but his ability surpasses that of many full professors. He is researching gears and has already become well-known in his field all over the world. I'm sure you'll need to talk to him someday, so I'll introduce you to him."

Nukiyama then asked his assistant to find Naruse and ask him to come to his office.

"No, wait a minute," Kiichiro said, motioning for the assistant to remain seated. "Don't call him in. I'll go and introduce myself to him."

While it was customary for the younger man to introduce himself to the older, Kiichiro felt that under the circumstances it was only fitting to introduce himself to Naruse. After all, it was he, Kiichiro, who was the student in this case. He asked Nukiyama to accompany him, and the two walked into a slightly unkempt laboratory to visit Naruse. Naruse was truly astonished. Not only was he being visited by a friend of his professor, whom he greatly respected, but a much senior man known throughout the world for having perfected the Toyoda Automatic Loom. This man had gone out of his way to come to his laboratory to meet him in a display of truly rare courtesy.

At the time, Naruse was also lecturing at Yonezawa Technical School. When he had first come to Yonezawa, he had researched the administration records of the famous intellectual, Yozan Uesugi. Uesugi was known for having spent his life in search of a solution to the poverty caused by clan government, and had invited Hirasu Hosoi from Edo to teach him about government affairs. Until that time, Hosoi was known only as an expert on urban affairs.

This person is like Yozan Uesugi. It's only natural that with someone like this at the helm, Toyoda Automatic Loom Works is bound to be held in high esteem everywhere, Naruse thought to himself, promising to someday repay Kiichiro for his gesture of respect. His present long tutorial with Iwaoka stemmed from that promise.

Iwaoka completed his forty-day crash course in the science of gears and returned to Kariya around December 10. When Iwaoka made his report, Kiichiro was greatly relieved to find that he'd made the right decision and that Iwaoka was now equipped to understand the hypoid gear design. Kiichiro said, "I'm really glad we didn't go ahead and risk further time-consuming mistakes."

Kiichiro's profound respect for Naruse's brilliance culminated in an invitation to lecture at the factory for one week, beginning on January 6, 1935. Already enamored of Kiichiro's strength of character and visionary genius, Naruse accepted without reservation.

It was the beginning of a rare mutual admiration between two inventor\engineers. On the way to the Kariya factory, Naruse prayed for Kiichiro's success. On the morning of New Year's Day, after leaving Sendai, he made a stop at his birthplace in Chiba Prefecture where he stayed for four days. He took a room at an inn and performed his ablutions in the sea every day.

It was Naruse's belief that exposing one's skin to the cold winter air and soaking the body in the cold seawater cleansed the spirit and the mind. As he performed his ritual, he contemplated Kiichiro's quest.

In the Ford factory in Detroit, a car is produced each minute. It is said that there is no way that Japan can compete with this, but I wonder if that's really the case? No, I don't think so. One should not be deceived by quantity. The key to all of this is to have each part be correct and have the technology to assemble them; this requires superior technical skill, but it also means mastering the fundamentals, such as establishing the most efficient production system. Once these fundamentals are in place, quantity will take care of itself. We could better Ford's production rate by a factor or two, producing a car every thirty seconds, or even by a factor of three, where one car comes off the line every ten seconds. There is no reason to believe we can't beat what they do in America! All we need are good solid fundamentals and adequate technical skill.

Then Naruse went to Kariya. As soon as he arrived, Kiichiro gave Naruse a personal tour of the automobile factory. They stopped at the surface grinder, a machine tool for planing metal to very fine tolerances. One of its features involved the use of a special cutting oil to reduce distortion caused by high heat during the grinding process. Realizing that this was the most high-tech machine in the plant, Naruse asked the operator, "How precise is it?"

"It's not as precise as we expected. We're having problems with it," the operator replied.

Standing next to Naruse, Kiichiro suddenly took off his jacket, rolled up his shirt sleeves and without saying a word, stuck his arms into the cutting oil. He mixed the oil two or three times with his arms, then scooped up a handful of slimy material and threw it onto the ground, exclaiming, "Are you saying that you can grind with precision in this?"

The technician turned pale and, with his cheek twitching, lowered his head. Kiichiro was silent. He wiped the oil from his arms with a handkerchief and went on to the next area.

The slimy substance Kiichiro had "taken a bath in" was sludge that built up from pollution of the oil by particles left behind by the grinding process. No wonder the surface grinder lacked precision. Nothing more needed to be said. The machine tool operator definitely got the point.

"That's the caliber of technicians we have here," grumbled Kiichiro to Naruse, as they walked to the next station. "It's a serious problem. What is very bothersome to me is that these men always want to stay *indoors,* and not get their hands dirty. They like to remain in the comfort of the technicians' office, a room away from the factory floor. I always tell them to stand in the middle of the factory, even if they don't have anything to do."

Naruse found it odd that Kiichiro should feel this way, for his impression was that the technicians of this factory were very close to their work. He did, however, experience firsthand one of Kiichiro's great strengths. Now that Kiichiro had rolled up his sleeves and stuck his hands into the oil, the other young technicians had no choice but to follow his example. For many reasons, Naruse could deeply appreciate this "nothing-is-beneath-me" quality in Kiichiro. Naruse himself had been born into a samurai family, which lost status in the aftermath of the Meiji Restoration. He, too, experienced poverty in childhood. Without an education, his father had worked at a very low income as an elementary school substitute teacher. There were nine children in the family, Naruse being the oldest. Faced with such hardship, Naruse took care of all household matters from the time that he was a student in elementary school, thus allowing his mother to work at home to supplement the family income. He also did everything from gathering firewood to pickling the vegetables. He even paid his own way through middle school by growing wheat and other produce.

After graduating from middle school, he taught for awhile as a substitute teacher. Then he entered Sendai Technical School, and continued to support his own education by working as an assistant kendo teacher in a local school. By the time he enrolled in the engineering department of Tohoku University in Sendai, his years of common labor had taught him the value of getting his hands dirty. It was the same quality and philosophy he saw in Kiichiro.

Kiichiro must have inherited this from Mr. Sakichi, thought Naruse to himself. *The beliefs of the father are being filtered through the son, which is why Kiichiro will succeed, even in a business as foreboding as automobile manufacturing. Kiichiro's cars will surpass American-made cars, and there will be a day when he'll be exporting them to America.* This enthusiasm for Kiichiro and his project made Naruse's week-long lecture an enjoyable one indeed.

From Naruse many of Kiichiro's engineers acquired a basic understanding of gears. It was also learned that more equipment was necessary for further progress to be made, especially a particular milling machine cutter called a hob. At the time, hobs were being used in Japan to machine the gear teeth for warships and tanks, but one small enough to make automobile gears didn't exist anywhere in the country. Not to be daunted by such a small obstacle, Kiichiro simply ordered his crew to use a Chevrolet gear for the time being. They would worry about acquiring or building their own hob later. Though everyone was satisfied with Kiichiro's decision, it didn't go without notice that the make-shift solution was yet another reminder of the great disadvantages the project was working under.

Technical obstacles were not the only ones faced by the Automobile Department. As it became clearer that completion of the prototype was a long way off, critics of the project had a field day. Kiichiro was assailed from all directions, both inside and outside the company. Anxiety over the drain on the corporation's finances was mounting, and money was the hot topic of the day.

It was generally known that, before passing on, Sakichi had expressed a desire that the one million yen patent royalty payment from Platt Brothers was to be used as seed money for Kiichiro's research. That fund had been exhausted long ago. First, machine tools were tremendously expensive, as were the travel budgets eaten up in the process of acquiring them. The average piece of equipment carried a price tag of anywhere from 50,000 to 60,000 yen, and there were not just ten or twenty of them. In addition, the Kariya Automatic Loom Works compound was buzzing with new facilities like the automobile pilot plant and steel mill, all of which ran up high labor, energy, and maintenance costs. With the gradual but steady increase in personnel at the Automobile Department, the number of people it directly employed now rivaled that of the Automatic Loom division. And employees of the Automobile Department worked regularly until nine or ten o'clock at night, which meant there was overtime to pay. By now most of the original increased capitalization of two million yen had also already been spent.

The money situation caused a great deal of internal strife, as employees of the Loom Works began to grumble:

"....Those guys at the Automobile Department haven't earned a cent, yet they're paid more than we are!"

"....We're working to keep them fed, yet they're wearing real leather shoes!"

Frustration and resentment glowed fiercely in the loom workers' eyes for another reason as well. As the Loom Works became more mechanized and modern, production steadily rose and the common wage scale was lowered proportionately. Paid on a per piece basis, workers were actually making more per day as a result of increased output, but they were making less per piece. Of course, this was seen as a grave injustice and blame was placed on the financial drain of the Automobile Department.

"Whenever one building of the factory goes up, our salary goes down 10 percent."

"No, it's more like 20 percent."

"At this rate, our company will be eaten alive by the Automobile Department and we'll all be unemployed!"

The Automobile Department began to feel like an island surrounded by a sea of critics. Prejudice was apparent everywhere. Whenever Iwaoka, Shirai, or the other engineers went to Director Okabe to get approval for payment of an invoice for the purchase of materials or equipment, again and again he'd refuse to sign it.

"We really need this piece of equipment. If we don't have it, then starting next week, we must let over ten people go," Iwaoka would insist. If pressed hard enough, Okabe would reply, "Then I will order it. If I let you guys buy it, you'll end up buying the most expensive equipment around."

Okabe would then go to Osaka to purchase the machine Iwaoka requested. His frugality, however, would inevitably cause everyone headaches. If the department needed a specific machine -- for example a turret lathe produced only by a specialized manufacturer -- Okabe would end up buying an inexpensive, outdated lathe from an unknown supplier.

Kan and Iwaoka would join Shirai in complaining to Okabe, telling him the machine he'd ordered was completely useless for their purposes. Okabe would only get angry and flatly refuse to send it back. Eventually he would soften, and the correct machine would be ordered, but not without a lot of bitter grumbling: "You guys from the Automobile Department are way too extravagant!"

Whenever he was completely stonewalled by Okabe, Iwaoka would approach Kiichiro with his request, at which point Kiichiro would always agree to pay for the necessary machine out of his own pocket. Seeing this new machine up and running in the plant, Okabe would erupt in a fit of anger: "Who told you that you could buy this! Put it away!"

And away it would go. Iwaoka and Shirai were too busy to argue with the crusty old curmudgeon; instead they kept an eye on where the machine was placed in the warehouse, and they would return at night and retrieve it. They'd assemble it and work with it until Okabe noticed and demanded that it go back to the warehouse once again. After they did this two or three times, Okabe would give up and stop coming around.

Kiichiro remained silent but he was well aware of the situation. He also knew how deeply loyal Okabe was to the Toyoda family and how much pride he took in his technical know-how. By the same token, Kiichiro recognized that Okabe's know-how was outdated and that he was often stubborn when it came to buying new equipment. Okabe was a minor inconvenience, but certainly not a threat. The real threat, as Kiichiro knew, would be wearing new suits and acting in an arrogant manner. He would have to face these men sooner or later.

In the end, I'm all alone, thought Kiichiro. *Even if the Toyoda household goes bankrupt as a result of my quest to build an automobile, I will never give up!*

Kiichiro's brother-in-law, Risaburo, was steadfast in a resolve of his own. He was aware the times were changing. No longer could his company rely exclusively on building looms and spinning machines and expect to be successful. It was time to branch out into other products and entirely different industries. Yet he would not let go of the idea that a move into car manufacturing was much too risky for the Toyoda companies. Kiichiro's failure to meet his own deadline of producing the first prototype in one year simply reinforced Risaburo's convictions and antagonized his fears.

When Toyoda Automatic Loom Works officially started the Automobile Department, the plan was to build an automobile in a year, thought Risaburo. *That year has come and gone, and not even the engine has been perfected. Instead of manufacturing our own parts, as planned, were using parts from foreign-made cars. Rather than mass-producing bodies, the Automobile Department is still working on the first body by hand. The personnel list grows daily and the payroll right along with it. To make matters worse, the sophisticated machine tools turned out to be more expensive than expected. All in all, we're in a terrible fix. There is absolutely no guarantee that paying out money for months, even years, will deliver a marketable automobile.*

Risaburo wasn't the only one who was paranoid about the project. The firm's financial backers were getting uneasy, and Risaburo was beginning to feel pressure from members of the executive management of the Mitsui *zaibatsu*, bank officers, and the major stockholders of Toyoda Spinning and Weaving and Toyoda Automatic Loom Works. It was pressure he could manage well enough, but it did make life uncomfortable. Unlike Sakichi and Kiichiro, who were unaffected by the doubts, fears, and obstacles raised by those about them, Risaburo was, above all, "conservative." One wouldn't find him inviting censure, challenging tradition, or risking his security to pursue a great dream, as Sakichi had done and as Kiichiro was doing.

Gradually, I am beginning to become more and more like my father, Kiichiro would often utter to himself with a wry smile. At times he would spend entire nights lost in thought, mulling over possible ways of "cutting the Gordian knot" and breaking the logjam holding up completion of the prototype. Alone, he would slip quietly through a small gate into the branch factory of Toyoda Spinning and Weaving, unlock the door to his "secret room," sit down at his special desk, and immerse himself in contemplation.

On one such evening in April of 1935, he was mentally dissecting the engine and analyzing the intake and exhaust systems. He was passing time before a scheduled late-night test of a new engine manifold. The test was to determine whether the flashing problem with the manifold casting had indeed been corrected and whether the prototype engine could equal the power output of the Chevrolet.

It was nearly midnight and still a great deal of work had to be done before the engine was ready to be tested. Having observed the work for about an hour, but exhausted by lack of sleep over the preceding weeks, Kiichiro was retiring to the "secret room" for a brief rest.

As he walked to the spinning plant, Kiichiro was too lost in thought to notice young cherry trees in partial blossom. This was very unlike him. He was a nature-lover and an avid flower gardener. He had also built several ponds with his own hands and stocked them with goldfish and carp. These days he was too busy even to feed his fish.

Kiichiro sat down at his desk in the secret room, and closed his eyes. Too tired to sleep, he opened his eyes and looked around the room. In front of him was the circular loom that had been sent from Toyoda Spinning and Weaving in Shanghai after Sakichi's death. In his last years, Sakichi had devoted all his energy to developing this enormous, strange-looking machine.

As he observed the loom sitting mysteriously silent, poised to propel its shuttle in an endless, sweeping, circular motion, Kiichiro began to reminisce:

He developed this around the time I actually began to work on the automatic loom. I wondered for a long time why Sakichi started to work on such a machine.

The first time Kiichiro had seen the circular loom was during the winter of 1923. On arriving from Japan at the Toyoda Spinning and Weaving factory in Shanghai, he had been taken immediately to see the machine by his father, Sakichi. Sakichi had long been fascinated by circular movement, and had experimented with a rotary steam engine with several features similar to a turbine. He had, in fact, received a patent on this engine in 1914.

Sakichi's excitement about the loom was evident from the moment he shared the machine with his son: "This is what I'm working on now," said Sakichi. "It's a circular loom. I started thinking about this machine when I was young. Fifteen or sixteen years ago -- just before I had received the first patent for the automatic shuttle-changing device -- I was awarded the patent for this loom. At that time all of the details hadn't been fully worked out. Now I'll definitely complete it."

Sakichi's cheerful expression as he pointed out features of the device to his son reflected none of the many bitter years of frustration and derision he had endured nor the resentment he felt toward the abusive bankers and financiers. What Kiichiro remembered now in the quiet of his "secret room" was his father's serene, self-assured nature; a nature belied by the furrows of worry carved into his face.

Kiichiro recalled that Sakichi had talked about wrestling with the problem of power: "To eliminate the power loss inherent in the shuttle's constant reversal of direction, the shuttle of this loom is designed in such a way that it moves around the rim of the cylinder by centrifugal force. In other words, it is close to perpetual motion, and this loom will continue to effortlessly weave cloth in this way."

At the time of this statement, the young Kiichiro had just graduated from the university and was studying the automatic loom. Armed with a knowledge of mathematics, engineering, and physics, he thought the circular loom impractical and found his father's words about "perpetual motion" empty and foolish. Yet the story of how Sakichi had come upon the idea for a circular loom continued to fascinate him.

It all began with a young boy growing up in the country and a process for cleaning beans. To separate the good beans from the bad, Sakichi had learned a method for rolling the beans around the rim of a tilted tray. The lighter, insect-infested beans would remain at the center of the tray, while the heavier healthy beans would move to the outer edge. This motion evolved into the circular movement of a shuttle supplying thread. The bean tray essentially was the cylinder. When this was moved on a slanted axis, the shuttle would be set in motion by centrifugal force and would continue to revolve in perpetual motion. The shuttle would join the warp yarn hanging in the shape of a pouch and weave a wide, cylindrical piece of cloth. This was the homely beginning of an idea that would consume much of Sakichi's life as an inventor.

Young Kiichiro was skeptical from the very beginning about the scientific validity of a circular loom, and especially about the notion of perpetual motion. As he grew older, however, the fervor of his father's pursuit began to haunt him. Why had Sakichi put his heart and soul into such a silly invention? And why did various experts feel that Sakichi was truly on the track of something? For the most part, Kiichiro's early resentment of his father intervened before his curiosity could take him closer to an understanding of Sakichi's quest.

Now the many unanswered questions were coming back to Kiichiro. *I simply can't ignore Sakichi's work as idle fantasy. I wonder what this dream of perpetual motion truly meant to him?*

From his "secret room," Kiichiro could faintly hear the roar of an engine. The new manifold was being tested. His eyes were closed, his mind was shuttling back and forth between the past and the present. He could see his father's face, calm and filled with joy. He could feel his contempt for Sakichi evaporating. Sakichi was a rare dreamer who made things happen.

Then suddenly, Kiichiro was awakened from his revery by a different memory. When visiting Sakichi at his summer house, about a month before his death, Kiichiro asked him about his feelings regarding the manufacture of automobiles.

"Oh yes, automobiles," the old man said as he smiled. "They operate on perpetual power. Just like my circular loom, they are machines that run on infinite roads. You should make an automobile." There was no further explanation.

Kiichiro remembered his own eyes filling with tears, convinced as he was that his father's illness finally made him completely senile. Even Hatako and Aiko had said, "It's a shame that an honorable man like Father has become senile to the point that even his attendants are starting to make fun of him. It's so sad to see him this way."

As he held the image of his wife and sister crying on that by-gone afternoon, Kiichiro recalled a passage from Sakichi's *Diary of an Inventor:*

Western civilization is based on machinery. The development of machines was a result of the invention of the steam engine. The steam engine, however, requires coal, and coal has always been too expensive to run our country's industries. Somehow we had to develop another source of power. Therefore, I decided to concentrate my research on centrifugal or perpetual force (also known as the inventor's demon). For a long time, I suffered because of my innocence. My many experiments always ended in failure, and the prospects for success were growing poorer. This perpetual failure made me realize that my child must not lack what I have lacked -- a systematic education. Even if one were to succeed, members of the younger generation who lack an education will find it difficult to acquire funds for research. This is the lesson to be learned: one must not think that whatever one works on must be easy or original. But one must continue to work on it. Careful thought must be given....

Kiichiro opened his eyes slightly and looked at the circular loom again. Against this peculiar shape with the tilted cylinder, he could see a strange and faint image of Sakichi.

So, that's it! Kiichiro said softly, as though waking from a deep sleep. *Father meant that he himself or other individuals like him are the infinite source of power. He used the loom to tell this story to me and to future generations!*

Sakichi did not succumb to continuous failure. He sacrificed his life to develop the loom. As his offspring, I am sacrificing myself and risking everything to build an automobile. This is what was given me by my father, and what was given my father by his father, from one generation to the next, from era to era.... This is the perpetual motion of progress and improvement. This is what Sakichi was trying to point out through the allegory of the circular loom. Although the loom by itself has no meaning, as a symbol of human desire and destiny, it can be called one of the most noble objects! That is why I will....

At that moment, a loud knock on the door interrupted Kiichiro's train of thought.

"Mr. Toyoda, Mr. Toyoda!"

"The engine is purring and it's churning out an enormous amount of horsepower."

"Okay, tell them I'll be right there," Kiichiro answered, glancing once more at the circular loom as he rose from his chair.

When he entered the pilot plant, the very air seemed to swell with joy. Hovering around the engine, tense with overflowing energy, eyes glittering and faces contorted in glee, were Kan, Iwaoka and ten assistants.

"We've finally done it, Mr. Toyoda," Kan shouted joyously, pointing excitedly at the dynamometer.

"Please take a look. See how the torque increases! It's already exceeded sixty horsepower! It must be close to sixty-two, sixty-three!"

As the engine made its throaty roar, the needle of the dynamometer flickered slightly, edging upwards and hovering well past the sixty horsepower mark.

"Good job. I'm very happy," Kiichiro smiled. "From this moment, please begin the assembly of the full prototype. You should be able to complete it in a month."

Still smiling broadly, Kiichiro started with Kan and went down the line, shaking every oil-soaked hand.

Chapter
6

PREDICAMENTS AND REINFORCEMENTS

The anemic engine problem conquered, assembly of the Model A1 prototype was begun in earnest. At the same time, on April 21, 1935, a ceremony honoring the founder of Toyoda Automatic Loom Works and Toyoda Spinning and Weaving Company was held in the courtyard of the Nagoya headquarters.

The large courtyard was packed with hundreds of people, including the most prominent citizens of the area. At one end of the courtyard, a drape covered an object near a podium. Kiichiro sat in the front row next to Sasuke, Sakichi's brother and president of the company. The ceremony began with a speech by Risaburo, followed by congratulatory addresses from other Toyoda executives and guests.

When the drape was removed by Sakichi's two beaming grandchildren, a bronze bust bearing Sakichi's serene expression was greeted with a burst of applause. Mounted on a white marble pedestal, the bust depicted Sakichi dressed in formal Western-style attire, his chest adorned with the Imperial Merit of Honor.

According to the Shinto rite of offering a sprig from a sacred tree, Risaburo, Kiichiro, and Sakichi's widow, Asako, placed their sprigs upon the pedestal. Asako was wearing a conservative dress with a simple hair style. She seemed shy and gentle, even delicate, and appeared in sharp contrast to Kiichiro's childhood memories of her.

As he watched her perform the rite, Kiichiro shivered involuntarily. *What a formidable woman she is!* he thought. *This person created that bust! Fifty years ago she was an ignorant young daughter of a poor farmer in some forgotten rural town. Yet by grit, shrewd intelligence, and sheer determination, she kept the shop and family going in the brutal early years. Because of her, Sakichi could dedicate himself to his inventions.* Kiichiro was not an easy person to impress, but Asako's iron will and stamina never failed to astonish him. Not by the wildest stretch of imagination could she be described as an affectionate mother. She was strict, the fabled stepmother who found something everyday to carp at. Those close to her knew that being stern was Asako's way of teaching self-reliance and mental toughness. No one was exempt from this philosophy. Asako treated Kiichiro's half-sister Aiko -- Asako's own daughter -- precisely as she did all the children, including their cousin Eiji, the second oldest son of Sakichi's brother, Heikichi.

The unhappiness Kiichiro experienced as a result of his stern upbringing contributed to his dour, reticent character as an adult. His natural mother, Sakichi's first wife Tami, also nurtured a harsh and unforgiving resentment in Kiichiro toward Sakichi for neglecting his responsibilities towards his son and herself. Now that Sakichi had departed this world and Kiichiro had come to know firsthand the ordeals his father had endured, his bitter contempt for Sakichi had vanished. He had also come to see Asako in a different light. Kiichiro now realized that she had sacrificed herself and her children for the sake of the Toyoda household. Without her, the family's survival and prosperity would never have been possible. Despite the tears and loneliness he had suffered at the hands of Asako, Kiichiro profoundly admired her uncommon, ever unique, metamorphosis from poor farm girl to respected dowager. When Sakichi finally had become president of the factory, Asako adapted herself with aplomb and intelligence to her new role as "the president's" wife. Later, when Sakichi's reputation had spread far and wide as head of the Toyoda *zaibatsu,* Asako was appropriately dignified, but never cold and arrogant. Though she had relinquished any direct involvement with company affairs, she always retained a good head for business. Both in Nagoya and in Shanghai, her dignity and intelligence earned everyone's respect.

Lost in admiration for this bust of Sakichi, Kiichiro felt he understood Asako even better than before. Perhaps he had never fully grasped the nature of her dedication to her husband. Here that dedication stood immortalized in marble and bronze. Determined all the world should know of Sakichi's accomplishments, Asako had studied sculpture for several years with an artist named Nishiyama Watanabe. From the very beginning, she worked on nothing but sculptures of her late husband, telling Watanabe, "I have no objective nor interest to create anything but a sculpture of Sakichi."

Watanabe's artistic philosophy made it easy for him to empathize with Asako's desire. As he told her, "What is essential is to focus on something, to pursue it without reservation; to do that is to enter the realm of purity and be directly shown by the gods how to create an expression."

This person devoted her life to elevating a man named Sakichi to the level of a god, Kiichiro thought.

He marveled at the economical and graceful lines that so simply captured Sakichi's essence, his determination and indomitable spirit. But the sculpture was also an image of Asako's own essence, the tenacity which echoes Sakichi's stubborn pursuit of invention.

Asako sculpted some ten works of Sakichi in all, but this one was special. She had worked on it from the evening of the fifth day after Sakichi's death on October 30 of the previous year, and in a burst of creative energy, had completed it on November 10, just eleven days after he died.

If she can do that, there's nothing that I can't do, thought Kiichiro. *Hardships may find me, but I will make automobile manufacturing a reality. I too will tred the thorny path that Sakichi and Asako took.* The unveiling ceremony brought Kiichiro's ambition into even greater focus, and he resolved to spend that night working on the prototype.

The first Model A1 was finally completed in early May. It was a joyous event, but not as euphoric as it would have been had more of the automobile's parts been original Toyoda productions. As it was, only the engine block, cylinder head, transmission case and similar housings, a few accessories, and the car's body had not been borrowed from imported models. And with the exception of the castings, most of these items had been relatively easy to make. The more demanding components -- chassis, gearbox and differential gears -- were genuine Chevrolet parts. The building of a completely domestic vehicle lay in the future, and would require the endurance of an industrial marathon runner.

A ceremony celebrating the completion of the first prototype was held nonetheless. As soon as the last bolt was tightened and the hood closed, a tent was put up in the courtyard of the pilot factory. As a fitting tribute following the celebration, Kiichiro and his closest assistants drove the new car to the burial site of Sakichi's ashes. They wanted to share their accomplishment with the man who ultimately had made it possible.

Later, Kiichiro, his wife's brother, Shinsaburo Iida, and Risaburo Oshima drove the car to Tokyo. Traversing the Hakone Pass invited a few difficulties, but a proud telegram was sent back to headquarters anyway proclaiming, "We have just crossed the Hakone Pass."

Upon arrival in Tokyo, the car was driven to Kumabe's laboratory in the Engineering Department at Tokyo University for a detailed inspection. They also wanted to discuss another project which had been started in March, shortly before final touches had been given the A1. The project referred to was construction of the Model G1 truck; a high priority project intended to ensure Toyoda's position once the government moved to subsidize vehicle production. Using the 1934 Ford truck as its model, the Automobile Department established these guidelines for the G1's development:

> *(1) Since a version of the 1933 Chevrolet engine has already been built for the A1, this engine will be utilized.*
>
> *(2) Since the Ford's frame is solidly built, it will serve as the model for the G1's frame. The front axle will be patterned after the Chevrolet, and the rear axle after the Ford. In view of Japan's poor roads, four-wheel independent suspension will be employed; that way, even if an axle shaft breaks, the truck will not fall apart.*
>
> *(3) Other parts will be selected on the basis of the relative strengths of the various American models. The body will be made manually, which will eliminate the need for a forming press and thus reduce lead time.*

A sheet metal factory for production of the G1's body was established in early June. A few days later, upon return from one of his frequent trips to Tokyo, Kiichiro startled his engineers by telling them, "We won't spend time working on a truck prototype. We must move directly into production and be ready to formally introduce the truck and start marketing it this year."

Kiichiro's assistants were speechless. No one doubted that Kiichiro was bold and displayed the calculated daring of a true engineer, but this was ridiculous. Even his most ambitious engineers and managers could not believe what they were hearing.

"Design, manufacture, and sell it before year's end?" Kan gasped, his eyebrows raised in astonishment.

"Isn't that being a little unreasonable?" asked Oshima with a deep frown.

Only six months remained in the present year and the team was still technologically immature. Kiichiro's plan spelled certain disaster. But it was Kiichiro's wish, which meant that production of the G1 would begin at once.

At once would also begin six months of working from dawn to midnight, seven days a week. Six months of fumbling and blundering through design and assembly of the G1. Six months of solid stress and worry for Oshima and his crew. Kan and Oshima felt it their duty to inform their leader that he was asking for the moon. Perhaps the continued endless pressure brought about by production of the A1 prototype had caused Kiichiro to completely lose his judgment.

As usual, there was much more to the situation than met the eye, and Kiichiro had perfectly good reasons for what appeared to the others as intemperate lunacy. If they only knew the dire consequences of not succeeding with truck production in such a tight time frame, they would not be standing with their mouths agape or grumbling under their breaths. Kiichiro did not attempt to explain, instead telling everyone firmly, "I have decided on this. We must do it."

"Yes sir," answered Oshima and Kan tersely, still not entirely reconciled to being asked to do the impossible. But they made no further attempts at discussion. Whatever Kiichiro's reasons, he would not go back on his decision and the two men knew this.

From this point forward, Kiichiro spared neither his men nor himself, working until the middle of the night, troubleshooting when needed, urging his workers and assistants on. He rarely left the factory. He would catch a few hours sleep and then be back at work, his badge of leadership the grease and oil that soaked his clothing, smudged his face, and darkened his hands.

Simultaneous with work on the G1 truck, final preparations continued for the A1 prototype. With this dual drain on its resources, the Automobile Department saw its funds quickly dwindle. Outlays now began to eat away at the operating capital of its parent companies, Toyoda Automatic Loom Works and Toyoda Spinning and Weaving.

According to calculations of Toyoda Spinning and Weaving Managing Director Tojiro Okamoto, the Automobile Department had spent in excess of five million yen. In Japan today, three to five thousand times that amount would be required for the venture -- an astronomical 1.5 to 2.5 billion yen. This helps to put into perspective the enormous risk being taken to give birth to a domestic auto industry.

Fortunately, the person charged with guarding the Toyoda concerns was Okamoto. A long time trusted friend and head clerk for Sakichi Toyoda, Okamoto hailed from Nagoya and was five years older than Kiichiro. Upon graduation from a municipal trade school, he had studied in America and had graduated from New York's Eastman School of Business. He then took a position with Mitsui and Company and spent considerable time on assignment in the United States. While there, he became very familiar with the automotive industry, a familiarity which allowed him to see the potential for such an industry in Japan.

Okamoto was an amiable, reasonable person, but he could be tough-minded and resolute, like Sakichi and Kiichiro. Okamoto also shared a similar progressive and visionary quality which allowed him to see the value of taking risks.

As major shareholders and members of the board of directors came to express their apprehensions and discontent, Okamoto would frequently reply, "Why don't we look at it from a long-term perspective? Automobile manufacturing will definitely develop. Toyoda-related companies haven't as yet been even slightly affected by financial constraints." Getting no satisfaction from Okamoto, the critics would then take their complaints to Risaburo.

To combat the critics complaints, Risaburo relied on the opinions of two men in the firm who influenced him the most; Seki Yada and Taizo Ishida. Yada had been Nagoya branch manager for Mitsui Bank before joining the Toyoda *zaibatsu*, and Ishida, Risaburo's brother, was the auditor of Toyoda Spinning and Weaving.

Yada had graduated from Keio University and currently lived in Nagoya. He was educated and literate, and by virtue of published works -- his writings often appeared in local newspapers -- he was one of the area's leading literary figures. Nearly ten years older than Risaburo, he was almost sixty years old.

Risaburo asked Yada what he thought about the automobile project: "Ten million or twenty million yen would not be sufficient to start automobile production. That's why Mitsui and Mitsubishi have stayed out of it. If we're dragged in by Mr. Kiichiro's pushy recklessness, who knows how many millions of yen will be used up?

"Now I hear that Mr. Kiichiro wants to change to mass production of trucks without even building a prototype. Excuse my saying so, but I think that's just like throwing money down the drain. If we persist in this, the Toyoda business we've worked so hard to build since the death of Mr. Sakichi will be destroyed."

Although Yada's words bristled with suspicion and anger at what he saw as an inexcusably rash commitment, they also reflected his sincere concern and dedication to the company, considerations that touched a responsive chord in the already alarmed Risaburo.

Like Yada, Taizo Ishida had banking experience and was determined to see the Toyoda enterprises stay financially healthy. Although Ishida realized that the drain on Toyoda's resources could not continue forever, his view of the situation was more temperate than Yada's. He was of the opinion that the time had not yet arrived to scuttle the automobile project.

Ishida came from Chiba Prefecture. Born in 1888, he was the fifth son of a middle-class farmer named Sawada, a relative of the Kodama family to which Risaburo and his brother Ichizo belonged. Ishida graduated from primary school in 1902, but since he didn't have the money to go on to middle school and no land to become a farmer, he was at a loss for an occupation. Casting about for something to do, he was offered a position by Mitsui and Company as a management trainee in its China office. It was better than nothing, but for an ambitious youngster with little education, it didn't offer much hope for a worthwhile career.

Shortly before Ishida was scheduled to depart for China, Ichizo Kodama told him, "It's silly for you to take a job in China. You should go to school. I'll talk to your mother and send you to middle school, so come home with me to Hikone."

Despite the fact that his family had gone bankrupt during the post-Meiji Restoration period and was poor at the time, Kodama convinced Ishida to come home with him. This must have caused a great deal of trouble for Kodama's mother. The death of her husband had left her alone to feed three hungry boys - - Risaburo, who was four years older than Taizo and attending middle school at the time, Keizo, who was the next oldest, and Ichizo. And now there was Taizo Ishida. Despite her many disadvantages, she never complained.

Ishida's stay with the Kodama family was the beginning of a life of good fortune. Even when things went wrong, they would always turn out well for him in the long run. Bright but headstrong and impetuous, Ishida rarely studied. His preference was athletics, not academics. In his fifth year at school, he was named captain of the rowing team, which took him even further from his studies. Only his keen intelligence and ability to learn quickly permitted him to graduate. Eventually he decided to continue his education but felt he could not burden the Kodama family any further. His only alternative was to find a school without tuition requirements, and he applied to the two military institutions, the Naval Academy and the Engine School. When both rejected his application due to his height, he tried to enroll in the Fisheries School. Once again he was "too short."

Ishida had no choice but to return to his hometown. There he secured a position as a substitute teacher. For a talented young man burning with desire for success, the prospect of spending the rest of his life as an elementary school teacher was not an attractive one. So Ishida decided to become a merchant and packed off to Kyoto, where he went to work for a foreign-owned furniture store. He soon quit the furniture business and married shortly after. Mrs. Kodama had recommended him as a suitable husband for a member of a local well-to-do family. Upon becoming an adopted son, he took on the name of his wife's family, Ishida, and lived a short while in Hikone near the Kodama family. He took a position with a Tokyo dry goods firm, Ichibashi Shoten, owned by a relative. Ishida's job was to pull an eight-wheeled cart and sell his wares as far away as Chiba and Ibaraki Prefectures. It was hard work and especially difficult on hot summer days, when perspiration would stream down his face and salt would dry in streaks down his shirt. He stayed with the job as long as he could and then returned to Hikone.

During this time, Ishida's friend Kodama had become the general manager of the cotton department in the Osaka branch office of Mitsui and Company. Through his connections, he was able to help Ishida get a job with Kaneka, a well-known cotton cloth wholesaler in Nagoya. The president of Kaneka was Kensaburo Hatori, a business tycoon who had started his career as an apprentice. It was during his employment at Kaneka that Ishida began to acquire an acute business sense.

Years later, following the panic of March, 1920, when Kaneka was on the verge of bankruptcy, President Hatori committed suicide and willed what assets remained as repayment for his debts. Ironically Kaneka did not collapse. Led by manager Tsunejiro Sanron, the store employees worked together and succeeded in rebuilding the company.

That experience provided a valuable education for Ishida. He learned the power and cruelty of money and business, and he learned the nature of responsibilities and self-sacrifice necessary for teamwork, all lessons that would never leave him as his career moved forward.

Ishida's success at Kaneka won him a manager's position at a newly-opened branch office in Shanghai. Fate was once again working in his favor. Through his "good angel," Kodama, Ishida met Sakichi Toyoda, the founder of Toyoda Automatic Loom Works and Toyoda Spinning and Weaving, and his life would never be the same. Sakichi quickly took to this bright, ambitious young man and visited with him frequently. Each time Sakichi would ask him:

"How's it going? Are you making a profit?"

"Yes, some," Taizo would reply.

"Some isn't good enough," Sakichi would snort. "You're a businessman...you have to earn a lot of money, and from the profits you earn, you must give us inventors a big chunk to fund our research. If you don't do that, Japan will never become prosperous."

Those words evoked a memory dating back to Ishida's very first days at Kaneka. An old man dressed in a rough-woven cotton kimono and carrying a cloth bag walked into the store and sat down without saying a word. No one paid attention to him and he just sat there in silence. After a while, President Hatori spied the man and said, "What can I do for you today? Do you have some business to take care of?"

"Uh-huh," was the man's laconic reply.

"Is it money again?" asked Hatori.

"Uh-huh."

"How much this time?"

"A lot. About 250,000 yen," the old man replied.

Neither said another word as Hatori wrote a promissory note and the old man took it, stamped his signature on the piece of broad cloth, put the note inside his bag and left the store.

Ishida learned later from his co-workers the old man was the well-known inventor, Sakichi Toyoda. Though his curiosity regarding Hatori's and Sakichi's exchange that day was never satisfied, Ishida inferred from later conversations with Sakichi in Shanghai that the promissory note must have been related to research funds.

It was a topic often in Sakichi's mind, as he would reminisce to Ishida about living on rice and gruel in order to continue work on his inventions. The personal setbacks suffered as a result of insufficient research funds and the stinginess of the business world were favorite themes and made deep marks on Ishida's impressionable mind.

"That's why those who go into business must earn a lot of money and channel part of it to inventors," Sakichi would say, "not out of charity, but because they are making an investment in their future and will profit from whatever is invented. Unless that's done, Japan and her people will never be well-off."

These were the words Ishida heard as he consulted with Risaburo over the company's financial woes caused by the Automobile Department. But Ishida had another consideration as well. Risaburo was more than a friend to him. Indeed, he was like a brother, as Ishida had been "adopted" into the Kodama family and lived with them while going to school. By the time Risaburo married into the Toyoda family, Ishida was moving up in Toyoda Spinning and Weaving, where he eventually attained the position of head clerk. Through business as well as personal connections, Ishida and Risaburo remained close. This made it difficult for Ishida to say what he truly felt regarding problems caused by the automobile project.

"Automobile production takes an exorbitant amount of money," Ishida began, conceding the obvious, but showing respect for Risaburo and his worries. "If we start with inadequate preparation, then production will suffer a setback, and if the Automobile Department were to go bankrupt, Toyoda Automatic Loom Works and Toyoda Spinning and Weaving would go bankrupt, too. In other words, both you and Mr. Kiichiro must be prepared to stake your very lives on the success of the Automobile Department."

With Risaburo nodding sagely, thinking that perhaps his head clerk was sympathetic to his cause, Ishida deftly reversed directions: "However, invention and business growth are the keys to making future profits. If the spinning division earns a satisfactory profit, then we should gladly have Mr. Kiichiro utilize it."

As a look of annoyance flitted across Risaburo's face, Ishida thought to himself, *Oh well, I've never learned to keep my mouth shut and it's a little late for this old dog to be taught new tricks. Besides, he asked me. And that is what I really believe.*

"All right, I understand what you've said," Risaburo answered in a half-serious, half-joking tone. The words of "his brother" stung like thorns in his heart and added to the already mounting confusion and resentment Risaburo felt toward Kiichiro's project.

This resentment would eventually explode on an evening in mid-June, about half a month after the announcement concerning truck production. Without any warning, Kiichiro marched into Risaburo's office and asked him to increase capital funding by three million yen to cover the truck production costs. It wasn't exactly what Risaburo needed to hear at that moment.

"You haven't been able to produce a single full-fledged prototype, and here you're asking me for money to produce a truck. Why are you always in such a hurry?" Risaburo thundered. "What makes you think you can build a truck that will even run?"

Ignoring the question, Kiichiro replied quietly, "Unless money is put in at the beginning, earnings won't come out in the end."

"You say 'capital increase, capital increase' so easily," Risaburo fumed. He was fighting to control the anger seething within his breast. "How much do you think you're going to need in total? How much do you think we have spent so far?"

"I don't know," Kiichiro answered. "But after this, ultimately I think increases in capital will no longer be needed."

"What do you mean by 'ultimately,' " Risaburo rasped. "Five million yen has already been spent! In addition, based on your request, we negotiated the purchase of some four hundred acres in Koromo."

"I heard that you backed out of the deal," Kiichiro responded.

"Yes. They kept trying to raise the price, and I didn't like the sound of it. So I backed out in April. But I hear that you have talked to them, and they've asked us if we're still interested in buying it."

As Kiichiro eyed him impassively, Risaburo paused momentarily. Then he continued, "If unlimited amounts of money keep flowing out, not only the Loom Works but also the Spinning and Weaving division will go bankrupt. The executive management of Mitsui and Mr. Yada have also expressed their concern in precisely these terms."

Kiichiro's eyes narrowed and a slight annoyance came into his voice: "In spite of the fact that bankers don't create anything by themselves, it's always been their trade to butt into other people's business and give advice."

"What the hell!" exploded Risaburo, his face turning purple with rage. Blue veins stood out on his aging forehead.

"Kiichiro, can't you give this some careful thought? I...we...have a responsibility to our late Dad."

"I **have** given this careful thought. And anyway, Sakichi would not object to what I am doing. In fact, he would applaud my efforts to build an automobile," Kiichiro said with calm self-assurance.

"What!!???"

"You might as well get used to the notion that I'm not going to abandon the project. There's simply no turning back now. Please honor my request for additional funds," Kiichiro said. He then turned and left the room.

What a pain he is! thought Risaburo, clenching his teeth and smiling grimly.

As president of the company, it was within Risaburo's authority to simply order Kiichiro to suspend the project. But there was no assurance that Kiichiro would obey such an order. Stubborn as only he could be, Kiichiro might defiantly move forward, and in so doing cause a sharp rift in the company and totally destroy the unity of the Toyoda family.

Risaburo could be very authoritarian and uncompromising, and many feared him for that reason. But when it came to confrontations with Kiichiro, Risaburo's authority crumbled. He felt a nagging sense of helplessness not only because Kiichiro was "the true son" of the founding father, but also because he was an intimidating personality in his own right.

"Is anyone there?" Risaburo barked in the direction of his secretary's desk outside his office. "Call Okamoto immediately and tell him to come to my house tonight!" The secretary immediately picked up the phone and passed the order on to Okamoto.

That night, when Tojiro Okamoto arrived at Risaburo's residence, he was greeted with a proper bow by two neatly dressed maids at the entrance. *As usual everything is so very proper here,* thought Okamoto, smiling to himself. He knew that every evening, when Risaburo left the office by chauffeured car, his secretary called his residence to notify Aiko and the domestic staff that he was on his way home. This gave the mistress of the house a chance to prepare all of her maids, who would line up at the entrance to greet Risaburo with their polite bows as he came in the door. Failure to properly observe this ritual would leave Risaburo sullen and grumpy. To Okamoto, such ceremoniousness seemed as useless as gilding cherry blossoms with gold, for he himself was a simple man of simple customs, an attitude he had acquired directly from Sakichi Toyoda. But Okamoto was courteous and never made the slightest disclosure of his feelings about empty decorum.

As soon as he was shown into the extravagant waiting room, Okamoto was greeted by Risaburo, who was dressed informally. Risaburo motioned for Okamoto to take a seat and promptly sat down himself.

"Do we still have any funds left in Toyoda Spinning and Weaving?" Risaburo asked in the manner of a feudal lord questioning one of his subjects.

"Yes, funds are available. According to the last accounting report, business increased by one tenth, and eight tenths was paid out as dividends, leaving our cash deposits decreased somewhat, though our securities have increased at the same rate."

"That," Risaburo mused, "is probably a result of issuing the stock certificates to raise funds from the Automatic Loom division to fund the Automobile Department. If the Automobile Department goes bankrupt, then that stock issuance will end up being a total waste. The financial report is based on how one closes the books, and what I'm asking for are the implications. Aren't we somewhat tight on cash?"

Okamoto was ready with an answer, but paused momentarily to show respect for Risaburo's question. He knew the finances of the Spinning and Weaving operation down to the last yen. He also knew that Toyoda Spinning and Weaving had contributed 1.15 million yen of the total 2 million yen needed as seed money for Kiichiro's Automobile Department. Even at that time Okamoto knew the project would cost much more than anticipated. He was aware of the enormous risks involved, but he felt relatively certain the Automobile Department would not drag the Toyoda companies into bankruptcy.

For this reason he answered, "No, we are not in financial danger. We have loaned a large amount to the Automobile Department, so it's only natural that we feel some financial pressure...."

"Can we still give out more? I keep on telling Kiichiro to put an end to it, but he doesn't think about the consequences and moves ahead recklessly. It's becoming a very great problem," Risaburo said, shaking his head.

"I see," Okamoto murmured, nodding reflectively. "But hasn't that been the Toyoda way ever since the late Master's era? I, myself am a timid person. Every time the late Master ventured into a new business, I would shudder. I would frantically total up the figures on my abacus, but by the time I finished the Master had already moved ahead. My calculations were of no use."

"This is different from Dad's ventures!" Risaburo erupted, once more turning purple with rage. "Dad's work was very small in scale. The task of building an automobile is so large it doesn't compare. If our investment in automobiles fails, we'll be totally devastated!"

"Please excuse me, but aren't the two the same?" Okamoto replied, his voice serene as usual. "Although the scope of his operation was small, in the beginning the late Master barely had any organization or capital to work with. This time the task is large. But we already have the organization and the capital behind us. We also have a solid workforce trained by the late Master, we have advanced technology, and we have the strong solidarity of our workers. Losing everything due to failure? That is no different today than it was in the late Master's day." Okamoto smiled cheerfully as he spoke, but his words constituted a frustrating counterargument which elevated Risaburo's temper and left him with little more to say.

"Then as soon as possible," Risaburo replied lamely, "I will deliver to you the detailed figures of the Loom Works division." Seeing this as an opportune moment, Okamoto rose, bowed politely and left the room, walking over to Kiichiro's house nearby.

Dressed in her everyday clothes, Kiichiro's wife Hatako greeted him with a warm smile and obvious pleasure: "Mr. Okamoto, how nice to see you. It's been a long time."

"Please excuse me for neglecting to call first. Is Mr. Kiichiro in?" Okamoto felt much more relaxed when he came here. It was just like visiting Mr. Sakichi; nothing had changed and he could feel comfortable here.

"Yes, he is here. Oh, what is he doing now? He has such bad manners. He is playing with the children," Hatako said with a laugh as she ushered Okamoto into the living room.

Gracious, as always, Hatako is such a personable wife, thought Okamoto. He remembered Sakichi being overjoyed when Hatako joined the Toyoda family as the wife of his son. At the wedding, Sakichi had clapped his hands, saying: "Her name is *Hatako*, her age is *Hatachi* [twenty], and we run a *Hataya* [loom shop]! There is nothing more auspicious for the future of our family than this!" Hatako also came from a very well-known and respected family, the Takashimaya Iida.

"Dear, Mr. Okamoto is here," said Hatako, sliding open a living room door. Kiichiro was dressed in a dressing gown, hunched over his drawings, which looked like blueprints. Surrounding him were his four children, noisily asking him questions. His oldest daughter, Yuriko, was a sixth grader in elementary school; his eldest son, Shoichiro, was a fifth grader; his second daughter, Wakako, and his second son, Tatsuro, were still in preschool.

"Are you in the midst of a lesson?" Okamoto asked.

Smiling cheerfully and motioning with his head, Kiichiro offered Okamoto a seat opposite him. With the same smile he signaled for the children to leave.

"May I ask what you are drawing?" asked Okamoto in his usual quiet voice, smiling as he sat down.

"This is a design for a helicopter."

"Helicopter," Okamoto repeated, "Are you also planning to build those?"

"In due time. The helicopter is unlike the autogiro that we often see flying around. It is a totally new design. By altering the propeller angle, it can be made to go forward, backward, and sideways, and it can hover perfectly still. Moreover, it can ascend and land vertically. This is a drawing of the mechanism controlling that propeller angle...."

With Kiichiro about to launch into a lecture, Okamoto turned his palms outward and said, "Well, well. I'm certainly not knowledgeable about such things."

Kiichiro was perceptive and dropped the subject. With the courtesy due the revered head clerk from Sakichi's era, he asked, "What can I do for you?"

"It's about the expenses of the Automobile Department, which are currently of great concern to the *secondary residence* -- especially in connection with your recent decision to immediately begin mass-producing trucks. I have told him that as long as you, sir, will be doing it, I am confident of success. But as for the *secondary residence*, perhaps it would be best to give him a little more explanation."

In the Toyoda household, the *secondary residence* referred to Risaburo's residence. The term *main residence* referred to the residence of Sakichi and Asako, while Kiichiro's residence was known as the *new residence.*

Give him an explanation? Risaburo wouldn't understand if I did give him an explanation! Kiichiro was about to say this, but caught himself and withheld the comment. Okamoto was obviously not his adversary, but Kiichiro thought it better to be temperate and avoid the possibility of offending or alienating him.

"I worked for a long time under the late Master and I believe that if the Master were alive today, he would do things just as you are doing them. I'm certain that the Master would say that it's all right for Toyoda to risk bankruptcy if that's what it takes to succeed. What really matters is that an automobile industry must be established in Japan. I did what little I could do to assist the Master and hoped that Toyoda would in some way prosper. I have continued to make whatever efforts I can despite my limitations and my attitude toward the Toyoda concerns has not changed. I have a great desire to see a Japanese automobile industry become a reality, but I would hate to see the company divided over our own auto project."

Stirred by the sincerity behind Okamoto's words, Kiichiro listened attentively.

"I feel sorry for Mr. Risaburo," continued Okamoto. "His is a much more painful situation than yours. So I ask that you please have a heart-to-heart talk with him about your reasons and plans for going ahead with large-scale truck production."

Does Risaburo really deserve such sympathy and consideration? thought Kiichiro. *He is a braggart and a stuffed shirt who only knows how to preserve what has already been created. Risaburo lacks courage and is incapable of seeing past the present. But if Okamoto feels sorry for him, perhaps I should be less harsh.*

Kiichiro's prejudice toward Risaburo was deeply influenced by impressions formed much earlier in his life. Kiichiro, whose unhappy boyhood had been spent in poverty, saw Risaburo as a spoiled and pampered child. For all he knew, Risaburo played with his new toys in a towering mansion and rode his shiny new bike on a manicured lawn. Admittedly, this was a romanticized view, but one that Kiichiro could not free himself from. In reality, Risaburo came from far more humble beginnings. His family was not well-off and he did not enjoy the advantages of the aristocracy. Moreover, he was much more sensitive about his situation in life than Kiichiro gave him credit for. Risaburo was painfully aware that he was only "the adopted son" of the Toyoda family and that Kiichiro was the true son of Sakichi. This was a constant aggravation for him, like a pebble in his sandal.

For this reason, Risaburo often undervalued his real worth to the Toyoda companies. Because he had owed a great debt of gratitude to the patronage of Ichizo Kodama, who had climbed to an executive management position with Mitsui and now served as chairman of the board at Toyo Menka, Sakichi had gladly welcomed Kodama's brother into his family as the husband of his daughter, Aiko. As the adopted son, Risaburo entered the Toyoda business and quickly proved to be an attribute, as much for his competence in business as for his family ties to Mitsui and Toyo Menka, upon whom Toyoda depended heavily for its livelihood. Risaburo was proficient at managing the company's resources and helped to guide Toyoda toward stable growth. Yet he always secretly harbored the notion that he was of minor importance compared to Kiichiro. Whereas Kiichiro was free to risk the company's future on his and his father's "crazy dreams" about the automobile, Risaburo felt restricted to guarding the company's stability. That he acted as the autocratic patriarch of the Toyoda family was often only a cover-up for his more real insecurity.

As Kiichiro's understanding of Risaburo's situation broadened, his prejudice softened. But it was still difficult for him not be put off by Risaburo's presupposing arrogance, whether the result of a cover-up or not. Okamoto's present sympathy for Risaburo's plight, however, was helping Kiichiro to maintain a considerate perspective.

Yes, perhaps I should feel sorry for Risaburo, thought Kiichiro, mulling over what Okamoto had said.

At the same time, sensing that Okamoto could be a valuable ally in turmoil over finances yet to come, he decided to disclose to this discreet clerk information that might prove useful to him later on. Normally a man of few words, Kiichiro launched into a lengthy discourse:

"Risaburo and the others are completely unaware of various conditions which make the move into truck production even more critical than ever. These conditions are complex, which is why I have continued to be very vague about the subject. You are aware, of course, of the debate over the Law Concerning the Manufacture of Motor Vehicles?"

"Yes," replied Okamoto, "I know something about it. To promote domestic automobile production, the government plans to offer subsidies and protection to domestic manufacturers. Among other things, they will also lay down the rules regarding production levels for Ford, GM, and other manufacturers."

"That's right. The military is the main instigator of this plan. It all started about two or three years ago. Then suddenly in the spring of last year [1934] things started to speed up. Since relations with the United States and England have deteriorated due to the Manchurian Incident and other problems with China, the military wants to somehow build a strong Japanese automobile industry. The Ministry of Commerce and Trade holds the same opinion and previously tried to establish a large automobile manufacturing company consisting of a union of *zaibatsu* and existing domestic automobile companies. They also toyed with a number of other approaches, but none of them succeeded.

"On the subject of controlling foreign companies in Japan," Kiichiro continued, "the military and the Ministry of Commerce and Trade are worlds apart. The military favors restricting the market to domestic automobiles by enacting import restrictions. The Ministry of Commerce and Trade, on the other hand, favors a plan that would preserve a degree of freedom for importers. Essentially, the two groups have gone in totally opposite directions. That is why I was invited last summer to meet with a high-ranking official of the military."

"Really?" Okamoto asked. "This is the first I heard of it."

"That's right. Until this moment, I haven't spoken about it to anyone. To start with, a school friend of mine, named Kaoru Ban, is an expert in manufacturing for the Ministry of Commerce and Trade. It was Ban who reported to high-ranking officials of the Ministry and the military that Toyoda was test-building an automobile and had plans to mass-produce it.

"Because none of the *zaibatsu* and Japanese car companies were interested in becoming part of a large domestic automobile conglomerate, the military was at loggerheads with the Ministry of Commerce and Trade over what to do next. When they heard about our automobile project, they showed immediate interest. They secretly called me, and I told them candidly that what Toyoda intends to do is to independently mass-produce a passenger automobile like Ford and Chevrolet. We are not expecting government assistance or protection. As far as funding is concerned, even if it means spending several million yen, we will deal with that ourselves for at least the next five years. We do not plan to become dependent upon and especially not to restrict ourselves with government policies."

"I see," said Okamoto.

"The military official laughed and told me to reconsider. Then he asked me might we be willing to consider building trucks. He seemed almost to be pleading."

"Is that so?..." remarked Okamoto.

"I was careful not to commit myself to anything, but the next day I went to Karuizawa and gave it great thought. To build an automobile is a colossal undertaking. It will take much longer than I originally anticipated. To ease the financial drain that is causing everyone so much concern, I asked myself, why don't we try building trucks? After all, the government and the military are nearly begging us to do this. It will gain us valuable time. And that is why I called in Mr. Oshima and asked him to design and build a truck prototype."

"I see. Now I understand," sparked Okamoto.

"But the new factory that Ford is planning to build in Yokohama this year is not an inexpensive one like a knockdown assembly plant. We now know that they are making preparations for a large, totally integrated plant, equipped with everything from a steel mill to a parts manufacturing division. If and when this happens, there won't be any chance for domestic manufacturers to compete. Our country's efforts to promote domestic automobile manufacturing will have all been for naught.

"The people at the Ministry of Commerce and Industry were caught completely off-guard by Ford's move. Perceiving it as an immediate threat, they put aside their differences with the military and joined forces to revive the Automobile Manufacturing Law -- this time as an emergency issue."

Okamoto's eyes lit up and he continued to listen intently, determined to not miss -- nor to repeat -- a single word Kiichiro had to say.

"The Manufacturing Law, of course, puts a freeze on production of foreign automobiles in Japan. With regard to Japanese automobile manufacturers, the government will provide substantial assistance to a select group of small, highly capable companies. The only qualification is that these companies will also have to build trucks in addition to automobiles."

"I see," Okamoto said, leaning forward as he sensed that Kiichiro was nearing the crux of the matter.

"According to the preliminary report I heard earlier this month [June], the government will soon make a decision about who qualifies for the program. Only those companies that have built or are capable of building automobiles will have a chance of being chosen. Once this decision is made, no other Japanese companies will be permitted to produce automobiles, the only exception being small-shop, specialty auto makers. Furthermore, the few companies chosen will be given enough governmental assistance for them to beat the foreign competition in this country."

"When do you think this law will come into being?" Okamoto asked.

"By this summer a decision will likely be made by the Cabinet. Then, by this fall at the earliest, and by January of next year at the latest, a bill should be introduced in the Parliament. Because the government and the military are of one mind at this point, passage of the bill is inevitable. This means that by the end of this year and certainly by next spring, the bill should become law."

"In other words, we have half a year to about ten months to get something accomplished?" checked Okamoto.

"I believe so."

"That's why you...that's why you suddenly decided to rush into truck production!" yelled Okamoto, shedding his normal calmness.

"That's right. The only problem is that we haven't proved that we can produce a single automobile, let alone mass-produce them. And yet if we don't succeed before The Manufacturing Law is enacted, we'll never be permitted to build automobiles. All our hard work and investment will have been wasted. What complicates matters even further is that the grace period is only six months."

"But can't you ask them for more time?" Okamoto interjected. "They want a domestic automobile, right? Then when we've made the necessary preparations...."

"No," Kiichiro interrupted, "that won't do. Just as we are racing against time with this Manufacturing Law, the Law itself is racing against Ford. Before Ford completes preparations for their new, massive factory, the Manufacturing Law must be enacted. Unless that is done, we'll have no choice but to grant permission to Ford, which will mean a big loss for the government and the military. They don't have the luxury of waiting for Toyoda. We're still an unknown entity"

"Then, why don't they...." Okamoto started to say, the muscles in his face tightening. "Then...does such a Japanese automobile company exist...one that can deliver the quantities expected by the government and the military?"

"Yes," replied Kiichiro. "At least one company is close: Nissan Motor Company. You are, of course, familiar with a man named Yoshisuke Ayukawa?"

"Certainly," Okamoto answered. "Isn't he the founder of the Nissan company and something of a corporate wizard?"

"Exactly," Kiichiro said, nodding. "This Mr. Ayukawa came from Yamaguchi Prefecture. His father was the head of the Mori clan. After the Meiji Restoration, he worked at a company called Senshu Company, owned by Kaoru Inoue, one of Japan's most powerful politicians and adviser to the Mitsui family. After that, he went back to his hometown and did little of anything. Yoshisuke's mother, Sumi, was Inoue's older sister and she was married to Kusuyata Kimura, a high-ranking member of the Mitsubishi executive management. Sumi's sister, Kiyo, was the wife of Fusanosuke Kuhara, a member of a very honorable family. Reportedly, Yoshisuke lived at Kaoru Inoue's residence while he was attending Tokyo University. At the time, Inoue was one of the most powerful financial men in Japan, so politicians and important members of the financial community -- Eiichi Shibuzawa, for example -- were constantly parading through his house."

"Really?"

Answering Okamoto's rhetorical question with a nod, Kiichiro continued, "Consequently, Yoshisuke Ayukawa was exposed to the top men of Japan's financial and political circles very early on. In addition to having excellent connections, he is bright and aggressive. It was Ayukawa who brought the Dat Motor Company under the Nissan umbrella and who built a large factory in Yokohama. But his real stroke of genius came when he bought the complete facilities of an American automobile manufacturer named Graham-Paige. In one fell swoop he was able to create a fully equipped, modern automobile manufacturing facility by importing the plant to Japan. That clearly demonstrates his ability and commitment to automotive mass production. Mr. Ayukawa has pledged to establish every type of industry Japan needs to be self-reliant, starting with the heavy industries. He claims to be doing it for the good of the country and the people and denies any desire to become rich in the process. I'm sure there's a streak of idealism there. But you can rest assured that if there's a success in the making, Mr. Ayukawa has his hands in it.

"At one point, Mr. Ayukawa was plowing ahead with a plan to team up with GM in a joint venture to produce a Chevrolet, parts and all, entirely in Japan. What killed it was the deterioration in relations with the United States after Japan seceded from the League of Nations, and the intense opposition of the military.

"This time around, he's planning to move ahead and independently manufacture automobiles on a mass production scale. Moreover, he's got a tremendous head start. Nissan can already meet the Manufacturing Law's criteria by virtue of cars produced under the merger of Ishikawajima Motor Company, Dat Motor Company, and the revolutionary Kaishinsha of Japan Automobile Company.

"Can you see what we're up against? If only one company is chosen to produce automobiles, you can bet the government, the military, and Mr. Ayukawa himself think that company will be Nissan. On the other hand, there's an old saying about putting all your eggs in one basket, so I'm hoping the government will be wise and select more than one company to produce cars. After all, Nissan has not yet acquired the technology or experience needed to mass-produce automobiles. Still, I'm sure Mr. Ayukawa will quickly change that. He's a first-rate engineer. And if no Japanese company meets all of the government's requirements by the time the Manufacturing Law is passed, Nissan will likely still be chosen.

"I see," said Okamoto with a deep sigh. "I understand quite well now. Then will we be ready by the time the law is passed?"

"It is not a matter of will we be ready -- we **must** be ready. We have no choice," Kiichiro answered grimly.

Nodding in agreement, Okamoto responded, "Then, as I said previously, why don't you talk this over directly with the *secondary residence?*"

"Unfortunately, I cannot tell him what type of information I've received nor from whom," said Kiichiro. "In all good conscience, I cannot name any of my sources. But unless I do, my plan to manufacture trucks seems like just another of my hair-brained schemes. Yet if I try to discuss this with Risaburo without disclosing everything, I'll just muddy the waters and complicate matters further. No, the race against the clock is too tight to risk delays by involving Risaburo in my thinking.

"The sensible thing for me to do is to move ahead and ignore the criticism. Even if I'm labelled reckless, I won't waver. There's no other way but to remain silent and stay on course," Kiichiro concluded.

"I fully understand," Okamoto responded gravely.

The two of them bowed their heads and remained silent for quite some time.

Finally, Okamoto raised his head and spoke very deliberately: "For the time being, though, can't we produce just trucks? If we must also produce a passenger car, it'll be hard on me and on our pocketbooks. If the military wants trucks, why don't we concentrate on them exclusively? That way we're assured of a market and we can somehow come up with the funds."

"Will the Spinning and Weaving division give us the funds?" Kiichiro asked in a casual tone.

"No," replied Okamoto, "but I'll find funding somewhere in the company, even if it means we ultimately go bankrupt. I'm sure the late Master would want it that way. Besides, there are other sources we can tap. Please be patient for perhaps ten days to two weeks."

"Oh, thank you. I will be waiting to hear from you," said Kiichiro, closing his eyes for a few moments. Then he added, "Passenger cars are my dream. I definitely want to produce them. But I know that it's impossible to build them right now, so, for the time being, we'll focus on trucks.''

If Kiichiro understood what Okamoto meant by ''other sources,'' he gave no sign. Kiichiro continued to talk for a while about the design of the truck and what remained to be done. Okamoto listened intently, interjecting ''I see,'' ''Yes, yes,'' and ''Hmmm'' at the appropriate places. Then he went home in a good mood.

While Okamoto was talking to Kiichiro, Risaburo was still sitting in the waiting room, stewing about Okamoto's comments to him. Okamoto's arguments were dispassionate and plausible. But the more he brooded, the more convinced Risaburo became that the head clerk was leaning in favor of Kiichiro. He had been made a fool of by this crafty old accountant. Enraged, Risaburo shouted, ''Aiko!''

Hearing his yell and afraid he might be ill, Aiko appeared almost instantly from the room next door. Though fifteen years younger than Risaburo, Aiko appeared as solicitous as a mother calming a frightened child. ''Is something wrong?'' she asked.

''I'm going to have Kiichiro declared incompetent! If we let him continue to run rampant, the House of Toyoda will collapse!''

''I'm not sure I understand,'' Aiko said quietly.

''Trucks! Without discussing it with anyone, he made the unilateral decision to start manufacturing trucks,'' Risaburo sputtered. ''He's already spent five million yen trying to build a car! What am I? His errand boy? He doesn't even have the common courtesy to consult the president of the company. He makes a fool out of me. I can't...ah....''

Risaburo had worked himself into such a rage that he lost track of what he was saying.

''But....'' Aiko started to say something, when Risaburo blurted out:

''He is insane!''

''But I've heard that Father was also called that by everyone when he was young,'' Aiko said.

Risaburo stared at her in total surprise; for the first time since they had married, Aiko said ''but'' to him.

She spoke in her normal voice -- quiet and serene -- but there was an air of determination in her words.

It's all right even if Toyoda does go bankrupt, thought Aiko.

Sakichi had left an enormous bequest to her and Risaburo in his will. To Kiichiro he had left all of the assets that had accrued in the Toyoda family before Sakichi's time -- the fields, mountain forests, the house and the estate in Kosai where Sakichi was born.

Except for special bequests, what Sakichi acquired during his lifetime was split among the three, half going to Kiichiro, and the other half to Risaburo and Aiko. That included Sakichi's shares of stock in Toyoda Automatic Loom Works, Toyoda Spinning and Weaving and related enterprises, the real estate in Nagoya, Kariya and other areas, and substantial bank deposits.

By today's standards, such a division of wealth would be considered normal. For the times, however, it was revolutionary. The customary arrangement under the old civil code was to award the total inheritance to the oldest son, which would be Kiichiro; nothing would go to his brothers or sisters. But Sakichi's deep love for Aiko lay behind his departure from custom.

Aiko happened to be in the next room when her husband and Okamoto were talking. When she overheard the angry comments Risaburo made about her brother, she shook her head ruefully.

By any social standard, Risaburo and I have been blessed. After Father's death, Risaburo immediately became a director and president, and was given a large salary. He now occupies the "secondary residence" which is far more affluent than Kiichiro's "new residence." Why then does Risaburo have such insecurities about Kiichiro? Why won't he cooperate with my brother?

Aiko felt very sad. From the beginning, because of the differences in their personalities and circumstances, Risaburo and Kiichiro were incompatible, but they both made an effort to be cordial and polite to each other. Ever since the automobile project began in earnest, however, their relationship had steadily become more strained, which filled Aiko with anxiety.

Listening to her husband's conversation with Okamoto, Aiko had walked over to a display shelf and picked up a small, plain, old wooden box. She opened the cover and poured the contents on the table. Out rattled twenty or thirty small shells, each one a memory that came flooding back to her.

It was on an early day many years before, when Aiko was still a preschooler and Kiichiro was attending elementary school, that Kiichiro had picked up these shells for Aiko during a field trip to the seashore. Sakichi was hard at work on his loom and Asako was so engrossed in running the business that the two children were feeling severely neglected. Without Kiichiro, Aiko would have felt totally alone and abandoned.

Kiichiro was a kind and thoughtful brother. Since household finances were tight and there was no extra money to buy dolls or toys, Kiichiro handmade many of Aiko's playthings. When bamboo dragonflies became popular, he went to the bamboo groves several miles away and chopped down bamboo shoots for making countless dragonflies for Aiko. At first, his craftsmanship was crude, but by the time he was done, he had perfected the toy. Aiko's dragonflies remained airborne much longer than anyone else's.

Aiko also remembered coming home one rainy day. She had tripped over a rock and broken one of her *geta* (clogs). Instead of going to her mother, who would have given her a scolding, she had gone straight to Kiichiro.

"Here, give it to me," Kiichiro had said.

After inspecting the broken heel, with Aiko following right behind, he took the *geta* with him into his father's workshop. The shop had everything one needed for woodworking -- hammers, saws, planers, hand drills and chisels, carving tools, and various planks and rectangular shaped pieces of wood. Kiichiro selected a wood scrap a little larger than the heel, clamped it in a carpenter's vise, and began shaving it to size with a small hand planer. When the size seemed right, he sanded the heel to a smooth finish, fixed the clog and gave it to Aiko to try on. It was a bit too high, and caused her to limp.

Though Aiko never complained, Kiichiro said, "No. Let me have it again."

As he planed and sanded it a second time, Aiko snuggled happily against her big brother, watching him as he worked, his hands dirty from the wet, muddy *geta*.

My big brother will do anything for me, Aiko thought blissfully.

Kiichiro had done much the same thing when he brought home Aiko's seashells. Seeing how happy she was playing with them, Kiichiro smiled and asked her, "Do you really like these shells that much?"

"They are Aiko's treasures," she replied.

"Okay. Then I'll make a treasure box for you," he told her.

Kiichiro went straight into Sakichi's workshop, found a solid piece of fine-grained cherry wood. He even carved an arabesque on the cover and finished the box with dark brown lacquer.

Although Aiko and Risaburo were wealthy enough to buy the most skillfully crafted treasure box to fill with expensive treasures, the box of seashells always sat in a place of honor on Aiko's shelf. These were Aiko's true treasures. The shells were now chipped and worn and had long since lost their luster, but in every precious one resided a memory of her brother during their lonely childhood days.

When Aiko had heard Risaburo loudly complaining about the money Kiichiro was spending on the Automobile Department, she was nearly moved to tears. Upset that Risaburo was reacting this way, she whispered to herself defiantly; *If my big brother is going to make it, then it's sure to be the best automobile in the world.*

Now, standing face to face with her irate husband, Aiko said calmly but firmly, "They say that even Father was called a lunatic, a good-for-nothing. But Father won out despite such criticism. I fully understand your concern, yet Kiichiro should do as he thinks best."

Aiko normally went out of her way to placate her husband, but this was something very different. She had faith in her brother and was determined to protect him, no matter what the consequences would be for her insolence.

"Fool! Even you're against me!" Risaburo shouted angrily.

Aiko had never contradicted him, even when he recognized he was clearly in the wrong. But he wasn't wrong in this case. Kiichiro had to be stopped, or they would all become paupers as the Automobile Department sank the company into bankruptcy. Risaburo also knew he would never be able to convince his wife of this. Still furious and now frustrated at his wife's resistance, Risaburo felt a deep sense of inadequacy and personal failure. He hung his head in silence as Aiko sat down opposite him and gazed at him with sad eyes.

Perhaps I never will be able to understand what runs in the blood of the Toyoda family after all, Risaburo thought, his frustration giving way to self-pity and leaving him close to tears.

Risaburo had given every bit of himself to protect the Toyoda interests. Didn't the prosperity of the parent firm, Toyoda Automatic Loom Works, and the development of the Toyoda Spinning and Weaving subsidiary mean anything? If he was now standing firm in protecting the Toyoda interests, could that be seen as a betrayal of the Toyoda family?

Perhaps Okamoto was right after all, maybe Risaburo was one to be pitied. He was the one shareholders and bankers upbraided whenever they had complaints, and now they were complaining all the time. Certainly that deserved a little sympathy.

Eyes still ablaze, his face pale and directed at the floor, Risaburo remained seated without saying a word. The gray hair on his balding head seemed to stand out, making Aiko feel for a moment that Risaburo looked like a man in his seventies rather than in his mid-fifties. She wanted to speak but remained silent. Nothing more was said that evening and the incident was not mentioned again. On an evening in June some two weeks later, just after the end of the rainy season, Kiichiro received a telephone call from Okamoto. Akitsugu Nishikawa had just returned from Shanghai and had invited he, Risaburo, and Kiichiro to join him for an evening at the Yayoi. By the time Kiichiro arrived, Okamoto and Nishikawa had already been seated and were waiting patiently. Kiichiro was escorted to a seat in the alcove where he always sat when visiting the Yayoi.

"The *secondary residence* will be arriving shortly," Okamoto explained quietly with a smile.

Seven or eight beautiful *geishas* were seated in the room, serving their guests *sake*, and playing the *shamisen*. Everything had been arranged by the host, Nishikawa, to be open and friendly, certainly not an arrangement conducive to secret consultations.

As Nishikawa began to speak about recent conditions in Shanghai, Risaburo entered, guided by *O-su*.

"What is this?" laughed Risaburo, eying the *geishas* and remarking jovially. "What's the occasion worthy of having so many beauties lined up in here?" Chuckling at his own joke, he moved to take his place in the upper seat as Kiichiro shyly avoided his glance, fiddling with his cigarette box.

Rising from his seat, Nishikawa bade Risaburo welcome and said, "It's been a long time. Since our last meeting, I have heard many good things about what you are doing. This is a happy occasion."

Puzzled, Risaburo replied, "Mr. Nishikawa, may I ask what you mean by 'happy occasion?' What is there to be so happy about?"

Nishikawa had been with the Toyoda organization longer than anyone, with the exception of Sakichi himself, so Risaburo spoke to him with polite respect. Nishikawa responded to Risaburo's question in a roundabout way:

"Well, during his stay in Shanghai, the great Master spoke frequently of the role of the automobile in civilizing Asia. Yet he was very distressed to see that every automobile that arrived was made in either the United States or Europe. It was his feeling that Japan must devote its energies to developing an automobile industry to rival the United States. The Master thought about this continually.

"Now I hear that the Toyoda Group has finally taken the lead in Japan by deciding to produce automobiles. I was overjoyed to learn that the first prototype has already been built and is in operation. Were he alive today, the Master would be very happy indeed, and this is why I referred to this evening as a 'happy occasion.' "

Nishikawa paused momentarily and then continued in a serious manner: "The late Master always said that the son doesn't have to follow in the father's footsteps. Nor must brothers pursue an identical course in life. He always said that at least one son must explore new territory. That is why I want to commend Kiichiro for boldly venturing into automobile manufacturing. And I want to commend you, sir, for giving him your support and cooperation."

Nishikawa appeared a little choked up. He paused to clear his throat and then continued, "I don't know what to say, this is such an exhilarating development that it fills me with happiness. This is truly a joyous occasion."

The crafty Nishikawa took out his handkerchief and made a gesture to wipe his tears. This might have been overdoing it a bit, yet Nishikawa did feel strongly about the automobile project and its implications for the future of Japan. As he spoke, the *geishas* sat with their hands in their laps and listened quietly.

"You say this is a 'joyous occasion,' but we still don't know if we can do it or not. Besides, it's going to require an enormous amount of capital," Risaburo said, his facial expression now changed to one of obvious displeasure.

"Yes, that is certainly so," Nishikawa conceded. "But, let me tell you a story. When the late Master was first getting started and working on his inventions, we had a very difficult time coming up with funds. Asako was forced to frequent the pawnshop, as the banks refused to lend us much of anything. I went to the shrine every day to pray. Yet we survived and prospered, and that is my point. Unless we take risks, we never have a chance of achieving anything but mediocre success. That was the situation we faced when expanding our business into China. Money was tight, but we took the chance and succeeded."

Nishikawa spoke in a cheerful voice, but one which did not disguise the seriousness of his words:

"The late Master maintained that it was critical for Japan to establish good relations with China. As a sign of his commitment to this idea, he lived in Shanghai during his last seven or eight years, and asked to be buried in China. The late Master was a true visionary. Though the atmosphere between Japan and China is very strained at present and war may be imminent, in the future we will eventually heal our differences and once again join hands to end the domination of the Chinese continent by the British, Americans, Russians, and French.

"Sakichi believed this would eventually come to pass. When it does, I assure you Japan will throw off the yoke of Ford and GM, and Toyoda will sell automobiles in every corner of China and the rest of the world."

Having carefully set the stage and laid his groundwork, Nishikawa got to his main point:

"It was in 1910, roughly a quarter of a century ago, that the late Master resigned from Toyoda Loom Works. Just out of college with a degree in textiles, I was invited to accompany him on a trip to the United States. When we crossed the tall bridge that connects the island of Manhattan in New York with New Jersey, the late Master looked down at the endless stream of cars on the riverside road below and said they reminded him of rows of ants. He turned to me and said, 'Nishikawa, make sure you get a good look at those rows of ants. We produced an automatic loom and grew to the point where our name, Toyoda, became known throughout the world. I have wagered half of my life to complete this loom, but you young people must not forget the sight of those rows of ants. The automotive age definitely will come and Japan must be a part of it. You must apply the skills you've acquired in the loom business to building automobiles one day, and they must be better and there must be more of them than you see down there.' "

"I remember the late Master's words as clearly as if they were spoken yesterday. Thus for the past twenty-five years, I have felt great sorrow for not pursuing the manufacture of automobiles and following his wishes." Nishikawa again made a gesture to blot tears from his cheeks. Then he straightened himself in his chair and threw his shoulders back, as he continued to speak:

"So, I'm happy you have entered the 'automobile race.' Please excuse my forwardness, but if there is anything we can do to help with this venture, our services in Shanghai are at your disposal. That is why I dragged these old bones to this meeting today. I have heard from Mr. Okamoto that you are planning to increase your investment in the Automobile Department by three million yen. If I do not offend, please let me contribute that amount from my end of the business. It's the least I can do to redeem myself for not doing what the late Master had instructed."

So this is what Okamoto meant by "other sources," thought Kiichiro, as he looked at Nishikawa and smiled inwardly.

Nishikawa was a distant relative of Asako. Born in 1881, he was three years older than Risaburo, but had been with Toyoda many more years. It was Nishikawa whom Sakichi had told, "The industrial age has dawned. You should attend the Engineering School at Tokyo University or you will not go far in this new world." Nishikawa studied textiles, graduated in 1909, and spent the next two years learning the textile industry of the United States. When he returned to Japan, he became Sakichi's right-hand man, managing the business so Sakichi could concentrate on his inventions. It was also Nishikawa who had helped Kiichiro and Aiko to find better schools and who had worked closely with Sakichi on improving Chinese-Japanese relations. In China, Nishikawa was so well-respected that after World War II, he was asked by the Communist government to remain in Shanghai as a high-ranking government adviser. Nishikawa stayed in China until 1949 and conducted workshops on the manufacture of spinning and weaving machinery, broadening his own experience with the industry. Nishikawa was widely known as a shrewd business man and was a worthy opponent for Risaburo, as Kiichiro well understood.

When Nishikawa had finished his offer to underwrite recapitalization of the Automobile Department, Risaburo had responded with a simple "I see." His mood was very pensive and until that moment, he had convinced himself that the initiative was his and that Kiichiro had isolated himself from the rest of the world by his obstinacy. Now it became painfully apparent to him that he was the one who was isolated. Once again the world proved thankless for all of the effort he had put into the Toyoda business and into holding the Toyoda family together. Risaburo became sullen and quiet as Okamoto began to speak:

"Mr. Kiichiro has agreed to set aside development of automobiles for production of trucks, as trucks have an immediate market. Furthermore, the government is eager to provide financial assistance and protection. Over the next six months, a Toyoda truck will be designed, tested, manufactured, and put out on the market...."

As quickly as it had turned sullen, Risaburo's mood lightened and he seemed to show genuine excitement for this course of action. Smiling broadly, he said:

"Why don't we give it a try, Kiichiro? Let's quickly buy that land in Koromo and build the best factory in the world! Mr. Okamoto, it's all right if Toyoda Automatic Loom Works collapses, it's all right if Toyoda Spinning and Weaving goes bankrupt. If worse comes to worst, Mr. Nishikawa, please be prepared for the Shanghai company to join us in bankruptcy!"

Chuckling gleefully, Nishikawa said, "No need to worry. If bankruptcy had been a major concern, there is no way we could have kept up with the late Master for even one day."

Impulsively raising his *sake* cup, Risaburo shouted, "All right. Let's have a toast! To Toyoda automobiles! *Banzai!*"

Jumping to their feet, Nishikawa and Okamoto raised their *sake* cups and, with the *geishas* joining in, they swelled their chests with yells of:

"*Banzai! Banzai!*"

The emotion of the moment was so overwhelming that it moved even the stoic Kiichiro to tears. Nishikawa and Okamoto were relieved to see their plan had worked so meticulously. Now, all that remained was to make this very ambitious dream a reality, and that was going to be a challenge far greater than swaying Risaburo to their cause.

The *geishas* chanting their *banzais* had been carefully selected for this occasion because of their familiarity with the business magnates of Nagoya. No sooner than the party would end and news of Toyoda's decision to manufacture trucks would be leaked to the rest of the Japanese world. By the next morning, Toyoda's bridges would be burnt and there would be no turning back.

Before returning to Shanghai, Nishikawa gave Okamoto the promissory note for three million yen. The Automobile Department was truly on its way, thought everyone knew that many dark thickets lay ahead. At least Risaburo would not represent one of them. Not only had he become an enthusiastic supporter, but he took it upon himself to personally pave the way for Kiichiro's efforts.

The game plan for manufacture took shape as blueprints for the factory and vehicle specifications were worked out. According to the final production schedule, 150 to 200 trucks per month were to be rolling off the assembly line starting in January of the following year, 1936.

While harmony held sway within the executive ranks of the company and among the people directly working on automobile production, the successful coup at the Yayoi by no means quashed all opposition to the venture. Suspicion continued to smolder among the larger shareholders and banks, while internally, employees of the loom and spinning departments continued to grumble about "the free ride" accorded the crew of the Automobile Department.

As usual, Kiichiro took all of this opposition in stride:

"It is only natural for most of the large shareholders to question whether we can do it. Several years of man hours, hard work, and millions of yen have been expended and so far we don't have a single vehicle to show for it. It's the age old conflict between the entrepreneurs and financiers. Unless there is an entrepreneur with enough courage to build a car, no financier will undertake the venture. And yet, when an entrepreneur does come forth with courage and a dream, the financiers are hesitant to help without the guarantee of a profit. It's a wonder anything ever gets changed or improved."

As Kiichiro mused about the short-sightedness of the financiers, Risaburo came under heavy fire from investors. His mood was ambivalent, but for the most part his optimism for the success of the venture was strong enough for him to shrug off his critics.

Negotiations to purchase the Koromo factory property moved into high gear, and the increase in capital made possible by Nishikawa was doubled to six million yen through a decision made at a special stockholders meeting on July 9. Four million yen was granted to the Automobile Department.

In August of 1935, the long-awaited bill concerning the Manufacture of Automobiles was approved by the Cabinet and now only needed the approval of the Parliament to become law. The highlights of the pending legislation were: (1) the right to manufacture automobiles would be granted to a very small number of companies; (2) these companies would be publicly held companies, with majority ownership by Japanese, and not foreign investors; (3) these companies would be regulated according to government and national defense requirements; (4) rights previously granted to existing domestic automobile manufacturers would be honored, but no new rights would be granted; and (5) to establish a thoroughly autonomous industry (partly for reasons of national security) automobiles would be built only with domestically made parts. Those companies able to meet these requirements would receive special governmental subsidies.

The nature of this bill was as exactly as Kiichiro had previously reported to Okamoto. In clauses four and five, the national objective was clearly implied. Japanese companies would be brought on par with Ford and General Motors, and all companies would compete equally. In total, eleven companies would be allowed in the competition, beginning with Nissan Motor company and including Toyoda Automatic Loom Works, Ford, and General Motors. When word of the Ministry of Commerce and Industry's decision came, Kiichiro felt a heavy burden lifted from his shoulders.

But the news was bitter-sweet. Kiichiro had initially dreamed of mass-producing passenger cars and competing in the domestic and global marketplaces without government help or restrictions. Now that dream had vanished for the time being.

And so had the risk of financial failure.

The first Model G1 truck prototype was completed on August 25, 1936, approximately two weeks after the Cabinet approved the new bill. Work on the A1 had not been a total waste after all. Without experience virtually clawed and sweated from production of the A1 prototype, Toyoda would never have been able to move quickly enough to earn a berth in the new domestic automobile program. The fact of the matter still remained, however, that somewhere in the plant sat the remnants of Kiichiro's early vision gathering dust -- the three Model A1 automobiles produced to date.

Chapter
7

SIX TRUCKS

Amidst the flurry of activity to accomplish everything at once, no one noticed the cool breezes of September had arrived. Model G1 trucks were rolling off the assembly line of the Kariya pilot plant at a rate of two hundred per month. As testing and production were proceeding simultaneously, required corrections and modifications were done right on line. It was not the most desirable arrangement, but it was the best that could be done under the circumstances. The operative word for the truck production program was expediency.

It was during this period that Tojiro Okamoto was paid a visit at his residence in Nagoya. According to his business card, the callers name was Shataro Kamiya. When Okamoto was informed of this man standing at his front entrance, he rushed to the door and bowed deeply, saying, "Oh my, Mr. Kamiya! It's been a very long time! Please come in." Okamoto ushered his honored guest into the living room.

"I am sorry for neglecting to call on you sooner. It must be nearly twenty years since we last saw each other in Seattle," said Kamiya.

"I can't believe it's been that long. That must have been back in 1918 or 1919. How time flies...." The two men were in a jovial mood and soon settled into a long reminiscence.

They had met when employed abroad by Mitsui and Company, later to become Toyo Menka. Okamoto normally worked out of Dallas, Texas, but was on temporary assignment in Seattle, Washington. It was through the Seattle Branch Manager, Reisuke Ishida, who gained widespread recognition as president of Japan National Railways after World War II, that Okamoto met Kamiya. A similarity in personalities and common interests between the young men created a lasting friendship.

Ten years Okamoto's junior, Kamiya was twenty-one and just out of trade school. He was a cheerful, articulate, and hardworking lad and had already accomplished enough to prove his maturity beyond his years. His excellent service as a Mitsui representative in the United States won him a quick promotion to the company's foreign headquarters in London. While in London, Kamiya came to the realization that his chances of moving up further in the company were severely hampered by his lack of a degree from one of the elite Japanese universities, such as Hitotsubashi, Keio, or Tokyo. As a result, he resigned and founded his own company in London exporting steel goods to Japan. From its humble beginnings as a two-person operation -- Kamiya and a typist -- the export company grew into a work force of some thirty employees of varying nationalities. Unfortunately, the Great Depression saw the Kamiya Trading Company go bankrupt, at which point Kamiya returned to Japan.

Due to his superior bilingual skills and management experience, Kamiya was soon employed by General Motors of Japan, newly headquarted in Osaka. There he served briefly as a managerial assistant, only to be promoted to manager of GM's Tokyo office. Eventually, he returned to the Osaka headquarters as director of advertising, becoming the first Japanese appointed to an executive position in General Motors. Kamiya's meteoric success made for an interesting story and certainly one Okamoto enjoyed listening to.

"I would like to ask you something," Kamiya said to Okamoto looking him directly in the eye. "I have heard that Mr. Toyoda's company has just started manufacturing automobiles. Do you and your people have any experience in marketing?"

"No," Okamoto replied frankly, "none whatsoever. If you know of anyone in marketing that could help us out, please let me know."

"Well, at the moment, I don't have anyone in mind. But GM of Japan has just set up what they are calling General Motors Acceptance Corporation, a loan division for helping customers finance their autos. I don't want to work for foreigners forever. So I thought perhaps I could help your company set up a similar plan," said Kamiya.

"A Toyoda finance division,..." Okamoto puzzled, his eyes narrowing.

"Yes. You wouldn't need much capital. Since the company belongs to the Toyoda group and that's a name that carries a lot of clout in financial circles. The banks will be only too happy to give you funding."

Okamoto began warming to the idea. Only a month before, he had confronted Kiichiro with the issue of marketing. As Okamoto had put it, assuming they were successful in building automobiles, another major hurdle would still await them: "We must think carefully about how we are going to sell them!"

"Oh dear! I haven't given that matter any thought at all," Kiichiro had replied, staring wide-eyed at Okamoto.

Okamoto chuckled to himself: *It's just like Mr. Kiichiro to concentrate on the technical matters and forget about everything else.* He could well anticipate Kiichiro's solution to the problem.

"Let's finish the car first," Kiichiro had said. "We'll think about selling them later."

It was just as Okamoto had suspected. Nothing more was said on the subject.

One of the reasons Toyoda Automatic Loom Works lacked a solid retail marketing strategy lay in the nature of their business. As a manufacturer of a single high-priced item, their market was a relatively limited universe of large and small textile companies reached through independent wholesalers. Because they too sold directly to wholesalers, Toyoda Spinning and.Weaving could offer their sister company little-or-no assistance in marketing the automobiles.

Gazing at his old chum of earlier days, Okamoto had a sudden flash: "Tell you what. Why don't you let me arrange a meeting with Mr. Kiichiro, Toyoda's senior vice president. He's in charge of the Automobile Department, and I know he's looking for marketing ideas. You might be able to provide just what he's looking for."

Kamiya nodded in agreement, and Okamoto rose to telephone Kiichiro. Kiichiro was indeed interested in Kamiya's management skills and strong sales background and asked for a meeting that very evening.

The meeting took place in a nearby restaurant. As soon as Kamiya was introduced, Kiichiro spoke to him without preamble, as if he were addressing an old friend: "Perhaps you know more about this than I do, but Ford of Japan has ignored opposition from the Ministry of Commerce and Industry and the War Ministry and has purchased land in Yokohama, as recently as July.

"If they build a huge factory as planned, that means tens of thousands or even hundreds of thousands of cars will be produced there annually. From that threat alone, not to mention Ford's other operations in our country, it's possible the Japanese automobile industry will permanently lose any chance of getting a foothold in our own marketplace. This is why the government is hurrying to pass the Law Concerning the Manufacture of Automobiles. It will help to keep local expansion by Ford and General Motors in check. But it also puts a great burden on us. Because Japan lacks a competitive, domestic automobile industry, we must fight frantically to begin mass production of trucks in the shortest time possible."

"I see," answered Kamiya, comfortable with Kiichiro's directness. He had been exposed to much of the same behavior in America and was accustomed to a lack of formal greetings.

Kiichiro continued, "But Ford and GM are not simply ahead of us in production technology and facilities. I believe they also have well-established marketing organizations. You would know that better than I. But the point is, both companies have established dealerships in various prefectures throughout Japan and are already deeply entrenched in our Japanese society."

"Well, yes, that's true," Kamiya replied.

"That's what I want to talk about," continued Kiichiro. "As far as design and manufacturing are concerned, I'll do my humble best to see that the project succeeds. I'd better! I've wagered my life on this project. I've done all I can to bring on board every talented engineer I can find in Japan. But I have no knowledge of marketing, nor do I have any marketing experts to turn to. Frankly, Mr. Kamiya, I'm stymied."

"You are being modest...." Kamiya started to say, before Kiichiro interrupted: "Not at all. I am being very honest. Please, Mr. Kamiya, join our team and manage the marketing end of our business. Naturally, you'll be given a free hand to do whatever you think necessary."

"That is...." Kamiya began to reply before falling silent. He was thoroughly nonplussed by Kiichiro's directness and strange familiarity. In essence, Kamiya was being offered a full management position and unlimited resources to build a marketing department for Toyoda, and before that evening he had never even met this man called Kiichiro.

Seeing Kamiya somewhat overcome by the offer, Kiichiro went on: "I am asking you to do this for more than just Toyoda's sake. I'm asking you to do it for the sake of Japan. Unless Japan builds an automobile industry, other vital industries will never have a chance of flourishing. If nothing changes in the current situation, Japan will end up like Canada: Ford took the lion's share of the Canadian market by means of its knockdown production facilities, and the entire nation lost any opportunity for spawning a domestic automobile industry. Just as Canada has succumbed to foreign domination, Japan's industrial markets will be ruled by United States firms. Japan will permanently become an economic colony of the United States. Please give this matter careful consideration."

Kamiya was greatly moved, but Kiichiro wasn't saying anything Kamiya hadn't thought before. He had worked for an American car manufacturer and well understood their ambitions for cornering the world market. Without going into his own feelings, Kamiya politely concurred with Kiichiro and said: "Of course, that is so. Would you please let me tour the plant?"

"Of course," Kiichiro said, getting to his feet. "Let's go!"

Kamiya threw up his hands and smiled broadly: "No, no, not tonight -- tomorrow perhaps?"

"All right then, let's do it tomorrow," Kiichiro said, sitting down and immediately resuming the conversation where he left off:

"By the way, we'll be competing with proven vehicles from Ford and General Motors. Do you think there's a market for domestic automobiles?"

Smiling, Kamiya shook his head, no: "A market is something that must be created. Just as you have brought together engineers to create a product called an automobile, we must also bring together experts in marketing from all over Japan in order to create a market. There's no other way."

"I see," Kiichiro said thoughtfully. "I agree with that. Then please do it in that manner."

Kamiya stared wide-eyed at Kiichiro for a moment, thinking: *The rumors I've heard about Mr. Toyoda's straight-forwardness and swift decisiveness are an understatement. This guy is really incredible! He's already assuming I've accepted his offer. I like this job already.*

Kamiya suddenly chuckled to himself as he realized he, too, had been talking as though he were already a Toyoda employee.

The next day, with Kiichiro as guide, Kamiya toured the Kariya automobile plant. He was aware this was only a temporary pilot plant involved with building prototypes and that the permanent facility was still in the planning stage. Thus, Kamiya expected to see no more than five or ten units under construction. To his great surprise, this "temporary" factory was equipped with complete lab and testing facilities, as well as a full-scale steel mill. Instead of a handful of trucks under construction, Kamiya saw two hundred in various stages of assembly on the assembly line. As he met the members of the engineering staff, he was extremely impressed to hear the names of pioneers and grizzled veterans of the Japanese automobile industry, people like Takatoshi Kan and Higuma Ikenaga. Even the younger engineers like Iwaoka and Shirai already had a surprisingly good grasp of automotive technology.

After the tour ended, as Kamiya stood near the end of the assembly line, Kiichiro asked, "Well, what do you think?"

What do I think? I think this Toyoda venture will be a success. Kiichiro Toyoda will make it happen. He is a colossal man! thought Kamiya, filled with awe and excitement. He accepted the job on the spot, and Kiichiro responded by giving the new employee his marching orders:

"Good. Please start organizing dealers at once. I want you to handle everything."

Kamiya set to his task immediately. After a brief orientation, he returned to Nagoya and went to Daichimachi to see Noboru Yamaguchi, the manager of Hinode Motors, a General Motors dealership for mid-sized and luxury General Motors cars. Daichimachi was the area where Kiichiro had taken the young Iwaoka for an education in "foreign automotive dominance" and also where he first disclosed his dream of building Toyoda automobiles.

"Mr. Yamaguchi, I'm leaving GM," Kamiya blurted out the moment he entered the wood-paneled, Western-style manager's office.

"You're quitting? Why? If you leave, then what will I do? What will happen to Hinode Motors?" sputtered Yamaguchi in a panic. His height was about the same as Kamiya's, and while he could not be described as tall, he was solidly-built with an extremely wide chest and large hips that gave him a daunting, even somewhat intimidating appearance. At forty, Yamaguchi was two years older than Kamiya.

"Yes," Kamiya answered, head held high. "I'm through with working for foreign companies. I've decided to join Mr. Kiichiro's Toyoda automobile company and to stake my career on successfully marketing domestic automobiles."

Without a moment's hesitation, Yamaguchi exclaimed: "Okay! Then please take me with you!"

"Think carefully before you commit yourself. The future of sales is very uncertain. We don't know if these Toyoda vehicles will move," Kamiya warned.

"That's good enough for me," Yamaguchi answered jokingly. "If they don't move, then we'll push them."

"Well," Kamiya grinned, "if you say so."

"To tell the truth, I'm also at my limit with working for foreigners," Yamaguchi said. "Besides, when we leave, maybe Hinode Motors will become Hinoku Motors."

Kamiya appreciated the wit and smiled: "Perhaps you're right."

In Japanese, Hinode is the word for sunrise and Hinoku for sunset. What made Yamaguchi's play on words even more witty was the fact that Hinode Motors was notorious for being pressed for money and always on the verge of bankruptcy.

Telling Kamiya he didn't need to think it over, Yamaguchi repeated his decision, and they promised each other they'd take the next step together. Ironically, Hinode Motors would not collapse into Hinoku Motors, but instead would become the first dealership for Toyoda automobiles. Kamiya and Yamaguchi shook hands to seal their bargain and "tipped their hats" good-bye for now to Hinode, happy about the new destinies awaiting them. Kamiya felt elated to have such a solid beginning in putting together his marketing team.

Yamaguchi was indeed a good catch. Dubbed "the commander" by his close friends and associates because of his colorful nature and blithe spirit, he had been the hero of his high school baseball team. In 1916, it had been Yamaguchi who led Tokyo's Sakurabibayashi High School to the pennant during the second National High School Baseball Tournament, an accomplishment not to be realized again by a Tokyo high school for another sixty years.

Yamaguchi was Sakurabibayashi's ace pitcher and was named the game's Most Valuable Player for his accurate throws, timely hits, and runs batted in. At the time, the great baseball journalist Hashido praised him highly, writing, "Yamaguchi of Keio is the consummate ball player."

Actually, such praise was nothing new for Yamaguchi. Outstanding academically, he was often allowed to attend classes at Keio University though still officially enrolled in what was then called "middle school," the equivalent of today's high school.

After Yamaguchi graduated from middle school and entered Keio University, his father's business failed. The family was left without resources to continue their son's education. Eventually, Yamaguchi was recruited by Taipei Sugar Refinery, a national company looking for talented university athletes from Tokyo. Accompanied by Meiji University's Gensaburo Okada, he left for Taipei where he lived for several years. Upon returning to his hometown, he was recommended by a friend and hired by an import automobile dealership in Nagoya.

Financial insecurity at that time plagued the import automobile dealership business, and Hinode Motors was no exception. It was a familiar story. The downhill slide of a dealership started almost the day it opened, as the foreign parent company took on an increasingly larger share of the profits and treated their overseas dealers with indifference and neglect. Of course, they had nothing to lose. There was always another Japanese entrepreneur to take over the dealership once it failed, which it always did.

In the spring of 1927, Yamaguchi had gone to work for Yutaka Motors, then a Chrysler dealership. Not long after, Yutaka was approached by General Motors, then just beginning to build its dealer network in Japan. Whatever the offer, Yutaka Motors must have found it attractive, for it promptly left Chrysler for GM and took Yamaguchi with it.

General Motors in general was having greater success than Ford in establishing a "dealer network." Ford had gotten a head start, but GM had quickly taken the lead because of better organization. Actually GM had two networks: one for handling its low-end cars, such as Chevrolet, and another for its more expensive line. Yutaka Motors was chosen to sell the high-end line of Buicks, Oldsmobiles, and GMC trucks. Moreover, it was assigned a territory covering seven prefectures: Aichi, Mie, Gifu, Nagano, Fukui, Ishikawa, and the northeastern area of Toyama. It looked like an attractive deal to Yutaka, but GM undercut it by limiting the dealer contract to one year and setting an unreasonable sales quota. It was a high pressure tactic used by all of the foreign manufacturers. If a dealership failed to meet its annual sales quota, it was closed immediately -- no questions asked.

Generally, the consumer cost for a low-end car like a Chevrolet was a little over 2,000 yen, while Buicks and other high-end cars sold for 3,500 yen and up (both enormous amounts based on today's monetary exchange rates). To stay in business selling low-end cars was substantially easier than selling the high-priced lines. With twenty or thirty employees, a low-end dealer could survive on four or five sales per month, assuming that the average mark-up was 20 to 22 percent. The problems faced by a high-end dealer, on the other hand, were low demand and high-price, though no one was sure which came first. Since Yutaka was a high-end dealer, it had to hustle to make ends meet and was always faced with an uncertain future.

There were other problems as well. The typical dealership agreement stipulated the number of cars to be inventoried and the cost of each car to the dealer. The catch was that the dealer had to pay cash for every car arriving from the foreign supplier, which especially left the high-end dealer with perpetual cash flow problems. If sales slumped, the dealer virtually "got killed" by his inventory, not to mention the hole he had already dug for himself as a result of incredible start-up costs.

Like nearly all foreign automobile dealerships, Yutaka Motors found the going rough. After only a year, it changed hands to become Isao Motors, which had little more luck than its predecessor.

It was during the time that Isao Motors was near bankruptcy, that General Motors' Shotaro Kamiya became district manager for the northeastern region. Since Yamaguchi had made the transition from Yutaka to Isao Motors, it was there the two men met. Kamiya was a highly self-motivated district manager, and Yamaguchi quickly came to admire and respect this quality in him. Kamiya pursued every lead and didn't hesitate to negotiate firmly with his American employer. This was unlike other district managers, who fell prey to the lethargy and pessimism built into the system by indifference of the parent company. Once it became apparent that Isao Motors was about to collapse, Kamiya was instructed to lay the ground work for new ownership. His first contact was his old friend Yamaguchi, now the highest-ranking employee at Isao. Yamaguchi agreed to take over the dealership, but with certain stipulations. He made it very clear that General Motors would have to amend the dealership contract. Kamiya later remembered being somewhat taken aback by Yamaguchi's forthrightness.

"What do you mean by 'amend the contract?' " Kamiya had asked.

"Number one," Yamaguchi had answered, "all the employees of Isao must be offered employment in the new dealership. Number two, when a dealer's contract is canceled, normally the contract stipulates the new company must start from scratch. That's totally unreasonable. I want all sales credits and receivables transferred over to the new dealership. With that, the new dealership will have a little seed money and a good chance of survival.''

"I understand. Let me see what I can do," Kamiya had promised. Being a man of honor, he always stood by his promises.

Hinode Motors was soon established under new ownership, with Yamaguchi as its manager. Unfortunately, improvements in the contract weren't matched by improvements in sales, and like its two predecessors, Hinode Motors quickly became strapped for funds, prompting the derisive "Hinoku Motors" jokes.

As a last ditch effort to stay in business, Yamaguchi abolished fixed incomes and put all of his salesmen on commission. That way, if sales dipped, the dealership wouldn't go under trying to keep pace with salary requirements. It was a good idea, but the company was too far gone for anything to save it.

Yamaguchi had seen the end coming more than a year earlier, shortly after the Murodo Typhoon in September of 1934. As soon as he heard the GM plant in Osaka had been flooded and its inventory inundated by the typhoon, he immediately called upon Kamiya:

"With this, the day has finally arrived for the collapse of Hinoku Motors. If we don't have cars to sell for two or three months, we will definitely go bankrupt. What can you do for me?''

Shaking his head, Kamiya said, "First of all, I disagree with your assessment. Go look for yourself at what happened to the factory. There are cars all over the plant that haven't been touched by the storm. GM has simply perpetrated that story to collect on their insurance. These cars aren't flood-damaged. If you were smart, you would buy as many of them as you can.''

Needing to see for himself, Yamaguchi went with Kamiya to the factory. Just as Kamiya had said, many cars were standing only wheel-deep in water and were in perfectly fine condition.

Yamaguchi was in a panic to see dealers already negotiating for the undamaged cars, but again Kamiya calmed him down: "Those are low-end Chevrolet dealers. None of the dealers carrying mid- to large-size cars are here yet. Go back to your store quickly, grab your cash, and buy everything you think you can sell.''

Fortunately for Yamaguchi, the typhoon had not interrupted train service, so he immediately returned home, scraped together all available funds -- nearly 40,000 yen -- and hurried back to Osaka.

"The dealers are saying that Chevys retailing for 2,500 yen will be sold for 1,500 yen. Consequently, mid- and large-size cars should go for 1,700 or 1,800 yen. Let me handle this,'' said Kamiya.

With Kamiya's help, Yamaguchi was able to purchase large-size cars, such as Oldsmobiles, Pontiacs, and Bedfords, for an average price of 1,750 yen. Not one had anything more wrong with it than wet tires. Part of Yamaguchi's scheme was to tag and store the new cars in a nearby factory. That way no one would suspect he had bought them as "storm damaged" merchandise. He would then retrieve a few at a time from storage and drive them back to Nagoya, seeing dollar signs all the way.

To Yamaguchi's supreme disappointment, prosperity only lasted a short while. In less than half a year after the typhoon, Hinode Motors was again verging on becoming "Hinoku Motors." Yamaguchi could see the end in sight:

This is no good. The job of selling imported cars under foreign companies is a losing game, set up in such a way that a Japanese dealer can't make any money. I've been at it long enough to know the problem is not due to lack of dealer ability or effort. It's due to unfair management from abroad.

This was Yamaguchi's frame of mind when Kamiya came to tell him he had decided to leave General Motors and take a new position as Director of Marketing at Toyoda. Until then, countless Japanese dealers had had their contracts canceled by GM; now Kamiya and Yamaguchi were the first to turn the tables and drop GM.

As the new Marketing Department slowly gathered momentum, production of the G1 truck was moving ahead at a good pace. Toyoda had finalized plans to introduce the new line of vehicles at a special show in Tokyo on November 21 and 22 of that year. With Risaburo Oshima and the newly recruited Shotaro Kamiya in charge, the "roll out" was held in the Toshiba facility and was lively, well-conceived, and well-attended. Members from the Ministry of Home Affairs, Ministry of Commerce and Industry, Ministry of Railways, and the Ministry of War attended on the first day. In attendance the second day were executives of bus and truck companies, some 800 people in all for the two-day event.

The success of the show was at least minor compensation for the severe cut in pay Kamiya had undergone to take his position at Toyoda. Despite being recruited by Kiichiro himself, Kamiya's monthly salary turned out to be only one hundred yen, as compared to the nearly six hundred yen he was receiving from General Motors. When asked about the disparity, Kamiya laughed and said, "I have no complaints. I can live on this."

A good review of the show in the first issue of the trade magazine called *Friends of Automation* also helped to keep Kamiya's spirits at a peak:

At five A.M. on November 18, on a cool morning, stars still visible in the gathering dawn, drivers of Toyoda Trucks Number One through Five -- designed by Director Oshima -- turned on their ignition keys, stepped on their starters, and amid the smooth roar of all five engines and throaty blasts of their powerful horns, tramped down on the clutch, shifted into first gear, and one by one, started off on the road to Tokyo. The engine in each vehicle operated smoothly as they traveled through Okazaki and Toyohashi and crossed over Lake Hamana, arriving in Hamamatsu at 9:40 A.M. They passed through Numazu and, after a short rest in Mishima, finally came to the forbidding Hakone Pass. The sun that seems to set so quickly in the mountains had plunged out of sight and the stars had begun to shine. The engines of all five vehicles continued to run smoothly, laboring a little as they continued to climb, then moved through the pass and headed downward, arriving safely in Odawara. From there they were driven through the streets of Yokohama and finally arrived at their destination, the Toshiba Garage in Tokyo, completing their inaugural drive to Tokyo at 11:50 P.M.

Routine, smooth, uneventful -- all in all, excellent publicity. But was it accurate? Seisi Kato, who made the journey to Tokyo, recorded a slightly different version in his *Memoirs of the Marketing Department:*

Before we'd even reached the halfway point, the third arm snapped off at Nakayama Pass. Fortunately, we'd packed a spare one, so we were able to somehow manage. But we had various problems with the quality of metal and lumber used for the frame. Thinking back on it, that certainly was a dangerous trip. We made stops in a number of small wooded areas to adjust the engines. The adjustments should have been made, of course, with gauges, but we didn't have any; instead we had to go on instinct. We did, finally, arrive at Toshiba. But we were way behind schedule -- it was three o'clock in the morning on the very day the show was to open.

In the middle of the night, apparently make-shift maintenance was needed at Hakone Pass when handles came off several trucks. Only the cover of darkness and a stroke of good luck saved the Toyoda crew from extreme embarrassment. Unaware of the "real story," exhibit attendees marveled at what they saw, with many commenting that respectable vehicles could be built domestically after all. All the while, the Toyoda team held their breath that none of the repairs and flaws would be noticed.

What finally sold everyone on the Toyoda trucks was their price: "2,900 yen, factory delivered." It was reassuring to know that a Japanese manufacturer could beat Chevrolet and Ford at their own game -- by two hundred yen. What no one knew was the price had been carefully calculated by Kamiya, who explained his reasoning this way: "We will not be able to aggressively and effectively sell this vehicle by appealing only to people's sense of nationalism."

Kiichiro was not present for the first Toyoda Show. Wasting no time to bask in a moment of glory, he and Okamoto were already out of the country in Manchuria to locate potential sources of iron ore. Upon receiving Oshima's telegram reporting the show's success, Kiichiro breathed a sigh of relief. Another great weight had been lifted from his shoulders.

It was only six months earlier that Kiichiro had decided to take this huge gamble and switch production from automobiles to trucks. As he now recalled the brashness of his decision and the avalanche of criticism which followed, including rumors that he had gone insane, Kiichiro could still hear the painful doubts of his trusted friends, Kan and Oshima: "It is impossible, Mr. Toyoda. Producing trucks in only six months is totally impossible."

Perhaps even more painful than Kan's and Oshima's apprehension was Kiichiro's own awareness that the task was indeed impossible. And that is why, for this one time in his life, he was willing to sacrifice perfection for the sake of meeting a deadline. Only his closest ally, Okamoto, knew of the anguish this decision had caused Kiichiro.

Now, holding the telegram and sinking into the sofa, Kiichiro turned to the managing director of Toyoda Spinning and Weaving Company and said quietly:

"Mr. Okamoto, somehow we made it."

The success of the show was a just reward, but both men knew in their hearts they still had a long way to go. By early June, Toyoda trucks were in the marketplace. That provided the "actual results" the Ministries of Commerce and Industry, Railways, and War would be looking for, if and when the Law Concerning the Manufacture of Automobiles was ratified. There were still many unknowns, however. Though the appropriate bill had just come before Parliament, it likely would take a year before it would pass into law. In that year a lot could happen, and there were no guarantees Toyoda would be one of the few companies chosen by the government to manufacture vehicles, once the law was passed. Also, a rumor had been circulating for some time that Nissan had a lock on the selection process. In the event only one manufacturer was chosen, Nissan would certainly be it. Toyoda would be left in the cold.

During the long year that followed, all of Kiichiro's unknowns were removed, one by one. The outcome was indeed not solely in favor of Nissan: Toyoda's "actual results" were impressive enough for the company to stake its claim upon the future of Japan's auto industry.

My life-long gamble came to an end today. I have won, sobbed Kiichiro, suddenly drained of all energy and slumped over his office desk.

For the moment at least, the story seemed to have a happy ending and progress came very quickly. Hinode Motors became the first Toyoda dealer; the first dealer showroom received a gala opening on December 8. Down came the General Motors logo and up went a large blue and yellow neon sign reading "DOMESTIC TOYODA." Right below it appeared, "HINODE MOTORS."

At the main factory in Kariya a similar neon sign appeared above the roof of the third plant. At the center of the sign was a rendering of the air-cooled Model A1 automobile in bright yellow, its wheels revolving. Above the automobile in large blue neon letters was the word, "DOMESTIC," to the left of the car, "TOYODA," and to the right of it "AUTOMOBILE." Because the third plant stood adjacent to the Tokaido (Tokyo to Hokkaido) Railway Line, the sign proudly broadcast the company's new name to all of the people that passed by on the train everyday.

In July of 1936, Toyoda was officially changed to "Toyota" following a nation-wide contest to determine a new name for the automobile. The majority of respondents felt "t" sounded better than "d."

"The Toyoda Automobile Department" thus became "TOYOTA MOTOR COMPANY," spreading, according to contemporary reports, "great consterna-tion" as employees rushed to change the "D's" to "T's" on the big neon signs at the Kariya plant and the Hinode Motors dealership.

On the day before the grand opening of Hinode Motors, with general manager Yamaguchi supervising the preparations, sales manager Taro Hibi, parts manager Chihiro Sakai, and other company employees were dashing about, setting up displays, decorating offices, and checking literature, signs, and invitation lists. Busy though they were, they would periodically throw worried glance down at the corner of the showroom below.

The showroom floor was bright and clean. Two platforms were built to display a pair of new Model G1 trucks fresh off the production line. By dusk, however, only one platform was occupied; the other looked like a missing front tooth.

The previous evening, drivers had gone to the Kariya plant to pick up the two trucks. En route to the Hayashi Body Shop, where they were to receive a last minute polish, one of the trucks broke a rear axle housing when it hit a telephone pole. Yamaguchi was speechless when news of the misfortune arrived. Then he recalled his own comment to Kamiya when Kamiya had recruited him to the marketing project: "If they don't move, then we'll push them."

Push them is exactly what I might have to do, thought Yamaguchi, this time in a more serious vein.

Yamaguchi had quickly sent for a replacement vehicle from Kariya, and now it was at the Hayashi Body Shop being spruced up for the introduction. By the time the truck was installed on its rightful platform and Yamaguchi had returned for one final check of the showroom, morning light was just kissing the horizon.

Good weather and widespread interest cooperated to make the show a total success. The showroom was filled from the moment the doors opened in the morning to the time they closed that night. Among the attendees were people who had traveled from as far away as the Atsumi Peninsula and deep in the mountains of Kitashidara. All expressed excitement and wonder as they eyed the beautiful sight of a domestically-built truck, gleaming under the lights, every panel and part polished, down to the lug nuts on the wheels. Nor did any visitors miss the prominently displayed price tag, "Retail Price: 3,200 yen, Nagoya delivery."

By now Noboru Yamaguchi was an emotional wreck, though he didn't show it on the outside. From a promotional standpoint, the Grand Opening was a huge success -- beyond everyone's most optimistic expectations. But in the back of Yamaguchi's mind were all of the mechanical flaws and breakdowns that had plagued the project and now filled him with a gnawing anxiety. *Will this vehicle ever operate without breaking down?* Just when he should have been enjoying the sparks of victory, the truck's questionable reliability had him muttering to himself.

And indeed the question of sales was not helping to ease matters any. Hinode was still Toyota's only dealer outlet. That meant that every single truck rolling off the Toyota assembly line would roll onto Yamaguchi's list of worries. The trouble-plagued inaugural trip of the G1's, as well as the major breakdown during the short run to the showroom, made the challenge that much more worrisome.

Yamaguchi wrestled with the knotty question of how to most effectively sell his vehicles to actual customers. From experience, he knew that news of any problems, especially a break down in transit, would spread like wildfire. If he put these temperamental trucks in the wrong hands, the backlash could literally kill the company. *I must be extremely cautious in selecting my customers,* Yamaguchi thought to himself with a very heavy heart.

Similar concern was evident among members of Toyota's executive management, especially on the manufacturing side. When Risaburo, Kiichiro, Oshima, Kan, and Kamiya had shown up at the exhibit, the first thing Risaburo had nervously asked Yamaguchi was, "How is it going? Does the truck run?"

Yamaguchi could only mumble, "Hmm...yes...somehow...."

Realizing that worry only aggravated problems rather than assisting in their solutions, Yamaguchi began to focus on various courses of action. Each course always had two things in common with the others: how to target customers and how to establish a complete customer service program. These, then, would be the cornerstones of the marketing strategy he would propose to Kamiya. Not long after the Hinode show, Yamaguchi and Kamiya met to discuss the future of the marketing department. Yamaguchi began the conversation:

"For a new and untested product, popularity can be a dangerous thing. As word gets around, the need for dependability increases proportionately. Ninety percent of the people who came to our opening were just looking, though they expressed excitement about our product. The other 10 percent were serious about trying out one of our trucks. That 10 percent likely are very patriotic and would buy our product out of national pride, rather than confidence in its quality and reliability. But when the user starts driving a truck, he isn't driving it as a patriotic gesture; he is driving it for his business. Given our truck's present track record, once it is actually put into use, we'll be flooded with complaints about mechanical problems. That is why a comprehensive service program is so essential. It should be our number one priority. The effectiveness of that service is, of course, dependent upon the training and skills of the repairmen we hire. It will be tragic if, after such a favorable response to our trucks, public opinion turns against us and Toyotas are labeled as "no good."

Kamiya remained silent, nodding his head in agreement, as Yamaguchi continued:

"That is why, at first, we must go slowly and target those people who will never complain. These are the people totally loyal to the Toyoda family and its cause. That will give us time to work out the bugs so we can more safely broaden our market. That is why...."

Yamaguchi suddenly stopped himself, realizing he'd again fallen prey to his pet phrase, "That is why...." He was trying to get away from it, but old habits die hard. He began again: "Because of that fact, I want to ask headquarters to hold off awhile on pressuring us for sales results."

"I understand," Kamiya replied, "We'll do just as you have asked. And be assured that we agree with your opinions regarding our first customers. They must be eager to use a domestically made automobile and should be on friendly terms with the Toyoda organization."

The following day, Yamaguchi held his first board of directors and executive management meeting of Hinode Motors, at which time he presented the plan he had shared with Kamiya. After the meeting, he called his staff together to brief them on their duties and responsibilities. His first instruction to his salesmen was unprecedented at Hinode or any of its predecessors, and perhaps in the entire annals of salesmanship:

"Listen carefully. When you're trying to sell the vehicle, you must never say that our truck is better than other trucks. Unfortunately ours is inferior to any vehicle currently on the market anywhere in the world.

"You must ask them to buy it and use it because it's made here in our own country. Unless we sell it that way, the Japanese market for domestically-produced vehicles will be doomed and the monopoly held by foreign manufacturers will remain unbroken. We cannot jeopardize our efforts by overselling our product.

"As long as there are people willing to buy our vehicles, Toyota Motor Company will make every effort to improve them. Eventually they will give us a vehicle that is number one in the world. That is why you must appeal to your customers to use this Toyota vehicle for the sake of this country called Japan and this nationality called Japanese. You must never say such things as 'this is better than an import.' It's flowery language and will certainly turn out to be a lie."

"In return for our customer's good will, we will provide unwavering service. Regardless of the mechanical problem, we will go and repair it anywhere, as many times as necessary, any hour of the day or night. The only way we can, in good conscience, hand the keys to this vehicle over to a customer is to back it up with our sincerity, honesty, and dedication. That is all we can offer. We must ask our customers to understand that, and we must also be uncompromising in our efforts to make good on our promises."

Until this time, car salesmen in Japan were seen as unctuous, glad-handing experts at using high pressure sales tactics. A "successful salesman" told half truths and made it his business to reassure customers that the very things most likely to go wrong would be "no problem." Whether he was simply making a virtue out of necessity or truly believed in "honesty in advertising," Yamaguchi was proposing to totally reverse the ethics of salesmanship.

Veteran import automobile salesmen on Yamaguchi's staff had the hardest time conforming to the new rules. Those who failed most often were given "desk jobs" or transferred into maintenance. Replacements were normally recruited from among company employees and fresh hires. Taro Hibi, an experienced accountant with no previous sales experience, was named the new sales manager, and bright, personable employees inexperienced in sales were groomed to become salesmen, as were graduates fresh out of trade school.

After exhaustive analysis, Kamiya and Yamaguchi decided to place only six of the introductory models. Two would be sold within the city of Nagoya, two in Owari, and two in Mikawa. Much thought was also given to the final customer choice. The two selected from Nagoya were Marutoku, a delivery company run by Tokuheiei Kimura, and a second delivery company, Masegumi, owned by a man named Mase.

Marutoku had done business for a long time with a porcelain trading company owned by Jisaburo Takito, former president of Hinode Motors. Because Takito asked this personal favor of Marutoku, they could hardly refuse to purchase the new Toyota vehicle. It was a favor they immediately regretted, as they watched their new truck break down like clock work, day in and day out.

Because they preferred to use domestically-produced goods whenever possible, the second company, Masegumi, was an easy sell. Mase himself took personal delight in knowing he would be one of the first to buy a Japanese-made vehicle. He acquired his truck at the end of December, and began using it on January 2,

1936, sending it fully loaded with confectionery goods for delivery in Osaka. No sooner had it left Nagoya than the truck's differential housing fractured and left the driver stalled in the middle of the road. The Hinode Motors employee who took the service call ran to the Kariya factory to get the necessary replacement parts and headed immediately to the site to fix the truck. Repairs were made and the driver managed to deliver his goods. But on the return trip to Nagoya, the truck broke a spindle just as it reached the top of a mountain pass.

Mase had purchased the truck with his eyes wide-open, alerted as he was to potential problems by an "honest" Hinode salesman. And being a realist, he had expected it to fall short of the imports in some aspects of performance. But not that far short and not in that many performance areas! His truck had two major breakdowns its first day on the road. "There is simply no excuse for such shoddy workmanship," fumed Mase as he indignantly stormed into Hinode Motors.

Unfortunately, Mase's tantrum was not an isolated incident for the Hinode staff, who were getting a priceless education in public relations.

One of the trucks sold in Mikawa was purchased by Amano Shokai, a seafood supplier located in Fukue on the Atsumi Peninsula. The proprietor, Kosaku Amano, needed a new vehicle to haul fish to market. Every morning before dawn, he would leave for Nagoya with a load of fresh fish caught near the Atsumi Peninsula, a trip that normally took four hours. On the return leg, he would carry sundries back to Fukue.

Singled out for his passionate patriotism, Amano bought his Toyota truck on December 28 and decided to use it right away. Because he owned five other vehicles, all new when purchased, Amano was prepared for small problems with his new truck. Most vehicles required two to three years of manufacturing before all the bugs were worked out, and Toyota was barely into its first year. Even with such an open-minded attitude, Amano was in for the shock of his life. On his first trip from Fukue to the peninsula -- only a short distance -- Amano was stalled by a broken chassis. Sure, the roads along the Atsumi Peninsula were rough, but a truck's chassis is its toughest part. "This is simply absurd!" yelled Amano, as he stormed into the offices of Hinode Motors.

Despite every problem imaginable, Amano stuck by his Toyota truck. Nearly every day he had a breakdown, often missing his morning market delivery, which meant the loss of a day's profit. And every day he cursed the vehicle mercilessly. Yet Yamaguchi's keen insight had been correct. The only reason Amano didn't abandon his Toyota for a foreign-made model was the uncompromising service he received from Hinode Motors.

During this period, the Hinode service representatives worked with precious little sleep. There were ten employees in all, including Masunori Takahashi, the manager, and his foremen, Tetsuzo Kobayashi and Shigekazu Tanaka. Takahashi tried to give his men a little respite whenever possible, but every morning and at least half of nearly every night was spent taking care of breakdowns and an occasional accident. As one employee put it, they were fortunate if they could even find time to smoke a cigarette. In what was considered a very smart move, Hinode Motors equipped one of its own trucks as a service vehicle. Fully stocked with tools and common replacement parts, it could transport an entire crew of service personnel to a breakdown site -- at least ideally speaking. More often than not, however, the truck was used in its own repair or was totally disabled in the shop.

Whenever time permitted, the servicemen humored each other with stories of their more ridiculous adventures. Each story was always better than the last. In one case, a serviceman had responded to a call from a truck owner in Owari. The truck simply stopped running and was stalled on the side of the road. After careful inspection, the serviceman told the driver, "I can't find anything wrong with it."

"Fool," yelled the driver, pointing at the truck, his face turning purple with rage, "the truck won't go! Isn't that proof that something's wrong with it!"

About to laugh, the serviceman caught himself and assumed a serious attitude; the driver was furious and clearly not in a joking mood. Upon inspecting the truck a second time, the serviceman discovered that the gas tank was bone dry. That was impossible claimed the driver. He had filled the tank before leaving Nagoya and had traveled only a few miles. Then the two of them spied the cause of the mystery -- a split in the gas tank's seam. The defect was in fact large enough to leave the truck without gas shortly into the journey, and it had gotten as far as it had running on fumes.

Proud of the dedicated and professional way his service team performed, but also aware that follow-up was only a partial solution to his problem, Yamaguchi told himself, *the factory must be made fully aware of the specific nature and frequency of mechanical failures.* He then began a record of breakdowns categorized according to types of technical failure. This he would send to the factory's engineers in an effort to pinpoint improvements. Yamaguchi didn't realize it at the time, but he was joining the age-old feud between the men who design the product and those who have to fix it.

The flow of Yamaguchi's "bad reports" was so steady and faithful that the engineering staff and workers at the Kariya plant fumed that "Hinode Motors was blowing everything out of proportion." When he heard that, Yamaguchi was irritated, to say the least. Then several circumstances developed that would sway the balance in his favor.

One cold winter evening, a report came in that a Toyota truck loaded with cotton goods had stalled in Suzuka Pass. The truck belonged to one of the Owari customers, a delivery company, and it was headed for dockside in Kobe to deliver goods for export.

When the customer phoned Hinode, he was desperate: "Unless we get there before the ship departs, we're going to be in deep trouble! Please send people from headquarters to take a look and see what you can do!"

Yamaguchi immediately had the service truck made ready and arranged for several "rental vehicles" as a backup. Then he promptly telephoned Risaburo Oshima at the factory in Kariya and asked him to go along to the breakdown site.

A major storm had hit Suzuka Pass and snow was still blowing and drifting when the repair crew arrived. The truck lay stalled in a snow bank and the driver was pacing nearby to keep himself warm. The problem was quickly attributed to a broken differential housing. Takahashi, the service manager, instructed the driver of one of the rentals to load his car with the cotton and head out with the owner for Kobe. Next Takahashi drove the second rental to a house located some two and a half miles away, where he arranged for rice to be cooked for his men and purchased a bundle of firewood. Then he returned to the breakdown site.

After building a fire, the crew jacked up the truck in the three-foot snow bank and set to work on the differential. The repair took all night in the freezing cold and the crew was exhausted when they finally returned to Nagoya late the following morning. Fate, however, had planned for them something other than a good long sleep. In their absence, the Hinode office had received an emergency call concerning an incident at a railway crossing on the Nagoya Railway Line at Kisogawa. Dead-tired, frustrated, and thoroughly fed up with delinquent trucks, the service group piled into the repair truck and headed out. When they arrived, they immediately saw the "incident" was no simple breakdown. There had been a serious accident and one person had been killed.

Apparently the truck had stopped at the crossing for a passing train. When all was clear, the driver restarted the truck and moved to cross the tracks, unaware that a train was bearing down from the opposite direction. According to an eye-witness, the driver had ample time to make it across the intersection, but the truck stalled right in the middle of the crossing. It was hit broadside and the driver was killed instantly.

From the twisted wreckage, the servicemen discovered that a faulty transmission had allowed the truck to pop out of gear. Before it could be re-engaged, the truck was struck by the train. It was a sad testament to the crude technology of the early trucks, and everyone was deeply saddened.

Oshima's presence at both of these incidents made him realize for the first time the full magnitude and gravity of the G1's endemic mechanical problems. With him as a spokesperson directly in the factory, Yamaguchi's meticulous record keeping and cry for improvements would definitely be heard.

Modifications became an ongoing process, but mechanical problems were so numerous and technology so slow to improve in the early going that serious defects plagued the first one hundred Toyota trucks to come off the assembly line. As truck sales grew, Hinode Motors became increasingly swamped with repair calls. Yamaguchi was busy day and night handling the increased repair load and spending much of his time apologizing to customers and, when necessary, negotiating replacements from the factory at Kariya.

It was a thankless job. The only guarantee Yamaguchi could give on his vehicles was the guarantee they would break down. He couldn't lie about his vehicles' quality, yet he was having a miserable time making sales by telling the truth. It took one of Yamaguchi's mettle to remain committed to such a difficult course, one that often left him exhausted from anguish. Yet he managed to hold Hinode Motors together and acted like a mother hen to his employees.

Because Toyota trucks were first marketed in December, the repair crew had winter to contend with. Often repairs were made in freezing temperatures, and it was not uncommon for work to be done during snowstorms and even full-fledged blizzards. In all but the most mild weather, Yamaguchi knew his service personnel would come back shivering from the cold. Snacks and rice cakes were always waiting, along with a hot fire in the stove. No matter how late at night, Yamaguchi would have warm sake and tea ready.

To keep a vehicle on the road the Hinode crew made every repair possible, but when no amount of nursing could restore a truck to health, it had to be returned to the factory. This continually brought home to Kiichiro the price being paid for the "mass production" he was aiming at. Like Yamaguchi, Kiichiro was also faced with a double-edged sword.

To beat the clock ticking ever closer toward enactment of the Law Concerning the Manufacture of Motor Vehicles, the G1 had to be built without any road tests. There was no other choice. The Toyota Motor Company had to have results or else the opportunity for a domestic automobile industry could be lost forever to foreign manufacturers. Also the future of all the Toyoda companies was at stake. Without success by Toyota Motor Company, the entire corporation might well sink into a financial black hole.

Kiichiro rarely left the factory during this early production period, going without sleep, checking progress on changes, lending encouragement to his hard-working engineering staff, asking questions and giving advice whenever he noticed someone having difficulty or looking puzzled.

"Regardless of how small the defect, you must stand back and re-examine it from every angle," he would tell his technicians. They had to get to the root of the problem. And this meant examining materials as well as design, but especially the tolerances of those parts that broke down frequently.

That's how, for example, the weakness of the failure-prone differential housing was pinpointed. Noting that it usually snapped along weld lines, the engineers closely examined the welding process and compared theirs to that of other manufacturers. It was the Chevrolet which showed them the necessity of electric welding, where parts are actually fused together. The gas welding method (known as "tack welding") used by Toyota left fracture lines between the welded parts, causing them to break away. While suitable for parts not subjected to great stress, tack welding was wholly inappropriate for such components like the differential housing. Because Toyota lacked the technology to switch to the electric welding process, their only recourse was to have the work done outside by Sumitomo Ironworks. That solved the immediate problem, and in time Toyota itself was able to master the new technology.

Impressed by Kiichiro's inexhaustible energy and the serious attention he paid to Hinode's failure reports, Yamaguchi decided to always notify Kiichiro directly when a pattern in mechanical failures indicated a fundamental problem in manufacturing. Whenever this happened, Kiichiro would drop whatever he was doing and respond immediately to Yamaguchi's call. Ever true to his belief in direct involvement, Kiichiro could be seen with his jacket off and shirt sleeves rolled, diving under the hood of a problem vehicle. By the time he was finished, he'd be covered with grease from top to bottom, always smiling as if Yamaguchi had just done him a huge favor, and saying, "Thank you for notifying me. I've discovered an important problem.'' It was due to this "working arrangement" between Kiichiro and Yamaguchi that manufacturing defects began to diminish.

While the factory was stepping up its improvement program, Kamiya was busy establishing a dealer network. The initial goal was to set up a network consisting of one dealer per prefecture. Kamiya concentrated on dealerships with which he had experience during his General Motors days. It was a solid plan, but the biggest single factor in making it work was the trust Kamiya had earned during his association with Japanese dealers, many of whom honored and respected, even idolized him, just as Noboru Yamaguchi had done during his time at GM.

As he had promised Kiichiro at their first meeting, one by one, Kamiya brought the veteran GM Japanese dealers into the Toyota franchise.

Helping Toyota kick off the New Year on a happy note, Taiyo Motors, a Chevrolet dealership based in Tokyo, switched to the domestic automobile maker in January to become the firm's second dealer. Taiyo was followed by KK Domestic Motors of Matsuzaka City in Mie Prefecture. Then in April, Osaka Toyota was established. To everyone's delight, the beat went on: in June, Dowa Motors in Manchuria signed a distributor contract, and in August, Kanto Toyota in Tochigi Prefecture, Shizuoka Toyota, and Hiroshima Toyota were established as Kamiya continued to weave a national dealer network.

Every dealership open house, and every exhibit staged to introduce Toyota's new and improving line was a success -- a success that could be attributed in large measure to the nationalistic trend of the times, aided by the Manchurian Incident.

Chapter
8

JUST-IN-TIME

In the fall and winter of 1935 while the Toyota truck was being introduced, factory manager Takatoshi Kan received two memos in succession from Kiichiro. The first one arrived right before the Tokyo Show, when Kiichiro was making preparations to travel to Manchuria. As usual, the memo had been dashed off with a pencil:

> *The monthly production plan of two hundred units will be revised to five hundred units. I would like to have an assembly plant designed and built on some sixteen acres. The site should face the Spinning factory to the north side of the Tokaido Railway Line.*

That would be easy. Kan had anticipated future expansion and set to his task immediately.

But the second note! It was a classic example of how history could be formed in so few words. Scribbled on a scrap of paper, the note arrived in the beginning of December, just before the first truck was marketed.

> *Please design a factory in Koromo that can regularly produce 500 passenger cars and 1,500 trucks per month.*

Two thousand units a month! How can that be written so casually as though it was a note for the gardener to plant a tree. Two thousand units a month amounted to an annual production of 24,000 units. That 2,000 was more than General Motors and Ford combined produced in Japan! Even translated into domestic American standards, that would be an enormous factory. Kan rubbed his eyes and read the note again, thinking he had misread it. No, that is what it said.

Perhaps in writing this, Mr. Toyoda made a mistake, thought Kan.

He'd check it out as soon as Kiichiro returned.

"Oh yes, you've got it right," answered Kiichiro matter-of-factly. "I'm talking about that piece of land in Koromo we've been debating about, the one you and I surveyed together. Well, we've settled the talks about acquiring a plot of some five hundred acres of land. We'll purchase it around the middle of this month.

"As you said when we looked it over earlier, it's scraggly land that only has shrubs and weeds growing on it, so it's not suitable for cultivation. That means we can always buy more later if we need to. Expanding what we haven't even built isn't something to talk about now, but as soon as we build the first factory to produce about two thousands units per month, I want to immediately start on a second factory to turn out ten thousand units per month. And eventually, I want to increase production in the first facility to 10,000, too, so that in the near future, we can produce 10,000 cars and ten thousand trucks or altogether, 20,000 units per month. With that in mind, please do a good job in apportioning the property."

"Yeah...ahh...yes," answered Kan, outwardly calm but inwardly overwhelmed, slightly giddy and light-headed. The current production target was 200 units a month and they were struggling under heavy stress to maintain a fifty-unit per month pace! Furthermore, while the engine of that vehicle could maintain speeds of 100 kilometers or roughly 60 MPH, the drive train and other parts kept bending or breaking. Those things should be corrected before expanding. And where would the capital come from? It was difficult enough to come up with the money to buy one machine tool, let alone hundreds.

Blissfully ignoring these circumstances, this guy is calmly ordering me to design an enormous factory geared to produce 20,000 per month! Why that amounts to 240,000 vehicles per year! All of Japan buys less than one tenth of that total in a year, and he wants to build about a year's supply each month! It's not enough to simply say that the scale envisioned is too large -- it's a total impossibility, Kan said to himself.

Kan was in shock. He couldn't even find words to reply, so he bowed and walked slowly back to the factory.

Once he had a chance to reflect upon the plan, Kan reassured himself that Kiichiro was not one to order something done unless it could be done. Likely, Kiichiro was making projections for the distant future. Yes, that must be it.

So, early the next morning, Kan went with a lighter heart to the new site and checked ground elevation, land forms, site orientation, slopes, water supplies, ground cover, soil composition, prevailing winds, and similar details of the property to begin preparations for the first of Kiichiro's new factories. To his surprise, the swiftness of his efforts proved none too fast, given the speed at which developments began to unfold.

By December 14, 1935, purchase of the property at Koromo -- the Takahara Plains -- was complete and soil preparation at the new 505-acre factory site began early in the new year. Kiichiro's secret work in putting together the technical talent and building technology allowed for quick advancement once he was officially ready to move. As the year began, the number of employees at the Automobile Department was close to three thousand. There also were key additions to the engineering staff, starting with Ryuichi Suzuki, an electrical engineering graduate and electronics expert from Hamamatsu University. Kiichiro had recruited him from Takaoka Manufacturing in Nagoya toward the end of 1934. Then there was Shoichi Saito, a graduate student under Nukiyama at Tohoku University. Saito, a mechanical engineering expert, joined Toyota in March of 1935. After him, several other university engineering graduates were added. With every addition, the table of organization began to resemble more and more the organized manufacturing scheme of a modern automobile maker.

On a cold day during the New Year holidays, shortly after the soil preparation had begun, the newly hired mechanical engineer, Shoichi Saito, accompanied Kiichiro and Kan to look over the factory site.

Koromo was roughly due east from the heart of Nagoya, and northeast of Kariya. The distances between the three locations were from twelve to eighteen miles. By road, though, the actual distances between the three points of this crooked triangle were much greater.

As he knew he'd be traveling frequently between Nagoya, Kariya and Koromo, Kiichiro finally decided to purchase a personal car. He selected a new 1934 Packard, a luxury car costing about 20,000 yen at the time.

For his chauffeur, Kiichiro employed a professional driver and former airplane pilot named Asano. When Kiichiro was not using the car for business, it was always available for family use. On Sundays, Asano would take Kiichiro's eldest son, Shoichiro -- still in grade school -- and his brother, Tatsuro, out for rides. Asano would run the big powerful automobile at speeds of sixty miles per hour or more over narrow, bumpy suburban roads with the youngsters spurring him on with cries of, "Faster! Faster!"

Riding along with Kiichiro in the Packard on his first trip to the factory site, Saito was surprised to find it was located in such a remote and inaccessible area. There was no direct train from Nagoya. There was, however, a branch line of the Natetsu Train which ran in the general vicinity, but the nearest station was quite far from the factory site.

I wonder how he plans to have thousands and perhaps tens of thousands of employees commute to such a remote, lonely, hilly area, thought Saito. Then he posed the question to Kiichiro.

"What did you ride in just now to get here?" Kiichiro replied, calmly answering the question with one of his own.

"I was offered a ride in your automobile," Saito answered. The ride had taken exactly one hour, and Asano had mentioned that it takes about the same time to drive there from Nagoya.

"See? In the future, company employees will all commute here by car," Kiichiro said, smiling. "By auto, thirty or even fifty miles is not very far at all."

With that, Kiichiro gestured to Kan to join them, spread out the blueprints, and launched into a review of the layout.

It took Saito several days to come to terms with Kiichiro's answer, and every time he thought about it, he felt his head spin. Only the bourgeoisie and people with considerable wealth owned personal cars. The idea that office and factory workers might own and drive them was too fantastic to even contemplate.

The more Saito began to think as Kiichiro thought, however, the more plausible everything began to seem. Kiichiro was not worried about the problem of commuting because, in his vision, soon everyone would be driving a Japanese-made automobile. And to make ready for that day required an enormous factory, which was unthinkable unless you were on Kiichiro's wavelength. Saito began to feel his enthusiasm for the project quickly returning. Yes, Kiichiro's thoughts lived where few others dared to venture -- in the future.

As work had come to be seen as the only life available to the Toyota crew, the wheels of domestic life were also endlessly turning. On January 29, 1936, Sakichi's widow, Asako, passed away. It was a sad moment for Kiichiro. Though he had felt anger and contempt for her in his early years, he came to respect her enormously in his adult years. He reflected now, *without Asako, there would be no Toyoda company. Given Sakichi's single-minded devotion to his inventions, without Asako there would have been no Toyoda family. She was the glue that had held their world together.* At her funeral, Kiichiro felt a deep personal loss and tears came from his heart.

Not long after, in March, Kiichiro moved his family to Tokyo. His eldest daughter, Yuriko, was entering Futaba Higher School for Women but, perhaps more importantly, he did not feel at ease staying in Nagoya, where the mood was very conservative. He had wagered too much to realize his dream of manufacturing domestic automobiles to be dragged down by a bunch of pessimists. Moreover, he could do more good promoting his ideas to the public in Tokyo. It was no secret that rural areas tended to be hostile to new ideas and slower to adopt new ways of doing things. Automobiles were widely regarded as frivolous toys of the rich and powerful and evoked a great deal of scorn among the masses. No, he would feel better in the more cosmopolitan Tokyo.

As it happened, however, it was difficult to tell whether Tokyo was his primary or secondary home. He had purchased a large plot of hilly land in Nagoya shortly before Sakichi died, and had built a mountain retreat where he could spend his Sundays thinking or relaxing. It was there that he continued to spend the bulk of his time away from work. But the official residence for now was Tokyo.

Upon moving from Nagoya, Kiichiro first rented a house in Akebono-cho in the Hongo district in Tokyo, but soon after moved to a new residence in a tall building in the Akasaka district. The building was located on a hill just past the brook where, today, the TBS (Tokyo Broadcasting System) Television Studio stands. In the mid-1930s, though at the heart of the city, the Akasaka district still offered a relatively tranquil setting.

As soon as he moved there, with the help of Shoichiro and his second son, Tatsuro, he built a concrete pond reminiscent of those he had built at his mountain retreat in Nagoya. Kiichiro's ponds always featured a fountain at the center, and a concrete waterway that ran to a large, shallow, level-bottomed pond which housed goldfish and carp. As Kiichiro was a "do-it-yourselfer," he spurned hired help and instead used only his children as helpers. He would prepare the foundation, wrestle decorative boulders into place, and mix and pour cement, sweating profusely with mud streaked all over his face, hands, feet and clothes.

To Kiichiro, in this environment was to know him for the simple man he was at heart. He loved to fish and therefore shied away from planting exotics in his "fishing pond." And his fishing equipment often consisted of a hook, string, and a hand-made pole, which he usually cut with his children from a willow. It was at times such as these that he felt farthest from the high-pressured world of automobile manufacturing and totally at peace with himself.

Soon after Kiichiro moved to Akasaka, Eiji, the second son of Sakichi's younger brother, Heikichi, graduated from the Mechanical Engineering Department of Tokyo University and came to live with Kiichiro's family. Since Kiichiro owed a great debt to Heikichi for making it possible for him to continue his education after he graduated from middle school, Kiichiro treated his cousin Eiji with great affection. Heikichi was the president of his own spinning company and planned to have Eiji inherit the business, but Kiichiro, after much pleading, was able to convince Heikichi to let Eiji work in the Automobile Department. The new addition was a perfect fit in Kiichiro's master plan.

Kiichiro instinctively knew then what others only learned in the wake of the marketing revolution after the war: that the necessary concerns of the moment often blind one to the important concerns of tomorrow. If a manager wants to see his company prosper, he must hold to a visionary philosophy. As Kiichiro once put it: "Those who manage factories cannot pay attention only to the job they see in front of them -- they must always be ready for the opportunity to continue research without regard to the task of the moment. Therefore, the company and the factory should be located in separate areas."

Acting on this philosophy, Kiichiro had Eiji find a laboratory in Shibaura and established it as the Toyoda Chemistry and Physics Research Laboratory. Ten university professors each from the science and the engineering fields were retained as advisers. Besides Eiji, the permanent lab staff included Shisaburo Kuruda, a graduate of the Electrical Engineering School who had designed automobiles at Mitsubishi and Hakuyosha; Tsunesa Sato, a math professor; Kuniei Kubota, a metallurgist; and Takeo Chiku, a battery expert. Hanji Umehara of Tohoku University, who later became the head of the Toyoda Central Research Laboratory, also did some research at the laboratory. In today's parlance, these men were Kiichiro's "think tank." They were free to research anything they wanted.

Kiichiro loved the lab and made a practice of spending an hour and a half there every morning. As soon as he arrived, he'd immediately collar somebody and start a discussion about that person's area of expertise. After finishing the discussion, Kiichiro quickly disappeared.

He did not, however, let Eiji get off that easy. "I want you to work on this," he would say, handing Eiji a torn scrap of paper with the problem written on it. While practical problems, these typically were beyond the established theories of automotive engineering, and therefore often quite difficult.

Eiji had two qualities that would forever endear him to Kiichiro. He was patient and tenacious. Regardless of the problem's difficulty, he'd take his time and never get flustered. When he tired of working, he'd put aside whatever he was doing and go to the airport next door to talk to the young employees of the newspaper aviation department, sometimes lending a hand in maintenance of the plane. He soon became fast friends with the people who worked there, and bummed joy rides on a regular basis as his form of relaxation during breaks.

Kiichiro and Eiji shared not only a similar work ethic, but similar personal habits as well. When Kiichiro went on a business trip, he'd often forget to shave and didn't mind wearing a dirty shirt and pants with shiny knees. When Eiji went to work at the Koromo plant, eventually transferred there as a section head, he'd wear the same old work uniform day after day. There was no denying the two were cut from the same mold.

Eiji also was a man of few words, neither gregarious nor given to flattery, let alone to customarily making a formal greeting. To those who did not know him, he was not readily approachable. That was probably due more to his preoccupation with ideas and the way he looked, for he was by no means unfriendly. While not overtly demonstrative, he was always straightforward, sincere, and loyal to friends and colleagues. Even to strangers, he was not haughty, but rather gracious in a reserved way. Once again there is a clear echo of Kiichiro. In fact, it is said that when Eiji grew older, he came to look like Kiichiro as well as act like him. Whenever he visited and however long he remained, Eiji was a valued guest in Kiichiro's new Tokyo household.

After Kiichiro had lived in Tokyo for some time, during one of his periodic trips back to Washizu for a visit, his aunt, Han, told him that his mother, Tami, was still alive and leading a very unhappy life. Han, Sakichi's younger sister, had married into a farming family named Makino in the same village.

Han felt deep sympathy for Tami, telling Kiichiro, "She is really unfortunate. Not only was she treated terribly by Sakichi but because he bankrupted the household, the rest of the Toyoda family ill-treated her as his bride. On top of that, she was criticized by her own family, and cried and cried when she had to leave you behind and return to her family. I heard that she remarried once, but she had no children. Apparently things didn't work out for her and now I hear that she's impoverished and living a miserable life in Kobe."

"I see," Kiichiro replied pensively, crossing his arms across his chest. At times when he was small, he would hide from his stepmother and cry, desperately yearning for his natural mother. Then there were times when bitterness would overwhelm him as he wondered why she had abandoned him. But, now, past forty and tempered by life, while a sense of loneliness remained, the harsh recriminations of his youth had vanished.

"My mother's address...can you find it out?" he asked after a pause.

"Of course," Han responded. "If I ask, I can find out immediately. What are you planning to do?"

Staring silently into the distance, then turning and gazing into his aunt's eyes, Kiichiro quietly said, "I would like to ask you to take some money to her. I will send it every month, but please don't mention that it's from me," Kiichiro said.

"I see. I think that's an excellent idea," Han replied, nodding her head and smiling sadly.

With a sadder but more loving heart, Kiichiro thought of Tami often in moments of reflection and during brief respites from work, which was moving apace at the new Koromo plant.

Kan's design and layout were well along, though it was a wonder he had any opportunity to work, given all the time he spent taking notes. Here are a few highlights from his records covering preliminary plans for the new factory:

(1) Most materials must be transported on the Mikawa Line, although small amounts can be transported by truck. (2) For safety and practicality, the building must be a one-story structure where function allows. (3) Since the railway spur runs along the west side of the site, the west side of the property must be utilized first. (4) The main offices should be located in a convenient area near the center of the property and facing the road. (5) The building housing the big stamping, punching, and forming presses must be built on solid, bedrock land, not areas that have been filled in, since in addition to bays for that heavy machinery, there'll be a steel mill, a big boiler room, and a foundry. (6) The ridges of the roof must run east-west to take advantage of the natural light. (7) The electric power station must be located near the center of electrical consumption to minimize the loss of energy through transmission. (8) The electrical cable for the factory compound will be installed in underground channels to ensure safety and minimize maintenance and repair costs. (9) The roads within the factory compound must be wide, paved, banked at sharp curves, and form unbroken loops since at times these roads will have to be utilized as a test course. (10) Worker cafeterias must be close to where they work. Since six to seven thousand people might be needed to operate this factory, we must build a number of cafeterias contiguous to the various work places. (11) In addition to the underground passageways for electric cable and steam and water pipes, each building must be connected by underground walkways. (12) The buildings must be made of reinforced concrete or be steel-framed structures. (13) Since an outside supplier will provide a substantial portion of our forging requirements, we can get by for the time being with a relatively small forge. (14) We'll be shipping out the vehicles as soon as they are finished, so there is no need for a warehouse to store them. (15) Water must be supplied through a deep well. The daily water usage for the factory will be over one million gallons, and we can estimate an additional 500,000 gallons will be needed for other uses. (16) The woods and thickets surrounding the factory area must be protected. Furthermore, along the western boundary line, trees must be planted to provide protection against the wind. (17) For safety, to meet insurance requirements, and to permit mass assemblies and meetings, a large, open outdoor area must be reserved in the middle of the property. (18) The floor of the factory, as a general rule, will be concrete; and it will have a straight-line roof. (19) The machining plant should be built on one floor; but to take ventilation and lavatory facilities into consideration, the floor must be partitioned into three areas. (20) Lavatories should ideally be flush-type, but for the sake of economy, that will not be possible.

To show the comprehensiveness of his planning, Kan went on to say that a small hill near the planned facility was ideally suited for a school, clubhouse, test track, movie theater, and luxury company housing.

Despite the fact that Kan was asked to do an architectural equivalent of "mission impossible," he not only pulled it off but as his notes indicate, managed to give serious, detailed thought not only to immediate requirements but also to future needs and possibilities. It would seem that all those Kiichiro had picked as his top managers shared in his farsightedness.

When Kan presented his initial outline of the plan, Kiichiro had only one comment to make.

"What is this?" he asked, pointing to the supply annex attached to each plant.

"Those are the warehouse staging areas for storing incoming parts and materials for each plant."

"We don't need them," Kiichiro replied, taking a red grease pencil and eliminating each one by marking it with a big red "X."

"But, we must have some of each of the parts shipped in by subcontractors on hand to be sure there are no interruptions in the production flow. They'll be sent from such places such as Nagoya, Kariya, or Toyohashi -- all of which are some distance away. If even one thing doesn't make it in time, then the whole assembly line has to stop."

"No, we must ensure that they arrive here on time," retorted Kiichiro, grimly shaking his head.

"This I call, *Just-In-Time*. It'll work out if right before it is to be used, each necessary part arrives at the appropriate place. It's harmful and wasteful to have them stacked up prior to being needed."

"But, isn't it true that the operating principle of the assembly line depends on a series of work stations with adjacent parts warehouses, arranged in the order in which the parts are assembled? At the current Ford factory, reputed to have the most advanced assembly line in the world, they do it that way," Kan insisted, adding lamely, "I really can't think of any other practical method."

"Please discard such ideas," said Kiichiro decisively. "Regardless of what method Ford is using, Toyota will do it the Toyota way. Unless we establish a method far superior to Ford's, we will never beat Ford. There'll be waste in everything if we follow Ford's method in which parts must be stored until they are needed. We must do the reverse, where the assembly line work stations receive, one by one, the required components *Just-In-Time*. Please turn your head 180 degrees and think in this manner."

"I see," Kan answered, but in truth still not grasping how it could possibly be made to work.

After mulling over the concept of *Just-In-Time* for a few days, however, Kan realized that Kiichiro was right. To build a parts holding annex or warehouse, a large, piece of land is needed.

Moreover, as business grows, the warehouse would have to expand accordingly, likely to the point where poor organization of materials would lend to production inefficiencies. That, coupled with obsolescence of parts due to design changes, would create a storage nightmare.

Finally, extra personnel also would be needed to oversee, store, retrieve, and keep track of the parts and the facility.

What an original idea! Mr. Toyoda has a brilliant plan, Kan thought.

To keep the assembly line operating smoothly, a precise schedule would be given to each parts manufacturer and strictly enforced. Unless a strict discipline was instilled *right from the beginning,* the process would not work. Kan revised his plan to eliminate all large parts warehouses but, with Kiichiro's approval, he included a small parts-storage room at each work station that could furnish replacements for defective parts or vehicles damaged on the assembly line.

Kan's awe over the brilliance of Kiichiro's concept was well-placed. The *Just-In-Time* system would not only work but go on to set the standard for assembly-line manufacturing in Japan and influence manufacturers worldwide. This departure from the established mass production systems followed by other auto makers proved to be the key that finally unlocked the secret interrelationship among quality, efficiency, and economy. Moreover, it would be a major factor in Toyota's meteoric climb in becoming one of the world's great automobile manufacturers...but not before the Koromo plant had been built.

The other parts of the plan were executed as Kan developed them. The Koromo factory, ranked number one in the Far East in its time, was built on the grand scale envisioned by Kiichiro. In addition to the production facilities, it included a building to house guests and press personnel, dining halls, lodging, and everything from an exercise field to a museum -- even a Toyota Technical University.

One would not suspect there were budget constraints in such an undertaking, but there were. In fact, only a portion of the elaborate conveyor system planned could be constructed and structures designed for the ceiling and upper areas were omitted. Actually these proved to be fortuitous omissions, as it allowed for future expansion and modification as needed. Much later -- after the war -- the open area of the ceiling was utilized to house a computerized conveyor system.

For awhile, progress remained on track. The trucks that had continually broken down were improved, and by the time Osaka Toyota officially opened in April of 1936, most of the mechanical problems had been eliminated.

That this was accomplished can be attributed to the fact that Kiichiro was a "practical dreamer," an excellent engineer with a broad understanding of science and technology, an excellent manager and a man willing to take enormous risks, and as the son of the founder of Toyoda, in a singular and perhaps unique position to do so. No better example of his willingness to do whatever it took to get the job done can be cited than when mechanical problems continued to plague Hinode Motors. It was Kiichiro who would come running immediately, anytime, anywhere, sleeves rolled, diving under the truck, and not just fix it but analyze the possible causes for the breakdown.

Once, acknowledging there was a major defect in the differential housing, he issued the order: "Throw away all of those housings and build them again." With that, he scrapped some seven hundred completed housings -- something no chairman of the board or salaried president would or could have so readily done.

He did not hesitate to do the same thing with other defective components. Because of Kiichiro's adherence to this mode of operation, improvements were made with unparalleled boldness and swiftness.

Looking back later, Kiichiro recounted that, "During that year, we made improvements in eight hundred areas."   Some might cynically respond with, "What? There were that many defects?" Others might consider it admirable that technical improvements on that scale had been made with such zeal.

However one judges the process, it was successful, and once the production of a nearly trouble-free truck was accomplished, it was possible to resume production of passenger cars that May.

On May 19, 1936, the Lower House of the Parliament finally passed the long-awaited Law Concerning the Manufacture of Motor Vehicles. The House of Peers approved it on the twenty-third, and it was promulgated on the twenty-ninth.

Ford of Japan tried to take advantage of the time gap between promulgation and enforcement of the law, and on June 9, submitted a petition to the Kanagawa Prefectural Office seeking permission to build a factory on the Asano landfill property it had already purchased at the Yokohama port. The application could not be rejected because it was legal, and the governor of Kanagawa Prefecture racked his brain over what to do.

To suppress that application, the government had hurried the passage of the Law Concerning the Manufacture of Motor Vehicles through both houses of Parliament. However, on July 10, it was first issued as Imperial Edict Number 170, and then as a Ministry of Commerce and Industry Order Number Six.

The edict became effective and was enforced beginning on the eleventh, preventing approval of Ford's application with no time to spare.

The law limited annual production by Ford and General Motors to 12,360 and 9,470 units, respectively, based on standards of actual production figures for the three year period ending August 9, 1935. That protected the investments by the United States firms while allowing development of a viable domestic automobile industry.

The passenger car Toyota resumed building in May was designated the Model AA. The front-end of the body was less rounded than that of the airflow-styled A1, but even by today's standards, its appearance was quite sleek.

On September 14, the Model AA was introduced at the Tokyo Trade Show at Toyota's *Commemorative Exhibit of the Domestic Toyota Automobile for the Masses.*

On the day before the show, the first meeting of the newly founded Committee for Domestic Automobile Manufacture was held, and its first order of business was to designate companies under the Law Concerning the Manufacture of Motor Vehicles. On July 23, the assembly unanimously decided upon Toyoda Automatic Loom Works, and two days later, chose Nissan Motor Company. They were the only two selected.

The news was relayed to the Model AA Exhibit Booth at the Trade Show, prompting Kiichiro to exclaim with a touch of satisfaction, "Finally, it has been decided!"

Although Toyota directors already knew of the decision, the official announcement was received with a great sense of relief that generated a joyful atmosphere at the Toyota exhibit.

Formal notification was delivered to the headquarters of Toyoda Automatic Loom Works on the nineteenth of the month in an announcement signed by Nobusuke Kishi of the Ministry of Commerce and Industry.

The official notification carried the stipulation that effective by 1938, all materials as well as components to be utilized in the manufacture of domestic automobiles must not be imported except under extreme circumstances.

Of course, the stipulation was unreasonable; it's one thing to have it as a goal but quite another to require it by law. Right from the very beginning, Kiichiro had made the "establishment of an automobile industry whose products are built entirely by Japanese brains and hands" his motto. But he always recognized this as being a long-term goal. Given the state of technology in Japan, having it even as a "long-term" goal was especially ambitious, and Kiichiro knew that, as did many others. The common perception among those who knew the industry was:

To make a car exclusively with domestic parts would be like erecting a building starting at the third or fourth floor.

For that reason, Kiichiro's priorities remained focused on the general situation -- how to ensure the autonomy of a public industry. If the only way to accomplish that was to use some foreign parts and materials, so be it. As dedicated as he was to creating a domestic industry, he did not insist on cutting foreign suppliers out of the picture. In fact, he had secretly started negotiations with Ford to share their technology, a move which put him in direct conflict with the new "national policy." There was simply no way around it.

In October, management acted on the idea Kamiya had advanced when first joining the company and established Toyota Credit Corporation. The new operation, capitalized at one million yen, would provide financing for automobile distributors as well as for individuals purchasing vehicles.

In addition, following approval of the third increase in capital funding by the board of directors in December, Toyoda Automatic Loom Works capital was boosted from six million to nine million yen.

The Automobile Department continued to make good progress. In the following year, in keeping with the prediction made by Akitsugu Nishikawa during the earlier "Yayoi Meeting," an automobile factory was built in Shanghai. By February of 1937, administrative offices and repair facilities were in operation and plans for an assembly plant in Shanghai and one in northern China had been approved.

To carry out those plans, construction preparations were quietly being made in China by Akitsugu Nishikawa and in Tokyo by Shinsaburo Iida, Hatako's brother and the individual who probably best understood Kiichiro.

Under Kamiya's direction, the establishment of dealer's in Japan was going well, with plans for a Toyota dealership in each prefecture by March of 1938.

Production of the modified truck, designated the Model GY, commenced in May. At the same time, the company began building a machine tool factory within the Kariya compound.

With these additions, the Automobile Department of Toyoda Automatic Loom Works now had a personnel list three thousand strong and had grown to such an enormous extent that its employees were now designated by department.

Moreover, where only a year or two earlier, banks, financial experts, and public opinion were predicting bankruptcy for the would-be automobile manufacturer, now the chorus changed to one of jealousy and envy. The prevailing "conventional wisdom" was that Toyoda would take the profit earned by virtue of the new national law and salt it all away in its family-owned Automatic Loom Works, essentially cashing in on a monopoly. To curb such rumors, Toyoda eventually would have to establish a new company and make a public offering of its stock.

From the company's perspective, going public was also a necessary move. Since the firm was legally required to quickly mass-produce trucks to government specifications, management had already moved ahead on plans to build its giant factory in Koromo. Kan's blueprints were finished and the building stage was at hand. Construction costs were projected at the enormous sum of thirty million yen, in today's economy the equivalent of several tens of billion yen. Although business was going well for Toyoda Spinning and Automatic Loom Works, an investment of that magnitude simply could not be financed privately.

Consequently, the idea of splitting off the Automobile Department and making it a separate concern quickly gained popularity, and a decision to designate it the "Toyota Motor Manufacturing Company" had tentatively been made.

Giving further impetus to the process, Japan was moving ever closer to an all out war with China. The Japanese army had taken Nanking, Hankow, and Canton despite fierce resistance by the Chinese, and further north, drove into Inner Mongolia and partially occupied the provinces of Shansi and Shensi.

With that as the backdrop, the movement in Japan to institute wartime economic controls gained momentum. At Toyota, the general consensus among management was: *If war spreads further, then any number of vehicles will be needed for military use. The demand for mass production of Toyotas will become much stronger. We must hurry and establish the new company.*

Spurred by the fever of events, the date of the meeting to establish the new manufacturing company was moved up to August 27, 1937. The motion was unanimously approved at the meeting and on the twenty-eighth, the new company was officially registered. On October 1, it started operations.

The headquarters of the company was established in Koromo, where the new factory was to be built. Its capitalization originally had been projected at 3.2 million yen, but that amount had to be reduced to 1.2 million yen. This reduction was the result of having to launch the company sooner than anticipated, and in line with the tradition maintained since Sakichi's era, capitalists, banks, and *zaibatsu* concerns were not to be trusted. That ruled out the idea of making a "far-reaching public offering of stock," which meant capitalization also had to be raised through loans from investors closely allied with the company. It also prompted an increase in the projected total loan from 1.5 million yen to an estimated 2.5 million and signaled company-wide belt tightening.

Risaburo was named president of the new company, with Kiichiro as vice president. Oshima and Masayoshi Takeuchi were appointed managers, and the board of directors, in addition to a few from outside the company, was made up of such individuals as Ikenaga, Ito, and Kamiya -- the top members of the team that had worked on the prototype. The Board of Auditors consisted of Heikichi, Kiichiro's uncle and lifetime benefactor; Okamoto, Okabe, and Nishikawa from Shanghai. Organization accomplished, the designated company rights under the Law Concerning the Manufacture of Motor Vehicles were transferred from the Automatic Loom Works, and the new company established its main factory in Koromo, with a branch factory in Kariya. A research department and a Tokyo branch store also were established in Tokyo's Shibaura Ward.

On September 29, two days before the new company started operations, a ground-breaking ceremony for the new factory was held at the building site at Koromo, where soil preparations had just been completed.

On the land where at one time, *tanuki* -- a Japanese badger -- and rabbits had lived and where mushrooms could be harvested in autumn, the sounds of hammers pounding on steel framework and an endless wave of trucks bringing in materials echoed across the shrubs and shook the overgrown branches of the thickets.

Kan and Saito never left the site during construction, and Kiichiro worked at his usual hectic pace. Often sweaty and dirty from manual labor, he could be seen working side by side with the night-shift or urging the work forward:

"We have to move ahead with construction, but actually we're moving faster with construction so we can quickly start production. Neither construction nor the move can be allowed to delay production."

The construction plan consisted of four largely concurrent phases. Phase one called for the assembly plant to be completed in February of 1938, equipped in March, and readied for occupancy by April. In phase two, the foundry would be completed in March of 1938, equipped in May, and made ready for casting in June. A June deadline for completion of the machine tool plant was phase three. And the final phase provided for company housing to be completed in February, 1938, and made ready for occupancy in June.

Kiichiro had ordered that both tasks of production and construction proceed simultaneously without any delays. Consequently, at the start of 1938, it was decided to move the equipment into the Koromo plant as soon as it had been completed. Some of the equipment had just recently arrived from the United States and other pieces were being moved from the Kariya plant. Every effort was being made to avoid upsetting production at Kariya. Truck production had been increased from four hundred a month to five hundred, and cars were rolling out at a rate of nearly one hundred per month. To make the transition without disturbing Kariya's production flow, Kiichiro came up with a detailed plan and made sure it was rigorously executed.

A split-second decision to use an approach he'd never heard of before and had no time to test may provide some idea of just how anxious Kiichiro was to complete the Koromo plant. It happened in February of 1938, when construction was running at its most feverish pace.

Responsible for overseeing the purchase of the equipment to outfit the new Koromo plant, Jiro Iwaoka had gone to the United States to see if he could move up delivery dates on some of the key equipment and to change orders for other equipment previously placed by Oshima and Kan. Upon his return, he was amazed to find clusters of steel-framed buildings rising up everywhere. With a jubilant spirit, Iwaoka immediately sought out Kiichiro and went to make his report and found him dressed in overalls and working alongside a construction crew.

"I've just returned. Pertaining to your orders...." Brusquely, without so much as a hello, Kiichiro interrupted Iwaoka, asking, "Did you see anything new?"

"Ah, yes, new things," Iwaoka replied, pausing momentarily as he mulled over the question. Then seeing the rows of machinery being brought in right under his nose, he said, "Oh yes. There's a new trend in the set-up of new machine tools in the United States. Many of them are built so they can just be placed on the plant floor without special foundations or complicated tie-downs."

"Really? That's great! It'll be more efficient," said Kiichiro, his eyes lighting up as he looked at Iwaoka and added, "You don't have to tell me the other things right now. Please have the floor of our factory made that way." With that, he sent Iwaoka off to the machine tool factory site.

Construction continued at a blistering pace and the new factory was finished just a hairsbreadth later than scheduled. By the end of September, the entire factory compound was ready for occupancy, and a month later, the move from Kariya was complete. All in all, there was an array of some forty plants covering a great area -- plants that gave raw materials new shapes, such as forging and casting; some for machining operations such as drilling, boring, tapping, reaming, countersinking, and grinding and honing; press areas for forming and notching body panels; paint finishing stations, and assembly lines. Affiliated with these plants were research and development labs, test areas, and complete health facilities. It was a historic moment, as Japan's first full-scale "monument" for the mass production of motor vehicles sprawled across the landscape.

Interestingly, history had produced, and was in the process of producing, its own ironic parallels. The same year Kiichiro had revealed his intention to mass-produce motor vehicles, Adolf Hitler had announced his plan for mass-production of the "Volkswagen." Then, almost on the same date Kiichiro succeeded in pushing the Koromo factory to completion, the ground-breaking ceremony for "Volkswagen City" was held. The parallel is striking in other respects. The German facility was built on a large tract of wasteland at Wolfsburg. With a population target of 90,000, the "city" would be built between a canal with one side consisting of a steam power plant and a factory compound, and on the other side, a residential community. Like Kiichiro's plant, it was a large-scale enterprise with highly original features, such as the plan to utilize steam emitted from the power plant to provide heat for the factories and residential housing.

The ceremony to commemorate completion of the Koromo Factory was held on November 3, 1938. Only those associated with the inner circle of the company were invited to the ceremony in which Kiichiro appeared clad in a factory uniform, offered his prayers at the shrine, and then solemnly read his speech:

My late father left behind as his parting wish that Toyoda build automobiles, and we have made that wish come true. We are gathered here to witness the birth of a domestic Japanese automobile industry.

It so happens that we have encountered an unprecedented time of emergency for the Japanese Empire, and under a pressing mission and deadline, we have built a factory in Koromo adapted to the national policy and thus have established a large-scale automobile factory.

As the Sino-Japanese conflict has greatly increased, the need for military use of motor vehicles has become greater. We have had to turn our eyes from peacetime to focus on the life blood of the national economy.

Motor vehicles are gifts of both peacetime and wartime, and play an increasingly important role in fulfilling the need for domestic transportation and further development of the continent. Our current task is to follow the orders of the government. We fully realize the supremacy of our duty.

Human beings must live by their duties. We must put aside our petty egos and work on larger ones. To ignore our duties is to ruin ourselves, to accomplish them is to promote ourselves. When one has the duty to take charge of something, one must do it with wholehearted sincerity. One must collect all the strength one can muster. In a chain, each link is connected to another, and this enterprise is like that. If, for example, one individual is careless, that may defeat all of the effort exerted thus far to build the complete factory. Even the movement of one pin is tied to the fate of the nation. There must not be any waste in any individual's task.

Here, each worker's wishes will be heard, and this important responsibility will permanently be carried on every shoulder. By acting this way, we will accomplish our duties. And by accomplishing our duties, we will make the effort to enhance the national prestige, and this national prestige will help lead to perpetual peace in the Far East.

To put this into practice, I expect everyone to accomplish each of his tasks. We must exert strenuous efforts and be totally dedicated to accomplishing these imperial wishes.

It was a fine piece of oratory written in an exalted style. As he read in his customary low voice, Kiichiro paused intermittently as tears welled up in his eyes. The animus for that speech came from dreams afar, the dream of his father which became Kiichiro's dream, and, through him, the dream of his beloved country and countrymen. To the very core of his heart, Kiichiro felt the deep pathos of a dream become reality.

Kiichiro turned and threw the master switch. The entire factory was brought to life at that very instant, and throughout the compound sounded the throaty roar of powerful machinery at work.

Chapter 9

THE FLAMES OF WAR

As the Koromo factory started operating in earnest, turning out two thousand units per month, the work force quickly grew to five thousand. Some of the factory and office employees moved closer to the work site, but the majority continued to commute from Kariya. The small privately-owned commuter trains were sagging under the burden of the daily mass migration to and from Koromo. Passengers were crammed together and understandably irritable. Railway officials were hard-pressed to come up with a solution to the congestion. Finally, open freight cars were pressed into service during rush-hours, but this did little to make commuting a pleasant experience. Without any lighting, the freight cars overflowed in the evening with factory workers carrying lighted lanterns. The trains were still over-loaded. In fact, they traveled so slowly that a person who missed a train at one station could run by way of a short cut and be waiting for it at the next.

All the factory workers received new uniforms and caps in an effort by management to kindle the team spirit and discipline essential to Kiichiro's *Just-In-Time* production method. Kiichiro reiterated what it would take for success:

"Everything concerning production must be Just-In-Time. Whether one misses a train by a minute or even just a second, they still missed the train. When one part for an automobile is late, whether one hour or one day, then that car cannot be completed. We must make sure that the part is there each and every time at the right place and at the right time."

This was the same concept Kiichiro had explained to Kan, with only one addition. A Supply Control Department would be established and assigned importance of the highest order. If, for example, there were fifty cylinder blocks, then there must also be fifty cylinder heads and fifty each of all the other related components. These were to be put at a designated place the night before. The Supply Control Department would be responsible for making certain that every component was present at its designated area and that the area would always be the same. This would eliminate any confusion.

According to the plan, parts would be inspected early in the morning by the Supply Control Department head. Kiichiro also made it a standing policy that everyone, at any time, regardless of where they worked, must immediately report *any* flaw, malfunction, or unusual circumstance to the proper inspector.

By "any," Kiichiro literally *meant* "any." His decree covered every conceivable thing from machinery malfunctions, improper placement of parts, and even such trivial deficiencies as leaky faucets in the bathrooms. Everyone understood that the major problems were to be covered, but the "little" ones also often had to be pointed out, at least at first.

When Eiji transferred to Koromo, for example, he was immediately assigned the duties of general inspector and instructed to report directly to Kiichiro. Eiji was very bright and assumed he understood what was expected of him. Yet he constantly found himself being reprimanded by Kiichiro for things he didn't know he was responsible for. Once, for instance, Eiji was checking out some parts when Kiichiro accosted him with, "Did you know that there are many small potholes in the road along the side of the factory?"

Startled, Eiji replied, "Yes, I saw a little bit of that before...."

"If you knew about it, why haven't you already had it fixed," Kiichiro demanded.

"What? Is it my responsibility to fix even the potholes in the roads," asked Eiji, taken aback.

"Of course," Kiichiro answered in an exasperated tone of voice, "everything is the responsibility of the head inspector. What do you think would happen if a parts truck hit one of those potholes? A car part could fall off and break or be damaged. On the assembly line, that would mean waiting for a replacement part. We can't tolerate stopping the assembly line whether the cause is a pothole in the road, or a piece of paper on the floor. You must give orders immediately, right there on the spot, to have any problem taken care of."

Kiichiro said often enough that he was putting his entire life on the line to build vehicles, and clearly he had no patience for anything but an all-out, highly-focused effort. Like a high-wire artist working without a net, he had absolutely no room for error. But unlike the high-wire performer, Kiichiro could only go forward. Kiichiro himself put it to his trusted friend, Iwaoka: "As long as we have shared so much this far, you should know there are no *back gears* on my vehicle. If, by any chance, I fail, I won't be able to start over and catch up, even if I were to kill myself trying. I have no choice but to succeed at everything I do."

And to succeed, Kiichiro had to be everywhere -- doing everything -- at once. As the company's organizational chart for 1939-1940 shows, Kiichiro was president, general manager of the research and the planning departments, and section manager of the "quality control department." Eiji is listed as the department's chief clerk and inspector.

The amount of diversity in titles and responsibilities which characterized Kiichiro's direct involvement was shared at that time by only one other person at Toyota -- Shotaro Kamiya. According to the same organizational charts, Kamiya was a director, general manager of marketing, and head of the service section of the marketing department. It was he who masterminded broad marketing strategies, as well as controlled the day-to-day workings of all customer-related aspects of the business -- customer satisfaction programs, repeat sales, and most importantly, repair services. In addition, he served as the Toyota representative to the Japan Motor Vehicle Distribution Company. This was a government-regulated company established in 1942 by a national decree. In other words, what Kiichiro was to manufacturing, Kamiya was to sales and marketing. It was under their stewardship that the company ran efficiently and fulfilled its goals. By 1939, the long-awaited production target of twenty thousand vehicles seemed to be within reach. However, global and national events were beginning to make such predictions somewhat precarious. Already, foreign nations were slapping various restrictions and controls on exports of machine tools, while military uses for such tools produced in Japan were receiving top priority.

Also by 1939, materials and fuel were becoming scarce. Not helping the problem any was Mother Nature herself. A serious drought had brought a dramatic drop in water levels in the more than one hundred main river systems which flowed from the mountainous interior to the sea and serviced all of Japan. Consequently, the availability of hydroelectric power was drastically reduced. Faced with these adversities, actual production for 1939 was a disappointing 14,018 units.

The following year only brought more of the same hardships. The production goal for 1940 was 22,000 units, but as procurement of materials became more and more difficult, the target was slashed to 13,500. Then in June, cutbacks in staff and hours were made. Though the supply of materials improved slightly, final production for 1940 was 14,041 units -- 541 units more than what was projected but only 23 more than the previous year's production. For all practical purposes, the company made no progress for a whole year.

At the January 28, 1941, shareholders' meeting, Risaburo resigned as chairman of the Board of Directors and Kiichiro was appointed as the new chairman and president, both in name and in fact. Concurrently, Hisagi Akai, a director at Mitsui and Company, was brought in and appointed vice-president.

Although Kiichiro now held the post that would have made his earlier "covert operations" unnecessary, it came a little late: the times were such that top executives of public corporations had little room to display their full abilities. The military now ran the government, and it left little doubt that its needs always came first. More and more, the manufacturing sector was brought under tight control. In January, the Ministry of Commerce and Industry issued regulations containing truck specifications for five different kinds of load-carrying capabilities. In February, as a recognized manufacturer of military vehicles, Toyota was allotted materials to produce them. At the same time, they were given the go-ahead to manufacture a passenger car -- the first in several years.

This was the "Model AE," also known as the *Shin-Nippon Go*, a five-passenger vehicle with 2,258CC displacement. The AE was definitely an automobile, but it was hardly the one Kiichiro had dreamed of mass-producing for the public. That automobile was still a few years away -- in fact, more than a war away -- but in the meantime, Toyota was gathering valuable engineering experience. In addition to the AE, Toyota produced many different automobiles during the war, nearly all of them luxury cars for high ranking military and government officials.

In March, the government fixed prices on Model GB trucks, and in June, specified prices for all vehicles while restricting sales only to approved users. As the purchase of trucks and buses was by permit only, those accorded permits placed their orders as soon as they received them. This meant that every vehicle moving off the Toyota assembly line had been spoken for.

Then came December 7, 1941 -- Pearl Harbor. On December 8, Japan declared war on the United States. Almost immediately, the automobile industry was saddled with the Motor Vehicle Regulation Committee, a control group created by the Key Industries Organization Order, effective December 24.

It was a bleak time. Everything was rigidly controlled by the war effort with individuality, creativity, inventiveness, and originality going by the boards.

The only event in which Kiichiro could take even a small degree of satisfaction during these trying times was an announcement of the monthly production figures for December -- 2,066 units. This surpassed the two thousand unit mark he had originally set and that had been attained only once before the war began. Annual production for 1941 was 14,611 units.

On January 15, 1942, an edict prohibiting sales of foreign-made passenger cars was issued. Actually the edict was ludicrous, as imports had come to a complete halt anyway. With the war ever-increasing the demand for domestic-made vehicles, production at Toyota reached 16,302 in 1942. It was carefully noted in the annual report that output had surpassed the pre-war record.

While the war was forging the immediate destiny of the Toyota Motor Company, it was also plotting a new future for all of the Toyoda-related manufacturers. Toyoda Spinning and Weaving -- once the primary business -- was combined with four other spinning companies in January, 1942, to form a new company called Chuo Spinning Company. Then in June of 1943, Chuo Spinning Company, now superfluous as a "peacetime venture," was merged with Toyota Motor Company, and essentially disappeared. Then the Toyoda Automatic Loom Works suspended manufacture of spinning machines and experienced a similar fate. Now subordinated to its one-time, spendthrift, troublesome, good-for-nothing "son" *the automobile maker,* the former parent firm was given the humbling task of manufacturing and assembling vehicle components and also producing a limited number of armaments.

Everywhere, even in Kiichiro's automobile company, the military inspectors began to creep in and take command. Eventually, everything fell under rigid military control. Kiichiro had no choice but to accept this state of affairs, but he didn't hesitate to show displeasure when military observers postured or threw their weight around. As long as the military representatives could understand reason, Kiichiro held no grudges. But if they were pompous bullies or inclined to make a public display of their power and importance, that was a different matter. Kiichiro's ire or the "ice" of his demeanor would make even the hardened military personnel shudder.

Kiichiro loved his country, but he thought the war with the United States was a calamitous mistake. In a memo written at the time, Kiichiro strongly expressed his convictions:

There is no way that Japan can win a war with the United States. We must stop such a foolish war as soon as possible -- even a day earlier than that. The military has mobilized the newspapers to print meaningless propaganda in order to fool the Japanese people into believing we can win the war. But what is the truth of our situation in comparison to the United States? In 1939, for example, automobile production in the United States totaled 3.59 million; Japan's was 34,500. In 1940, the United States turned out 4.47 million versus Japan's 46,000. That's the real truth of our chances of victory. We're out-ranked by a factor of one hundred. Even if we were to utilize our car engines to build airplanes, and the United States were to do the same thing, they could produce one hundred planes to our one. On the European battlefields of World War I, the German Army had 120,000 vehicles, while the Allied forces consisted of France's 97,000 vehicles, and the U.S.'s and Britain's combined 100,000. That difference of almost 80,000 vehicles determined victory. With a weapons ratio of one hundred to one against us, how much of a chance does Japan have?

Kiichiro's head-strong and rebellious days, when he disdained inequities visited by the West upon the East in general and Japan in particular, had waned with the on-set of the Sino-Japanese War, and ended with the war in the Pacific. In his growing wisdom, he was coming to see that it is indeed humane to settle competitions in arenas of sports and the global market place, and not on the world's battlefields. But being under the thumb of the military left him little to do other than meet the necessary manufacturing quotas of his country.

Through 1944, operations continued smoothly at both the Koromo and Kariya factories. Beginning in early 1945, airplanes were manufactured at a separate Toyoda plant. In China, prior to the war, the two main automobile plants in Shanghai and Tientsin were augmented by local repair facilities and branch offices established in Beijing, Tsingtao, Hsucho, Kaifun, Shichazhon, Taiyuen, Bawdien, and Houho. After the war began, repair facilities and branch offices opened in southern Asia at Taipei, the Philippines, Sumatra, Java, and Borneo. The establishment of these operations signaled the company was prospering, but the war-related nature of business had gradually gotten further and further away from Kiichiro's original desire and intention.

Kiichiro was filled with anxiety and began to quietly record his misgivings and observations around the time he took over the presidency of the company from Risaburo. His writings increasingly departed from his beloved and once almost exclusive technical topics to include ruminations on World War I and how the allies treated the defeated nations. He also recorded his strategies for managing the country after what he foresaw as Japan's inevitable defeat. Kiichiro took particular interest in the treatment and reconstruction of Germany after World War I and collected many documents dealing with the revitalization of German industry in the postwar period. As defeat was never a question in his mind, he was obviously drawing many parallels in an attempt to foresee how the allies would address the question of reconstruction of Japan's industries.

Considering the everyday business of manufacturing, Kiichiro loathed working under military supervisors. Often being openly at odds with them brought moments of peace to his soul. That's not to say his was heroic or outright mutinous behavior, or that he was putting his life in jeopardy. But his gestures were not meaningless either. Against the roar of the enormous totalitarian mechanism of the war government, it was difficult for any objections to be heard. Still Kiichiro never relinquished his dream of mass-producing an automobile for the common man. All he could do was bide his time and wait for times to change.

The picture grew darker and more grim for Japan with each passing year of the war. As time went on, Kiichiro became increasingly pessimistic about the prospects for regaining control of his business. At least one area of his life was improving, however. This period saw a marked change and decided improvement in relationships among family members.

When Kiichiro moved his family to Tokyo in 1936, his cousin, Eiji, moved in with them. Then in 1938, Risaburo's second oldest son, Daikichiro, also moved in, as he was attending Waseda University. Because of their various ages, Daikichiro was like a younger brother to Eiji, and an older brother to Kiichiro's son, Shoichiro, who was five years younger. Living under the same roof brought them very close together, and the great affection the three shared for one another radiated outward through the entire Toyoda family. Soon a conciliatory air was to be felt between the households of Kiichiro and Risaburo, muting the effects of the sharp words and hard feelings exchanged ever since the start of the automobile operations. Certainly Aiko, Kiichiro's sister and wife of Risaburo, and Hatako, Kiichiro's wife, were relieved to see the icy distance between their husbands and families melting.

As there was little for him to do now that the factory had been "usurped" by the military establishment, Kiichiro had a great deal of free time on his hands. He often went home to Washizu. His aunt, Han, had passed away in 1941, but her son, Bunjiro Makino, was taking care of the old residence in Yamaguchi village. Kiichiro's cousin Bunjiro was a small, quiet man, one year younger than Kiichiro, and he proved to be a suitable companion to the reticent Kiichiro. Now nearing fifty years of age, Kiichiro had always avoided small talk and "chitchat" in the past, eschewing any subject that did not pertain to business. But now, perhaps because his dream was on hold, Kiichiro found time for conversations with Bunjiro, relating some of his early experiences, personal as well as business.

Kiichiro's cousin was a good listener, and one clear day in May of 1943 at around ten o'clock in the morning, as Kiichiro sat reading the newspaper in the living room of the old residence, Bunjiro appeared in the yard.

"Kiichiro, I have brought a guest," Bunjiro called out cheerfully.

Glancing up from the paper, Kiichiro saw, standing behind Bunjiro, a small, frail-looking woman about seventy years of age, wearing a simple kimono and bowing her head. *It's Mother! It's Tami, my mother!* Kiichiro surmised immediately. He rose quickly and went to greet them.

· Smiling first at Kiichiro, then at Tami, Bunjiro quietly told her, "Please go in. Please take your time and have a nice talk. There is no need to be formal in this house." Taking the old woman's hand, he led her onto the veranda, looking up at Kiichiro, giving him a big smile, then turning to leave.

No one knows what Kiichiro and his mother talked about -- what they might have cried and laughed about. No one was in the house besides mother and son -- no one except the presence of the solitary scroll that hung on the wall as it had hung low these many years: the scroll, *a hundred ordeals, a thousand trials....*

Bunjiro returned to the house sometime after the lunch hour to find Tami already gone. Kiichiro was in an unusually jovial mood as he brewed coffee and then sat down and entertained Bunjiro with some of his experiences.

I was right. It was a good idea to let them meet, and judging by Kiichiro's high spirits, they must have had a pleasant conversation, thought Bunjiro, pleased with himself.

There seemed to be an understanding of the heart between the two men. Kiichiro remained silent about his visit with Tami, and Bunjiro did not ask, even though this may have been the last time mother and child would meet. It was a bright moment in an otherwise darkening world.

As the Japanese war effort deteriorated, taking several turns for the worse, materials became scarce at the Koromo automobile factory. Instead of building automobiles, the workers were busy digging evacuation shelters and laying in stores of potatoes. The military supervisory personnel had nothing to offer but empty ideology, threadbare slogans, and bluffs.

December 7, 1944, dawned much like any other day in December, cloudy during the morning, and then clearing. Taking Hatako with him, Kiichiro had driven to the old residence in Washizu in the morning. After lunch, while Hatako and Bunjiro were clearing the table, Kiichiro picked up an ax to chop firewood.

Around one-thirty in the afternoon, Kiichiro suddenly felt his legs give out. Dropping the ax, he grabbed hold of a nearby tree, panic rising in his breast as he grimly thought, *Oh no! It's the same as Dad's high blood pressure spasm!*

Regaining his legs, Kiichiro calmed down and began walking slowly back to the house for help. Suddenly he stopped, surprised to see that Hatako, Bunjiro, and the chauffeur were standing in the yard. Their faces were pale and grim as they looked about at various areas of the village.

"What? What's going on?" Kiichiro blurted out.

Hatako's face brightened as she saw that he appeared to be unharmed. She ran to him, crying, "It was a big earthquake, dear. Are you all right?"

"Oh, it was only an earthquake," smiled Kiichiro. "That's a big relief!"

What an odd thing to say, thought Hatako, glancing anxiously at Kiichiro for any signs of damage to his head.

He was still smiling broadly, but as he looked around, the smile faded quickly from his face. Small huts and walls of larger structures in the village had crumbled, and the eaves on many homes were hanging down.

"This is very bad. Some areas might have suffered extensive damages," Kiichiro said in a now serious voice tinged with awe as he realized, despite his relief at being spared his father's fatal illness, the situation was nothing to laugh about.

Noting that the house seemed to have come through the quake without damage, Kiichiro turned to Hatako and Bunjiro and told them, "Everything seems to be all right here, but I'm worried about the factory. You two stay here. I'm going to Koromo right away."

Telling the chauffeur to get the car ready and bring along a shovel and other emergency tools, Kiichiro quickly changed his clothes and got into the car, one of the popular Toyota Model AC's built at Koromo.

As they drove through Toyohashi, they began to see the damage worsen. By the time they reached Hekikai, they were seeing ravaged homes, stores, small businesses, and factories everywhere, some razed completely to the ground.

Driving was difficult, as fallen walls and other wreckage blocked the road.

"Please drive around twelve to eighteen miles per hour," Kiichiro told the driver, explaining that a slow-moving vehicle is much safer in the event of secondary quakes or aftershocks.

The advice was prudent. There were, in fact, a number of aftershocks that downed poles, trees, and walls all around, as Kiichiro and his driver swerved for safety. The ground trembled, but the car went on.

Every time an aftershock occurred, children came running wildly out of their houses, heedless of moving traffic and terrifying the two passengers, as they drove slowly on, steering clear of people and objects. It was a frightening journey to Kariya, especially as Kiichiro imagined what possible damages there might be at the Koromo plant.

When they arrived at Kariya, they saw that the straight-ridged roof of the Automatic Loom Works compound had fallen to the ground and that the prototype construction shop and an old warehouse had collapsed. The main parts of the factory, however, showed very little damage.

After a quick inventory, Kiichiro walked to the factory offices and entered, exclaiming to the first clerk he saw: "Koromo -- I wonder if it's all right!"

Smiling as he nodded yes, the office worker replied, "Koromo seems to be all right, but we've heard that the damage is extensive in Nagoya. The port area was devastated, and the aviation factory has been completely destroyed.

"One of the office workers had gone to the port area on a motorbike and just barely escaped being trapped by debris from the quake as he hurried back. He reports that the ground around the armament factory near the Nagoya port area shook so hard that segments jumped as high as eye-level and, right before his eyes, the enormous aviation factory compound just instantly collapsed."

The earthquake epicenter was located in the Sea of Kumano, and the event became known as the Southeast Sea Earthquake. Since Japan was in the midst of war, most of the damage was not publicly reported. Nevertheless, records show it was an enormous earthquake with a magnitude above 8.0 on the Richter scale in the Nagoya area. It was felt in places as far away as Tokyo, Osaka, and Kobe. In Aichi Prefecture where Nagoya is located, 998 deaths and 2,135 injuries were reported. A total of 26,130 homes were destroyed by the earthquake, and another 3,059 were destroyed by *tsunami* (tidal waves) raised by the quake. In addition, countless homes and other structures were damaged. In one rural area, a temple collapsed, and in another dozens of children died when the quake tragically demolished their orphanage.

That night Kiichiro stayed in Kariya. Its wrath spent, nature staged a beautiful sunset, as the western sky glowed with a rich, bright red. Very few even noticed as they dug through the rubble and prepared for the clean-up.

When Kiichiro went to Koromo the following morning, he was overjoyed to see that only one part of the factory roof had collapsed. The damages were much less than at Kariya. All day long, however, Kiichiro received reports confirming that the Nagoya factory complex -- the key strategic aviation factory in all of Japan -- had been completely and utterly destroyed.

With this, thought Kiichiro, *the war has ended!*

The earthquake had just hurried along what was to him an inevitability anyway. But now that he realized the day of defeat was in sight, Kiichiro felt a deep pain in his heart, like two waves of sadness colliding, one for himself and the other for his country:

Perhaps, my life, too, has come to an end.

The huge factory complex at Koromo that he had wagered his life to build, and that had consumed all of his energies and most of his waking hours, might be confiscated and destroyed by the victors.

Moreover, he himself might be tried and executed for his role in manufacturing motor vehicles for the military and also for producing aircraft, munitions, and war materiel. That he had no choice but to comply with the military establishment could very easily be overlooked by the conquering allies.

On the other hand, what if an automobile industry is allowed to exist after the defeat! It was too dangerous to think about even as a remote possibility. Yet Kiichiro's mood always brightened when he remembered how defeated nations had been treated in the wake of earlier wars.

I'm not going to build a truck factory under the controls and orders of the military. This time, I will try once more to fulfill my dream of mass-producing passenger cars for the public. This time, I'm going to make it come true regardless of how much I have to fight for it!

Still, there were too many unanswered questions to let his hope or determination rise too high. *I will spend ten, or if necessary, twenty days in meditation. I need to think this through very carefully.*

With that decision, Kiichiro boarded the crowded night train to Sendai, taking a seat in the corner. His plan was to visit his friends, Shiro Nukiyama and Masao Naruse, and to ask them to accompany him to the Mizuiwa Temple in Matsushima.

Chapter
10

RISING FROM THE RUINS

August 15, 1945....

On the morning of Japan's surrender, Kiichiro was at his residence in Setagaya-Ward of Tokyo's Okamoto District.

He had moved to this house, originally purchased as a vacation home, after his residence in Akasaka burned to the ground during an air raid on May 24.

Once a very tranquil area of Tokyo, Setagaya-Ward still displayed remnants of its earlier pastoral atmosphere. The large mansion was situated on 1.6 acres and had a chestnut grove and a large, shallow handmade pond in back. It was a setting which belied any hint that the rest of Japan was in a state of immense turmoil.

What was inevitable has finally come, Kiichiro uttered sadly when he heard the Emperor would address the nation at noon. The looming defeat had been fairly widely acknowledged for several days among the well-informed. Yet, when the actual time of surrender arrived, many could not believe it was true.

Kiichiro was better prepared mentally than most and spent little time bemoaning his country's fate. There was work to be done. Already he was wrestling with the question of how the automobile industry would be treated by the victors, as he was concerned about the many mouths he had to feed. All told, more than ten thousand people depended on the Toyota Motor Company for their livelihoods. What would happen to them if the Allies shut down the automobile factories?

Kiichiro carried this great weight in silence and otherwise tried to maintain an outward semblance of normalcy in his life. He had been in the yard since first light, weeding and caring for the chestnut trees along with his son Tatsuro and his chauffeur: "The Emperor's broadcast will be on soon," Kiichiro said as noon approached, and he went inside the house with Tatsuro.

The broadcast was short and to the point: Japan had lost the war. Kiichiro sat erect and crossed his arms as he listened; he still had a few green leaves from the chestnut tree clinging to the shoulder and back of his *yukata*. Turning to Tatsuro, he said, "Public opinion is that the Occupation Forces will tear Japan to pieces, but I don't think that's true. The Allied Forces have shown discretion in the past and there's no reason to believe they won't again. Nevertheless, no matter what happens, it's going to be a tough world to live in. We must work very hard."

Kiichiro went on at some length, telling Tatsuro about the treatment of Germany after World War I, and of that nation's resurgence. Then, standing up with his lips tightly pursed, Kiichiro called out to the chauffeur to bring the car around. After changing out of his work clothes, he departed for the Toyoda Administrative Offices. Through Hatako's connections, these offices had served as a temporary corporate headquarters and were located on the seventh floor of the Takashimaya Department Store in the Nihonbashi district. When Kiichiro arrived he was briefed about company-related matters immediately preceding the final surrender.

On the morning of the day prior to the Emperor's announcement, the Koromo factory had been strafed by American fighter planes and, in the afternoon, the foundry was hit by a bomb which blew off the entire roof. As damage inside the plant was extensive, a number of employees were needed to clean up debris, repair the roof, and begin structural renovation.

Eiji Toyoda, who had been at the plant the day of the surrender, went out into the courtyard of the main administrative office and stood alongside the military inspectors to listen to the Emperor's announcement blaring from speakers installed in the courtyard only a few days before. The previous evening, Vice President Akai had received a telegram from Tokyo, so Eiji and other members of the executive management had known the nature of the Emperor's address. However, the other employees, including the military staff, had no idea what was coming. As the Emperor began speaking in a diminutive voice, further affected by static, everyone strained to hear. Then they stood silent and dumbfounded by the message.

"What is meant by all of this?" asked one of the military inspectors as he turned to Eiji.

"You've just heard that we have decided to accept the Potsdam Declaration, haven't you? It's a broadcast that says we have lost the war -- we're quitting."

"I've never heard such a foolish thing," growled the inspector. His defiant face, clenched fists and rigid body seemed ready to fight. Shrugging his shoulders, Eiji looked at him silently for a second, then turned and quickly walked back to the office.

Everyone at the factory spent the afternoon cleaning up the mess left behind by the bombing. One part of the factory even continued to manufacture vehicles. But around three o'clock, as the shock wore off and truth seeped in, workers on the production line began to lay down their tools: "If we have lost the war, then it is useless to build trucks for military use." One by one the workers left and the factory gradually grew eerie with silence. Only the directors and other executives stayed behind, mulling over the company's future until after the sun had set on this long, excruciating summer day.

On the sixteenth, just a day after the Emperor spoke, throughout Japan towns had become deserted as though they'd been blown away. Other towns were becoming jammed with Allied military personnel busily moving in. At the Toyota factory, the number of workers that morning had fallen off dramatically. The original Toyoda Automobile Department employees still came to work, but most of the male and female students mobilized by the military, and others (including even a service core consisting of *geisha,* Buddhist priestesses, and convicts) failed to show up. Some members of the company's wartime military staff could not be found, and others appeared asking for travel money to return to their hometowns.

Around one o'clock in the afternoon, Vice President Akai called a meeting in the cafeteria for all managers. Since leaving Mutsui in 1941 to sign on with Toyota, Akai had skillfully managed the firm during the war. He dealt effectively with military and government personnel, earning the respect of all the company's employees. With the large cafeteria overflowing with people, Akai spoke briefly about the shock and sadness of defeat. Then raising his voice to be clearly heard by all, he said:

"As a result of the war's end, the time of the controlled wartime economy is over. It will be succeeded by a competitive, free market economy. This means that we will live in a world of open competition. We must make the effort to quickly resume production to meet the demands of the nation, restore our country, and eventually export overseas once more.

"Accordingly, today will be a day of rest to put our hearts in order. But, beginning tomorrow, we will return to our normal business activities. I ask for your cooperation and strenuous efforts."

Up to this point, the employees had been so quiet that Akai's voice rang throughout the huge room. Then, one man asked a highly emotional question in a half angry, half fearful voice that raised a stir in the assembly: "We don't know what kind of distress we may undergo when the American troops make their landing. Won't the commute be dangerous for female workers?"

Raising his hands to quiet the commotion, Akai answered in a loud, confident voice, "Such things will definitely not happen." Then he gave a vivid account of the humane behavior displayed by American troops in already-occupied Germany, and by Western allied forces in general following World War I. With that, everyone seemed to settle down.

The composure maintained by members of the executive management team, with Akai at the helm, was the key factor that saved the plant from anarchy and collapse. All in all the work force had diminished to seven thousand, down three thousand from its full wartime complement, but there were still plenty of hands to resume production.

Following the "day of rest" called for by Akai, the factory wheels began to turn again and, with the exception of the one day strike that would occur later, they never stopped.

One morning, two or three days after the surrender, Noboru Yamaguchi and Toshihide Koizumi, managing director of Aichi Prefecture Automobile Distribution Company, were chatting with two or three other managers.

Suddenly, a door opened, and a middle-aged man walked in.

Everyone fell silent. The man was wearing a neatly-pressed summer-cloth business suit, a clean starched shirt and tie, freshly shined shoes and he held a

Panama hat in his hand. From his appearance, no one might have guessed a World War had just been waged and lost. He certainly was not the visage of pessimism so clearly evident in the other men in the room. Yamaguchi and his cohorts were still unkempt and dishevelled from hours spent in the air raid shelters, their uniform jackets soiled with dust and soot from the bombings. Their faces were glum and hearts heavy with defeat as they had been talking about the future of Japan and its automobile industry. In short, they were a picture of exhaustion when the well-dressed man appeared.

"Oh, Mr. Kamiya!" yelled Yamaguchi, jumping to his feet.

The two men exchanged greetings and then Yamaguchi asked, "What are you doing here?"

"We've got to get back in business," replied Kamiya in a cheerful, quiet voice. "I thought I should first visit you to pay my respects."

By "back in business," Kamiya was, of course, referring to the business of marketing Toyota cars and a return to the pre-war sales strategy and organization. Shortly after the war had begun and the automobile industry became tightly regulated, the Japan Automobile Distribution Company was established. Kamiya was appointed its managing director, as well as Toyota's representative. At the same time, sales co-ops had been set up in each prefecture, and Yamaguchi was assigned Aichi Prefecture. As the headquarters of the Distribution Company focused primarily on metropolitan areas, Kamiya and Yamaguchi had only infrequent contact. Now Kamiya was proposing to turn that all around. Still a little nonplussed by Kamiya's demeanor and appearance, Yamaguchi realized he had not even offered him a chair. *That's right. The war has ended!* he thought. *That's right. We must get back in business. That's why Kamiya has gone out of his way to come and visit us and impress us with the fact it's a whole new ball game!*

As these thoughts changed from empty echoes to actual realizations, Yamaguchi felt tears well up in his eyes. It was a great relief to be lifted out of the fear and anarchy by such a clear direction from Kamiya: *how quickly one must adapt to new circumstances! Until yesterday, all Japanese automobile workers were wearing dirty national uniforms and all worked as a team in this one room; but from now on, Toyota will be Toyota, Nissan will be Nissan, and other companies will have their respective positions -- and all must face fierce competition in the stern and demanding global sales war!*

Yamaguchi felt his soul already taking off its national uniform and changing into a business suit. Even better, he had a sales management staff already in place -- the men who had worked under him for the last three years at the national Distribution Company.

First, there was Koizumi, who had been branch manager of Nissan's Nagoya office before being recruited into the new co-op by Yamaguchi. Though a highly respected and loyal employee, Koizumi had not been taken into Yamaguchi's confidence regarding Toyota's internal affairs. In fact, Yamaguchi had made a pact of personal silence with himself regarding all of the Nissan personnel on his distribution staff. Until now, Koizumi had been involved with low-level external negotiations, such as discussions with government offices and communicating with the headquarters of the Distribution Company. Now he would have to be given the full Toyota indoctrination, as Yamaguchi was not about to let him go. Nor would he let loose of his other valued Nissan-affiliated staff members. Fortunately, he had Kamiya's help in pulling off this minor "coup" against Nissan.

During his tenure as managing director of the Distribution Company, Kamiya had anticipated future competition and worked diligently, visiting all of the prefectural co-ops and getting to know everyone, Toyota and Nissan affiliates alike. For that reason, he was several jumps ahead when the war ended. Today alone, in six surprise visits identical to the one being paid Yamaguchi, Kamiya would capture six extremely powerful Nissan dealers and dealerships and substantially fatten Toyota's chances of success in the years ahead.

While Kamiya was soliciting his Nissan defectors, Kiichiro was in the throes of many changes, the most immediate being a change of residence from Tokyo to Nagoya. His stay in Tokyo, however, had done him some good. Using the Toyoda administrative office as his base of operations, he had been utilizing his wide information network to gather whatever information he could concerning the future of Japan and her industries, and policies that might be instituted by the Occupation Forces.

Of late, Kiichiro had a minimal role in the operation of the Koromo factory. Outside of a periodic show of authority as president of the company, he did little other than call Akai to issue orders. Akai was twelve years older than Kiichiro, composed and diligent and an ideal vice president.

Regrettably, Masayoshi Takeuchi, an outstanding administrative executive director who had been with the company since it started manufacturing operations, had been killed in March at his Nagoya residence during an air raid. It was a great loss to the accounting and labor departments and a lamentable casualty of war.

Along with the decrease in administrative duties, Kiichiro scaled back his involvement in technical matters. Perhaps not having Eiji around as a partner to "tinker" with had significantly lessened his desire and scientific impetus. It was hard to believe the Shibaura lab days were already ten years behind them. Eiji was now over thirty and already on the board of directors. How quickly times change.

At least Eiji hadn't changed much. He still had a round, boyish-looking face, and had neither grown haughty nor developed any affectation as a result of his advancement in the company. He continued to wear wrinkled clothes and looked very much as he did in his student days. This boyish exterior was deceiving to those who did not know him well. On the inside he was tough-willed and dedicated and he never failed to accomplish his task, no matter how difficult. He was definitely not one to be intimidated by a challenge. If Kiichiro was at all fearful of his diminished involvement, he knew the company was being steered by good people.

Eiji, Saito, and Ono are all there, Kiichiro often thought to himself. Shoichi Saito was a favorite pupil of Shiro Nukiyama. Kiichiro had recruited him right out of graduate school in engineering at Tohoku University around the time Eiji had joined the company. While Eiji drifted more toward design and quality improvement, Saito moved more in the direction of manufacturing and supervisory operations of the factory.

The third in this triumvirate of experts was Shoji Ono, a law graduate of Meiji University who had worked in the automotive parts area at Hakuyosha. He had joined the Automobile Department of Toyoda Automatic Loom Works right before Toyota Motor Company was established. Ono's expertise lay in materials procurement, purchasing, planning, and various business operations.

Kiichiro relied on these three men very heavily. They took part in the planning of Kiichiro's important affairs, and regardless of whether they had been clerks or managers, from the very beginning, they had been assigned to various director-level tasks. Unfortunately, their salaries were not commensurate with their levels of responsibility and Kiichiro was innocently at fault for this. Always so wrapped up in business, it never occurred to him that his three close proteges had lived on barely sustenance-level salaries of one yen and twenty sen per day (a sen being 1/100 yen). Not until Nukiyama pointed this out to Kiichiro was anything done about it. Finally, after three years of director-level responsibilities, Eiji, Saito, and Ono began to make more than a trainee's per diem salary.

One of Kiichiro's great skills was an ability to spot talent and then be able to recruit it. It was a skill that was now paying off by providing continuity in the company in an otherwise shaky and uncertain time. Kan, for instance, had become the managing director of Toyota Machine Tools, the operation he had founded as a subsidiary after it was split off from the machine tool division. Others also made lateral moves and became managers of other Toyota subsidiaries, but the flow of qualified people into the company always made for smooth transitions.

As soon as Kiichiro was settled in Nagoya, he went to the Koromo factory to see Eiji and Saito.

His message was clear and to the point: "From now on, it will be the era of the automobile for the general public. Please immediately start studying how to mass-produce small passenger cars."

If Eiji and Saito were surprised, they had good reason: the Occupation Forces were not totally in place and no clue had been given as to their policy toward Japanese industry. However, Kiichiro's reasoning was simple: if the Americans padlocked the factory, then that was that. But if they didn't, Toyota would be prepared to move forward. As Kiichiro wrote in his journal of that period:

If the factory is forced to close down, it all becomes zero. But one can't think about countermeasures when everything is zero. That's why the only thing I can think about for now is the day when automobile manufacture is allowed again.

Neither Eiji nor Saito showed the slightest sign of skepticism as Kiichiro explained what he wanted done. Speaking up boldly, Eiji answered for both "That'll be interesting. We'll start right away."

As the manager of the design and quality control departments, and as general manager of the manufacturing department, Eiji and Saito, respectively, had a combined control of all elements of Toyota production. They were accustomed to working very closely together, and this time was no different. Research on mass production of small cars began at once.

On September 2, Japan signed the instrument of surrender aboard the American battleship *U.S.S. Missouri.* That same day, General Headquarters (GHQ) was instituted as the supervisory authority for Japanese reconstruction. The first order issued by the GHQ was to dismantle the Japanese army and navy and to ban the armaments industry.

As various Toyota Motor Company divisions had been involved in the manufacture of planes and other armaments, the entire company fell under the GHQ edict. The factory was quickly ear-marked as a war indemnity and likely to be seized.

A general announcement went out to employees: "We must prepare ourselves for the painful path facing our company. All of our machinery and equipment might be confiscated, and we also might not be able to pay your wages. It is time for everyone to finally give some thought to their individual future circumstances."

As a result of the announcement, the number of employees decreased substantially. From the immediate post-war complement of 7,000, the number of employees dropped to 4,500 by September 15. This decrease simply saved management the pain of widespread layoffs.

By the end of October, the number of employees had dropped to 3,701, and virtually all of those who remained had been employees of the original Toyota Motor Company. They had been loyal from the very beginning and had cast their fate with Kiichiro under circumstances every bit as difficult as the present one.

On September 10, as the employment rosters were settling into their final groove, a general statement was issued by the Supreme Commander of the Allied Powers, General MacArthur, concerning the policies and philosophies for Japanese reconstruction. Among the points were payment of war reparations, dissolution of the *zaibatsu*, movement toward a deregulated marketplace, and the disarmament of Japan's army.

On September 22, GHQ Order Number Three mandated that armament manufacturers wishing to produce consumer goods must submit written petitions from the Japanese government requesting the change. Then on the twenty-fifth, a GHQ memo was issued, placing armament industries directly under GHQ supervision and clarifying what types of consumer goods would be permitted. As it applied to Toyota Motor Company, it allowed for the production of 1,500 trucks per month.

After determining consumer goods production targets for each factory, starting with Koromo, on October 10, Toyota Motor Company submitted its written petition for a government permit. Notes from a speech given by Kiichiro at that time reveal his guarded optimism for the future of his company -- and his dream:

Although limited to certain fixed types of businesses, the existence of a consumer goods industry has already been basically recognized. Furthermore, automotive industry production also has been allowed. Although it is not unthinkable that the situation could take a turn for the worse at a later time in which the Occupation Forces would confiscate all industrial organizations, that scenario is unlikely. Moreover, the chances of such a scenario unfolding are heavily dependent upon changes in international relations. And since that's unpredictable, it's useless for us to dwell on it.

So, focusing our thoughts on the near future of the automobile industry, we must do everything we can to reinforce it. The food situation in Japan is getting progressively worse every day -- the war of bombs and destruction has ended, but the war against hunger has become more intense. Japan has lacked sufficient food from the very outset of this war, but the main reason that situation currently worsens is an inadequate transportation system.

Revitalization of our railway system is important, but the ideal solution is to strengthen the truck transport system. If worse comes to worst, we could rely on carts pulled by oxen and horses.

Furthermore, the United States is a country that runs by motor transportation -- automobiles are as second nature there as "geta" [clogs] and shoes are in Japan. In view of that, plus the perception that the GHQ is responsible for solving the problem of Japan's famine, it's plausible that the United States will work on strengthening Japan's truck transport system as part of the solution.

Without a doubt, the automotive age will come to Japan in the near future. The motor vehicle will be pivotal to the promotion of the consumer goods industry and ultimate stabilization of the Japanese economy. Consequently, as motor vehicle manufacturers, it is our calling and our duty to help bring this about as soon as possible.

Kiichiro's insight was accurate to the letter. Though no one had access to what the Americans were actually thinking and planning, Kiichiro's uncanny understanding of the American mindset and culture gave his prophesies an unusual edge. In the aftermath of defeat, when experts were predicting confiscation of companies involved with armament production and severe punishment for heads of the *zaibatsu*, Kiichiro was reasoning with a keener intellect.

In October of 1945, with the ink on initial GHQ proclamations barely dry, Kiichiro summarized Toyota's course of action to the firm's executive management group:

We have finally come to the point where Japan will have to convert to a free market economy like that of the United States, and compete with the rest of the world on an equal basis. We must, therefore, reform our monopolistic system. The Japanese automobile industry has been nurtured and protected in a controlled economy -- in other words, it was reared in a greenhouse. Thus we cannot say that it grew on its own.

Moreover, viewed impartially from a global standpoint, Toyota is far from being a first class company. Needless to say, we have suffered a great defeat at the hands of war. But from a global perspective, we must view ourselves as a third class automobile company.

We will find it difficult to hold a clear course without foundering in the stormy seas of a free market economy. I believe that our ultimate success or failure will be determined by how this company -- despite the serious blows it has sustained -- makes the transition from a controlled to a free market economy. This will certainly require great effort and preparedness on everyone's part. In view of that, from now on I would like the basic operation of this company to be as follows:

First of all, this company will charge forth as one spear, specializing in automotive manufacturing. We will fight to the death.

Although there are many types of motorized vehicles, to become a specialized factory that wins not loses, to foreign companies, we will limit ourselves in the types of vehicles we will manufacture. If necessary, we will build factories where each one specializes in producing one thing; we will not present the appearance of being a giant, consolidated, entity, but one with many facets.

As soon as we agree upon this philosophy of specialization, we will pour our main efforts into domestic manufacturing and sales. Later, we will grow into an exporter.

Next, to achieve full specialization, we must build each factory according to its own special functions. Also, each factory will have its own accounting unit; this will not only foster conformance to free market economy notions, but it will also measure the economic efficiency of each plant. This system will eliminate the wasteful bureaucracy inherent in a highly centralized and regulated economy, and will be an important training tool for helping our people stand on their own in a totally private and free economy.

To the greatest extent possible, the management of each factory will be independent of the parent company. The factory complex will be split into more than five types of plants, such as the foundry; the forging plant; the body plant, including the forming presses and painting facilities; an assembly plant for large cars; and an assembly plant for building small cars. The small car plant will be separate from the main plant and will be built on a two-acre open lot on the west side of the compound.

After explaining the broad, basic directions the company would take, Kiichiro went on to articulate the details of his plan. He talked about ways to account for each machining and machine tool facility under direct control of the main plant, including metal-cutting and forming, precision grinding and honing, and surface plating and hardening. He not only discussed ways of apportioning operating costs to each plant, but also issues concerning research, design, and testing. He also talked about company and plant organization, outlining a new, detailed management policy dealing with everything from the invoice system through wages, accounting methods, and disposition of resources to the redeployment of employees among the different plants. Kiichiro then spoke about a three-year plan to upgrade equipment, his plan for implementing the "right man in the right place" concept, and the personnel shifts that would occur as a result of these changes:

"We will not be able to predict to what degree the world will become a global free economic society during the three year period wherein we will be dealing with these reforms. As for myself, however, regardless of whatever happens in the world, I plan to move ahead with these changes in the organization of the company as well as with the upgrading of our equipment and facilities. These efforts are, of course, not simply limited to those areas that have dealings with the outside but apply to all areas of the firm."

Though no one realized at the time, Kiichiro's clear and comprehensive charter for the post-war company would set Toyota on a course that would prove essential to survival and success in the global markets, which loomed more than a quarter century in the future.

The basic ideals underlying the specific elements of Kiichiro's presentation were the same as those Vice President Akai had spoken about in his address to the assembly after the Emperor's announcement of Japan's surrender on August 16.

What is remarkable about these concepts and this particular presentation, is that nowhere is there a single trace of wishful thinking, misguided sentiment, or the kind of pessimism endemic elsewhere in Japan during the frenetic period immediately after the war.

Comprehensive, yet flexible and adaptable to changing times, these fundamental ideals have remained the cornerstone of Toyota to the present day.

On November 2, GHQ ordered dissolution of the *zaibatsu* and the freezing of their assets. In the first round, fifteen *zaibatsu* concerns were affected, including Mitsui, Mitsubishi, Sumitomo, and Yasuda. At that point, it was not clear whether Toyota also would be named. The optimistic opinion that Toyota would not be so designated remained strong, but management did not break its silence on the matter.

Although their "transfer to consumer goods business" permit submitted on October 10 had not yet been granted, Kiichiro courageously instructed Eiji and his group to create a "design for the small car engine." This instruction came immediately upon the heels of GHQ's announcement concerning other *zaibatsu*.

The decision to develop a small car engine was a concrete link to the small passenger car study Kiichiro had made and talked about right after the war. Using the Adler engine from West Germany, and the Baby Ford engine from England as their models, Eiji and his research crew were to design a successful four cylinder, 1,000 CC side-valve engine, known then simply as "Model S."

Finally, on December 8, the long-awaited "transfer to consumer goods business permit" notification arrived from the Sixth Army Command Headquarters. Toyota would be permitted to engage in: (1) truck, as well as parts production at the Koromo factory; (2) electronic goods production at the Kariya factory south; (3) production of automotive parts and resumption of automotive repairs at the

Kariya factory north; (4) production of radiators, exhaust equipment, enamel steel goods, printing presses, and such other products as bicycles and farming tools at the Aichi factory.

It was good news, but bad news was not far behind. On January 20, 1946, the Indemnity Preservation Order was issued. In effect, the Aichi factory, including all of its production equipment and facilities, was being placed under Occupation control. Then on the twenty-sixth, the Koromo factory was placed under supervision of the United States Army 25th Infantry Division. The factory would be permitted to continue operating until a final indemnity order was settled, but all machinery and equipment was under threat of confiscation. Even worse, it was learned that the December 8 permit granting the transfer of business to consumer goods manufacturing was still under review.

From that point on -- 1946 to 1947 -- there were many twists and turns in GHQ policy, but several major demands remained steady: Among them were total dissolution of the *zaibatsu,* the designation of companies regulated by the Occupation powers, control of factories related to the indemnity issue, enforcement of the decentralization law, and the purge of *zaibatsu* leaders.

To avoid dissolution as a *zaibatsu,* each company of the Toyoda group undertook immediate measures. Toyoda Steel Works, for example, changed its name to Aichi Steel Works. Toyoda Machine Tools became Kariya Machine Tools. Risaburo and Kiichiro were no longer listed as owners or managers of any of the various companies.

The attitude of the GHQ, however, proved far more severe than it had been toward Germany after World War I, and certainly more harsh than Kiichiro anticipated. In September of 1947, Toyoda became the final company to be designated as a *zaibatsu.* Toyoda Sangyo, the holding company for the related Toyoda concerns, was no more.

On the bright side, all of the firm's employees passed the screening process designed to weed out war criminals. Not only had the Japanese army, navy, and air force been disbanded, but everyone associated with the conduct of the war was barred from holding public office and also from holding positions in firms under supervision of the Occupation. Thus, while a number of Toyoda companies fell under that restriction, none of its employees were purged.

Under terms imposed by various war reparations acts, a number of Toyoda operations were temporarily designated as subject to Occupation control, including the Koromo factory, Kariya factory south, and Kariya factory north. Toyota Motor Company, however, continued to petition for cancellation of this designation, arguing, "We have already received permission to transfer our business to production of consumer goods, and the Koromo factory has produced approximately 40 percent of the trucks for postwar reconstruction use." Finally, on August 16, 1946, the designation was removed from the Koromo factory.

Not until the Peace Treaty between the United States and Japan was signed in 1951 -- seven long years after Japan's capitulation -- was that designation removed from all of the firm's factories.

Chapter
11

SAD RETIREMENT

Throughout his career, Kiichiro had climbed a steep path learning the automobile industry from the ground up, mastering the technology, dealing with design failures, contending with massive criticism from family and financiers, and persevering the war.

Always a bold entrepreneur at heart, he was accustomed to bearing the responsibilities and burdens himself. Outside aid always meant outside interference and control. Yet as Japan became mired in the Sino-Japanese War and then in World War II, Kiichiro's independence was gradually eroded. Increased regulation by the military led ultimately to absolute control of Kiichiro's company by the government. Granted, the company grew by leaps and bounds during the war, but the price exacted for such progress was the very soul of Kiichiro's dream of mass-producing automobiles for the public.

The outlook for the immediate post war period did little to lessen Kiichiro's stress. Japan was in terrible psychological and economic shape, about to be reshaped in ways that would be just as drastic, if not more so than the 1868 Meiji Restoration. The actions and policies of the GHQ were difficult to predict, often appearing arbitrary, contradictory and susceptible to the influence of global political developments, especially the growing threat of a militant, communist Soviet Union. Throughout the confusion, however, it was relatively certain that Toyota would suffer for its contribution to the war effort. That the company had been entirely controlled by the military, and not by official Toyota Management, seemed to make little difference. Kiichiro knew full-well he might end up stripped of all he possessed and perhaps even imprisoned under measures designed to punish the "fomenters of war."

Yet his shrewd assessment of the fundamental logic of the situation and of American characteristics and ideals led him to believe (as history would prove) that at some future date Japan would be permitted to have an automobile industry. Moreover, he strongly suspected that he would not be "purged" if he received a fair hearing, which would mean a second chance for him to manufacture the automobile he dreamed of. If these things came to pass, he was prepared to move forward in high gear.

Up to, and through, the war, the Toyota staff had blossomed with superior engineers. Now Kiichiro felt more comfortable devoting himself to policy and management matters. With Eiji and Saito in charge of design and production, there was little to worry about. Moreover, they had been joined after the war by Hanji Umehara, the most talented and widely respected student of Kiichiro's friend, Professor Nukiyama.

Kiichiro was also fortunate in having Hisagi Akai as a vice-president. It was Akai to whom Kiichiro entrusted the day-to-day operations of the company. That freed Kiichiro not only to ponder the future of the entire automobile industry and develop strategies to deal with rapidly changing conditions, but also to spend a lot of time in Tokyo and elsewhere negotiating with Japanese government authorities and representatives of GHQ.

Toward the end of 1945, however, an unexpected calamity abruptly altered that set-up and plunged Kiichiro into a management crisis he was never quite able to resolve. On December 10th, Akai had been visiting the automatic loom factory in Kariya with Masao Naruse, Tohoku University professor and consultant to Toyota, and Tatsuji Wakamatsu, a Toyota engineer.

On their way back to Koromo, the car they were riding in broke down. A truck had been traveling not far behind, and the three flagged it down and asked the driver for a ride. As the truck approached a three-way divide in the road and was preparing to turn, Akai suddenly shouted to the driver to take a different turn and pointed his finger where he wanted to go. Startled, the driver swerved in the new direction, which sent the truck skidding sideways with its heavy load of metal castings. The driver frantically tried to recover control, but the truck plunged down a steep embankment. Akai and Wakamatsu were both hit in the back of the head by metal castings that came crashing into the cab. Both died instantly. Naruse and the driver escaped with their lives but were hospitalized for months with serious injuries.

The accident was tragic and the entire company mourned. Kiichiro took the blow very hard and felt as though he had lost half of himself in losing Akai.

Sixty-three years old at the time of the accident, Akai had been a veteran manager with astute knowledge of all aspects of the business. He was especially skilled in labor management, a talent that increased in worth as the complexities of modern business grew and as the labor situation suffered from the continued strain of reconstruction under the allies.

In the old days when the automobile company consisted of a tiny pilot factory at Kariya, Kiichiro was the "labor manager." He knew the name of every factory worker and talked to them frequently. He knew their interests, their concerns and what upset or irritated them. Though stern in his demands, he was very solicitous of their welfare, making sure their families were well-fed and had warm clothing in the winter. This was what it took to build good labor relations. At the early automobile plant, workers were more like a family than an entity to be "managed." The only labor problems arose from grumbling among workers in the spinning and loom operations who felt abused by the "wild spending" that went on to develop the first automobile prototype. But that was about the extent of it. Now that labor relations had become more subtle and complex, Kiichiro's family-style management was no longer appropriate or effective. He had depended heavily upon Akai, who was a skilled negotiator and adept in the "new labor psychology." Akai was particularly invaluable during the frenzied and uncertain times of the Occupation, when labor unrest continued to plague the company. He would be sorely missed, as would Takeuchi, who had been killed in an air raid near the end of the war. It was obvious to Kiichiro that the company was in for severe hardships unless suitable replacements could be found. In the meantime, counter-measures would have to be taken to fill the giant holes left by the tragic deaths of these men.

At the time of the accident, Kamiya was about to assume management of the sales division. Instead, at the Board of Directors' year-end meeting, he was appointed Executive Director. Even Risaburo Oshima, who had retired much earlier from that position, was reinstated as a director. Kamiya, of course, was a brilliant marketing man and Oshima an outstanding engineer. Each lacked broad administrative experience, yet they were resourceful and diligent. It was the best arrangement the Board could come up with, though it was openly conceded that it was a stopgap measure. There was virtually no one in the company with the talent and administrative skills of Akai and Takeuchi.

As Kiichiro sat at his desk trying to deal with the administrative problems that now troubled the company on a regular basis, he sometimes would lift his eyes from his papers, tilt his head back, and gently massage his temples and neck. His head felt heavy and, increasingly, he experienced weariness and growing depression. *Maybe it's due to my overworking again*, he muttered, annoyed and concerned, aware that the symptoms were common to high blood pressure and the same ones that presaged the death of his father. More than the loss of Akai and Takeuchi contributed to Kiichiro's symptoms. He had *always* pushed himself to his limits and beyond. At the time the Koromo factory was nearing completion, his blood pressure had risen to two hundred due to overwork. He had been able to somehow manage by taking a new medication obtained for him from Germany by Dr. Yoshiharu Nomura. Nomura was a friend from Kiichiro's high school days and Kiichiro had persuaded him to locate his practice in Kariya. Annoyed that these symptoms would reappear at this crucial time, Kiichiro was determined not to let them incapacitate him.

To keep his medical condition under contol, he had regular medical check-ups and treatment, a practice he started while still living in Tokyo, where he made regular visits to Yamao Clinic. When he moved back to Nagoya, he had his records transferred to Nomura Clinic and continued treatment there. At times when he was too busy to visit the clinic, he would take regular self-injections. Between the clinic and self-doctoring, Kiichiro managed to maintain a blood pressure of around 180. But as he found himself forced to bulldoze his way through prickly, unfamiliar matters that Akai had always quickly and ably resolved, the strain began to tell. Kiichiro remained as determined and strong-willed as ever. Yet he was older and less resilient, and both his health and his work suffered as a result.

Though his body's heart was aging, the heart of Kiichiro's dream continued to beat with unending youthfulness. Around the beginning of 1946, Kiichiro visited Kazuo Kumabe at Tokyo Technical University. His old friend had switched to that school in April of 1943, exchanging his professorship at Tokyo University for one at the technical institution.

Kiichiro got straight to the point: "I will start building the small passenger car prototypes that I was last able to consider doing about ten years ago. This time, I plan to actually build a passenger car, and I'm going to ask you to do it."

Cocking his head and pursing his lips, Kumabe replied, "If it were feasible, I would do it. But isn't production of passenger cars prohibited by the GHQ?"

"Of course," responded Kiichiro impatiently. "But that doesn't necessarily mean that it will always be so."

Nodding tentative agreement, Kumabe interjected, "I'm listening. Go on."

"I feel I have particular insight into these things. The United States is not very optimistic about her future relations with the Soviet Union, and that is why they're having second thoughts about destroying or sharply curbing Japan's industrial strength. There won't be much immediate change but, eventually, a passenger automobile industry will be allowed to develop. That's my firm belief."

"That is a possibility," Kumabe mused.

"Yes," answered Kiichiro emphatically. "That's why, even if manufacturing is impossible, I have decided to pursue another path. I'm thinking about research and testing that wouldn't be interdicted by GHQ -- I'm talking about looking at this with the big picture in mind."

The "another path" Kiichiro alluded to concerned Lieutenant Colonel Vanting, the commander of the Industry Regulation Committee of GHQ Economics Department. In the early days of the Occupation, the retired former president of Nissan and a good friend of Kiichiro's, Genshichi Asahara, had been barred from public or important private posts under the purge clause, even though he had long before retired as president of Nissan. Ironically, however, since Asahara had a Ph.D., knew several languages, and was an expert in the sciences, he had been appointed as an adviser to Lieutenant Colonel Vanting.

Like many other GHQ policies in the postwar period, the treatment of Asahara involved a blatant contradiction. Asahara had fallen under the "purge clause" because he was a talented individual associated with an operation producing war materiel...in other words, doing what his military government dictated. Like Kiichiro, Asahara had strongly objected to the war and there was nothing in his behavior during the war to suggest he was guilty of anything remotely resembling "war crimes." Still, he was purged, then ironically appointed as a consultant to the very people who purged him!

Regardless of how one views these painful contradictions, Asahara's consultantship with GHQ would prove fortunate for the future development of Japan's automotive industry. Through his inside contacts and Kiichiro's insistence, the lobbying to restore Japan's automobile industry would finally be successful. That happy circumstance, however, lay in the future; what Kiichiro was proposing to Kumabe was still under strict prohibition.

"Then is that why you're asking me to build a prototype?" Kumabe asked.

"No, not at all," Kiichiro answered. "I'm not just talking about prototypes. I'm asking you to *command* the project I have in mind; that is, to mass-produce small cars for the general public. Please immediately resign from the university and join Toyota as a vice-president. If you don't want to report to me, then you can be president, and I'll be vice-president."

"What on earth are you talking about," replied Kumabe, astounded at this totally unexpected proposal. The professor had been a consultant to Toyota ever since the company had begun building cars, but that was only a sideline. He was a university professor, not a businessman or industrialist.

"That won't do," he said, shaking his head. "A professor is an academic. Presidents and vice-presidents of companies live in a different world, a world run by the laws of economics and rules of commerce. I am deeply honored but must refuse. I will, however, accept your offer to build a prototype."

"I see," Kiichiro muttered, his bowed head and slumped shoulders reflecting his disappointment.

"Since Mr. Akai passed away, the weight on my shoulders has become a bit too heavy. Oh well, it seems there's nothing anyone can do about that. But regarding your concept of the car, please pursue the highest vision possible."

"All right," replied Kumabe, nodding his acceptance.

With that decided, Kiichiro launched into a discussion of his specific requirements for the passenger car prototype Kumabe would be developing. (1) The engine would have a displacement of 1,000 CC. (2) The overall length of the car, at 4,500mm or 177 in., would be slightly longer than the existing small car. (3) The structure of the car would be kept simple for reliability. (4) Fuel economy would be of the essence due to shortages that were a natural outgrowth of the Occupation.

That plan had been galvanizing inside Kiichiro's mind since November of the previous year, so he had already ordered Eiji's group to begin developing the engine. With Kumabe heading the project, work began in earnest on the new small passenger automobile, designated the Model SA, utilizing the design work already completed by Eiji and his engineering group.

The practical way to proceed would have been to design the car based on parts left over from wartime truck production. The manufacturing machinery was already in place, and with little make-ready, could have been moved into production. This would have helped to cut lead time and to hold down costs. But Kiichiro had something totally new in mind and did not want the project limited in any way by "trying to make do" or "forcing round pegs in square holes." No, the prototype would be built from scratch.

Later called the "Toyopet" after a nation-wide competition to name it, the Model SA embodied advanced design concepts and engineering excellence that would rank it as a milestone in Japan's mass-production automobile industry. That it was a masterpiece was a testament to the genius of Kazuo Kumabe. After all, it was Kumabe who "pioneered" automotive engineering in Japan, by being the first to lecture on the subject at Tokyo University in the late 1920s. The Toyopet, a two-door automobile with European airflow styling and a maximum speed of fifty-four miles per hour, was his crowning achievement.

The chassis consisted of a backbone-style frame, a first for both Toyota and the Japanese auto industry. In the conventional rectangular, ladder-like frame such as that used in the Toyota Model A1, the frame was interchangeable between trucks and automobiles. It was sturdy, heavy, and highly dependable, especially for trucks, where frame strength is necessary for increased load capacity. With cars, however, it inhibited design by obstructing doors, body panels, and interior layout. The backbone frame changed all that and was ideally suited to the unique requirements of automobile construction. While rarely utilized by American manufacturers, it had been the basis of the Volkswagen, to which Kumabe looked as his model for the chassis.

The Model SA's four-wheel, independent-suspension system was a perfect match for the poor roads in Japan at that time. It absorbed shocks well and provided as comfortable a ride as could be expected. The SA's (as its name suggests) was the S-type configuration Kiichiro had ordered Eiji and his crew to develop early on. Eiji had begun with no preconceptions based on old technology and, as a result, the final S-engine was totally innovative in its design. Durable and exceptionally long-lived, it was used in trucks and passenger cars alike until the 1950s when a new engine was developed for the Toyota Crown.

When the design and blueprints for the Model SA were nearly complete in June of 1946, Kiichiro once again asked Kazuo Kumabe to join the firm. This time, while still voicing reservations, Kumabe acquiesed, and Kiichiro was able to welcome him as an executive director. Eventually, Kiichiro also made good on his original promise to make Kumabe a vice-president.

About the same time he persuaded Kumabe to come aboard, Kiichiro also asked Masao Naruse to become a director. Naruse declined, however, insisting, "I am an academic. What I have done up until now consists only of jobs that spend money. The job of a company manager is the exact opposite of that; that job is responsible for earning money, and that is something I have no experience in doing -- and I'm not sure I'm even capable of doing it. If, in the future, you happen to expand the research facilities, then I will happily participate in such a project that allows me to spend money. Furthermore, I can promise you I'll take pleasure in spending that money in the most prudent, skillful, and cost-effective manner possible. But making money? I'm no good at that."

Kiichiro felt he was hearing the echo of Kumabe, and chuckled to himself.

That Kumabe finally accepted while Naruse declined is perhaps best explained by the different relationships each man had with Kiichiro. Naruse belonged to a younger generation. While he had great respect for Kiichiro, their friendship was based more on a commonality of interests than on comaraderie. In contrast, Kumabe was Kiichiro's good friend, an old school chum, and a long-time, night-on-the-town drinking buddy. In addition, right from the beginning, Kumabe had been adviser to Kiichiro's venture into automobile manufacturing. When Kiichiro appealed to him to help resolve the predicament occasioned by the loss of Akai, Kumabe probably felt it was the humane thing to do for a close friend. His major reservation had been, however, that he would prove a greater detriment than a help to Kiichiro. Unfortunately this reservation would eventually be confirmed. What Kiichiro needed most at the time, as Kumabe had told him, was a manager like Akai; all hopes and good intentions aside, he needed a bright, practical businessman. It was obvious that Kumabe would not be suited to handle Akai's tasks, since he was more like Kiichiro than Akai -- a thinker, a creative dreamer, a designer, and not a pragmatic doer. Despite this mismatch, Kumabe's worth to the company proved itself many times over in the masterminding of the Model SA.

The prototype was completed in January of 1947 and introduced at the first Toyota Dealer Meeting of the year. It had been ten years since Toyota had last built a passenger car. The warm reception and praise received by the SA was a glowing accolade to Kiichiro's spirit.

Riding high on the growing trend to reinstate international trade as GHQ gained confidence that its policies were nudging the nation in the right direction, Japan welcomed trade delegations from abroad. To provide these delegations with automobiles for their use, GHQ asked Toyota and Nissan whether they would be able to produce passenger cars on very short notice: could they provide fifty by the end of July? It was already May.

A resounding "YES" was heard from Toyota, and it wasted no time waiting for a reply. By utilizing stocks of materials left over from the war, overtime, and creative engineering, Toyota scrambled to meet the deadline. By July, fifty large Model AC passenger cars, plus four of its all-new, diminutive Toyopet Model SA automobiles, were ready for the road. With the lead car bearing a banner in English and Japanese -- "Toyota Trade Delegation Automobile" -- the column of fifty-four cars left the gate of the Koromo factory to the thundering applause of the entire plant.

There were other reasons as well for rejoicing. Perceiving an on-going need for automobiles for at least official purposes and pleased with Toyota's gumption, GHQ had issued an order on June 3, 1947, permitting the manufacture of three hundred small passenger cars annually. The maximum displacement was not to exceed 1,500 CC. GHQ simultaneously issued a permit for production of fifty large automobiles, which simply served to put an official stamp of approval on the project already underway at Toyota. That was the official signal everyone had been waiting for. *All right, here we go!* exalted Kiichiro to all of the workers at Toyota Motor Company. Although annual production of three hundred small cars amounted to a pittance for a major manufacturer, at least it indicated a loosening of GHQ's strangle hold on the Japanese automobile industry, which boded well for the future. With jubilation and relief, no one doubted that this would lead ultimately to full reinstatement of passenger car manufacturing.

Since preparations to produce the Model SA had been completed and it had been so well received by the firm's dealers, Toyota decided to introduce it in October. At this stage, however, some reservations and even direct criticism about some of its features were heard. The major assertions were that the Model SA was "too complicated" and "too luxurious." The SA did, of course, have unique, elaborate, and highly-advanced design features for its time. Along with its clean and elegant air-flow design, these features had, in fact, helped endear it to the men who would be selling it. The factory workers had a different opinion. Used to the simplicity of trucks, the SA's intricacies made construction difficult. With workers assembling the Toyopet slowly and deliberately to minimize mistakes, and with the higher costs associated with more sophisticated components, production expenditures for the SA were considerably higher than expected.

Coupled with the newness of the technology, these drawbacks gave rise to doubts about the viability of the SA as a passenger car for the common man.

Even Kiichiro was not immune to this rash of reservations: "When the driver-as-owner era arrives, then this car will be splendid. But for now, the strongest demand for it would appear to be in its use as a small taxicab. It's unfortunate, but perhaps we need to make it a bit simpler." Feeling the pain return to his head, he added, "There's nothing we can do about it now. Let's try again. By the time we get that done, the workers will have become more skillful and productive. That should solve both the cost over-run and morale problems."

Nodding agreement, Kumabe smiled ruefully. Like an archer shooting at a target, Kiichiro aimed high and overshot his mark. Now he had to lower his sights.

By April of 1947, the small Model SB truck had been completed under Kumabe's direction. The same length as the Model SA, the SB also used the S-type engine. Its only difference was a ladder-type chassis. Designed at a time when automobiles were scarce, it incorporated some of the characteristics of a passenger car as well as those of a truck, but one intended to carry light rather than heavy loads. Consequently, it included such practical features as more comfortable seats, more flexible springs for a softer ride, and a reduced steering wheel ratio to permit sharper turns. This small truck was well-received from the moment it first went on sale. With a ride and features similar to those of the SA small car, it became popularly known as the "Toyopet Truck." During the five-year period from its introduction until 1952, some 18,000 were sold.

As he pondered simplification of the Model SA passenger car, Kumabe looked at the SB truck for ideas. The result was the Model SC, a passenger car built on the SB's ladder-type chassis. The body also was changed from the European style utilized for the SA to one similar to the then-current American style. The SA had been a four-passenger, two-door auto; the new model SC was a four-door, five-passenger vehicle. Like all cars until the Crown series, it did, of course, utilize the same S-type engine. Its gears, transmission, drive shaft, and axles were the same as those used for the small truck, giving the SC both satisfactory performance and relatively maintenance-free operation. That made it suitable as a taxi and livery service vehicle, although Toyota did not recommend it for such uses. While the SC was well-received, it did represent a retreat from the highly-advanced and sophisticated Model SA passenger car.

The initial prototype of the SC was completed towards the end of 1947. However, orders for the SB truck dwarfed those for the new automobile, and production of the SC was halted after only three prototypes had been built. In February of 1948, with demand for light-duty trucks still strong, work was begun on the design of a new version of the truck, the Model SD.

Though from the frequency of the prototype changes it might appear that Toyota had indeed shifted again into high gear, production still remained very limited. GHQ continued to keep a very tight rein on the nation's economy, and particularly on automobile manufacturing. Kiichiro at least appeared optimistic about the future, arguing, "One must think of automobile prototypes as a training tool for human beings. They are very important for the future, so there's no need to give up hope just because actual production won't immediately occur." In these and similar words, Kiichiro consoled his engineering staff when all the work they did came to nothing as production was put off by GHQ. He urged them to share his belief that the day would yet come when the new Toyota would be produced in volume. As he talked, he'd massage away the pain in the back of his head, and many of his cohorts could not escape the feeling that his words were directed more at himself than at them. It was, after all, his dream of mass-producing passenger cars that once again had been put on hold. How could he not be bitterly disheartened by that in view of the fact a full decade had passed since he had begun the project in earnest?

While Kiichiro and his staff wrestled with these concerns, Japan's need for motor vehicles continued to far outstrip the available supply. This was very much as it had been throughout the three years since the end of the war.

The chaos accompanying defeat and the dramatic restructuring of the entire society were major factors in delaying production. Japan was in the process of becoming a country completely unlike what it was before the war. With the nation plagued by food shortages as well as wholesale loss of jobs and endemic economic distress, both the GHQ and the postwar Higashikuni Cabinet frantically sought ways to ameliorate the suffering.

Immediately after the war, moving quickly to avert catastrophe, the Higashikuni Cabinet authorized the release of 26.6 billion yen to cover temporary military expenditures. Disbursed during a three month period, this enormous sum was applied towards the payment of military retirement pensions and mustering out pay for demobilized military personnel. Debts to defense contractors were relieved and businesses were compensated for losses caused by cancellation of orders. While that money did keep the economy from grinding to a complete halt, it also had the effect of creating explosive consumer spending nationwide, especially in the cities. This was a backlash to the severe austerity endured by the general public during the war.

Unfortunately, the supply of goods and services did not increase commensurate to the massive funds being pumped into the economy. This would eventually prove disastrous to the country, but its immediate effect was to fuel a rapidly growing black market and to generate an illusion of prosperity. One good development to come out of the situation was the revival of shipping and exchange of commodities, an activity which had stagnated under war-time regulation. The efficient transportation of fresh food especially was a welcomed change.

The resurgence of shipping of course brought heavy pressure to improve the transportation system, which in turn created a heavy demand for all kinds of motor vehicles, including automobiles. It was a demand that was being sorely unattended.

Domestic production was so limited as to be, for all practical purposes, nonexistent, and Japan had neither the contacts nor the means to import more than a token number of foreign vehicles. Consequently, used cars were in enormous demand. The only problem was that most used cars were so "used" that they were beyond repair. In fact, 90 percent of the nation's privately-owned large passenger cars and 75 percent of its small cars were more than ten years old.

Pressure shifted back to new cars and began to build against the stone wall of GHQ. The solution was simple: make more cars. But it was a deceivingly simple solution, given the number and magnitude of forces working against it.

First and foremost was the vacuum in investment capital, the vital ingredient needed to rekindle the automobile industry. As individuals frantically withdrew or horded savings to buy food and other necessities after the war's end, inflation began a sharp upward spiral. Fears that assets would be confiscated by the allies simply reinforced the frenzy. This mad rush to withdraw savings effectively drained banks of funds available to finance business and industrial recovery, which shot prices of consumer goods even higher and added to the inflationary spiral.

Inflation fed further inflation, and the national spirit began to crumble. Labor disputes reached near epidemic proportions, as the sky-rocketing cost of living continued to undermine the wage scale. Consequently, businesses were hit by a two-pronged assault: tight money starved them for the funds needed to modernize, expand, and improve productivity, while labor discontent and strikes upped the cost of labor and took a further gouge out of productivity.

It was a simple but vicious cycle. Spiraling prices prompted people to spend money as soon as they got it. Rapid spending prompted more rapid price hikes, which prompted even more rapid spending. It appeared to be an endless problem.

To short-circuit the inflationary spiral, the government adopted tight money policies. A freeze was placed on war indemnity payments, which would reduce the amount of money in circulation. Also, certain companies were placed under strict financial surveillance to prevent exploitation of loopholes or misuse of scarce resources. Business loans were ended for all companies other than those given preference under the "priority production system," such as iron, steel, and coal producers. The net result of these measures was to create a severe shortage of both capital investment and normal operating funds for a majority of the nation's companies without accomplishing very much in the way of controlling inflation.

Toyota Motor Company was hit hard by the inflation and by government measures intended to control it. As one of the companies under financial surveillance, its resources dwindled virtually with each passing day.

The price ceilings set by the government to muzzle inflation suffered from the same malaise price control always develops: set prices too high and producers will make more, but consumers will buy less; set them too low and consumers demand more, but manufacturers produce less in an attempt to cover higher production costs. The latter is precisely what happened to Toyota and other manufactuers. They faced on-going, sudden, and sharp increases in the cost of materials and labor, yet could not raise their prices as a countermeasure. Even if the price celings were petitioned for and approved, half a year would be required for them to take effect.

By that time, labor and materials costs would have spiraled up enough to spill red ink all over the company's books. Convinced, however, that the automobile industry would eventually bounce back, rather than slashing employment rolls and cutting operations, Toyota attempted to maintain itself from 1945 on by gradually easing further and further into debt.

The extent of the firm's financial difficulties is reflected in its dealings with the network of Toyota dealers and its inability to deliver on some of its promises. Starting in early 1946, in anticipation of eventual permission to produce motor vehicles on a volume basis, Toyota worked at holding its dealer network together. In the fall of that year, an inaugural meeting of the Toyota Automobile Dealer Union was held in Nagoya and presided over by Noboru Yamaguchi, president of Aichi Toyota. In January of 1947, Toyota Motor Company then invited all the representatives of the new Dealer Union to Nagoya, for, among other things, an introduction to the Model SA Toyopet passenger car. The dealers liked the Toyopet so much that at their third meeting, held in February, they unanimously agreed the SA would be well-received by the public and submitted a formal request to Toyota to, "Please put that small car into production."

Already touting the new car to prospective buyers, dealers were chagrined to learn in April that the SB truck would be produced instead. Since the SB could be utilized as a passenger car as well as a light duty truck at a time when passenger cars were scarce, the dealers were easily placated. Besides, the SB could also compete against the Nissan Datsun. Everyone was again anxious, but the truck never arrived.

On August 26, Shiro Onishi, the general manager of Toyota's heavy vehicle department, attended the ninth dealer meeting in Nagoya, and members of the Dealer Union asked him what had happened to the production of the small truck.

Onishi answered that arrangements to produce the Model SB were nearly complete, and that the production schedule called for ten units to be produced in August, twenty in September, thirty per month from October through December, fifty in January, seventy in February, and one hundred per month from March on.

He then added, "To tell you the truth, the company is having financial difficulties. We must pay in advance for our materials, and gearing up for production also requires money. As soon as we are able to produce at a normal pace, we will immediately allocate vehicles to every dealership in the country. Prices have not been determined as yet, but we think they'll be in the 200,000 yen to 300,000 yen range. As a down payment for the first vehicle to be shipped to your dealership, I would like to ask each store to make an advance payment of 100,000 yen. When the vehicle is allocated to you and the invoice prepared, we will subtract the advance."

As one would expect, there was a lot of grumbling. Onishi was asking dealerships to make an advance payment on a vehicle that had not yet been built. But in the interest of accelerating production, those in attendance voted to have each dealership make an advance payment of 100,000 yen. Since there were forty-seven Toyota dealerships throughout the country, Toyota's working capital would be boosted by more than 4.7 million yen.

At least Toyota would have a little breathing room, but no one saw the arrangement as a long-term cure for the company's financial ills. Drastic cost-cutting measures were still imminent.

In May of 1947, management organized the Business Monitoring Committee. The committee's charge was to restrict overstocking of materials, dispose of obsolete parts that could be liquidated for cash, establish stringent controls, and halt disbursal of funds from headquarters to cover shortfalls at the various factories. Despite these stern measures, Toyota Motor Company continued to sink further into debt.

The situation was gloomy, but there were a few rays of sunlight to boost spirits from time to time. Toward the end of July of 1948, for example, a young reporter named "K" from the Nagoya office of a national newspaper came to Koromo with a proposal for his school chum, Kumabe: "Why don't you have the Toyopet race against the express train? That would be very interesting."

"I'm not sure I understand," replied Kumabe.

"Well, it seems that many people still don't believe an automobile built by a domestic manufacturer can provide high or even satisfactory performance. I happen to disagree. I believe that effective promotion of the domestic automobile industry is crucial to the future of every industry in Japan. Moreover, this Toyopet that you've worked so hard to create is, in my judgment, very advanced for its class. I want to improve the public's impression of the automobile industry by demonstrating in dramatic fashion the superior performance of the Toyopet."

"K" was very enthusiastic, but there was a "method to his madness." The editorial offices of the newspaper "K" worked for relied on an aging imported car that often broke down. While only an inconvenience for feature stories, interviews, and less time-pegged stories, it sometimes caused them to miss deadlines on fast-breaking news stories. The directors decided it was time for a change -- preferably to a brand new model. Having covered the introduction of the Toyopet and knowing the car inside and out through his old classmate, Kumabe, "K" recommended purchase of the versatile Toyopet.

After much heated discussion, the Toyopet was ruled out in favor of purchasing another used foreign car. "K" was supremely disappointed, convinced as he was of the Toyopet's quality and anxious to contribute to the national cause.

"Domestic cars will definitely come into their own in the future," the young reporter insisted when he told Kumabe of his paper's decision. "In fact, it's essential for the reconstruction of Japan that we cooperate to help it grow. That's why I have made a special effort to track the Toyopet's progress and have written so many articles on it. Continuing to buy worn out foreign cars is absurd!"

Part of the reporter's plan to change this absurdity involved drumming up a little more sensational press for the Toyopet. That was where staging a race between it and a locomotive came in.

According to his calculations, the Toyota car would win hands down. "K" worked out the route and then outlined his plan to Kumabe, smiling deviously all the while: "I will ask the stationmaster at Nagoya to be the starter. As soon as he hears the whistle signaling the train's departure, he'll fire the starting gun. Thus the train and the Toyopet will start at the same time. We'll also arrange to have the stationmaster at Osaka waiting on the platform there to verify the respective arrival times. That way, we'll know who won and by how many minutes. What do you think about the idea?''

"It sounds intriguing," mused Kumabe, grinning and nodding his head.

"Good," replied the newsman. "We'll handle such matters as negotiating with the GHQ and each prefectural police office regarding traffic control."

"Then by all means do it," smiled Kumabe. "Please discuss the details with Mr. Yamamoto. He's the publicity manager at the branch sales office right across from the Nagoya train station. I'll let him know you'll be coming in to see him about making the necessary arrangements."

"K" then shared his plan with Yamamoto: "To be fair, the Toyopet and the train must run parallel. The Toyopet will race against an express on the Tokaido Railway Line, and we'll choose a section of the railway that doesn't go over the Suzuka Pass. You'll arrange for a second car to follow along behind the Toyopet. To confirm that the race is fair and that the guidelines are strictly adhered to, I'll send a reporter and a photographer to ride in the second car. If the Toyopet breaks down in the middle of the race, that's it -- a replacement will not be allowed."

What remained to be done was for "K" to obtain the necessary approvals from GHQ, arrange for a reporter and photographer, and then choose the train and set the date for the race. Kumabe and Yamamoto were to line up the Model SC Toyopet "race car" and a Model SA "pursuit car." Drivers would also have to be selected. Preparations for the race began at once.

A fellow reporter assigned to cover GHQ was asked by "K" to obtain permission for the race. "K" then made arrangements with newsmen in Kyoto, Osaka, and other cities to report on various stages of the race. Finally, the proper prefectural police departments were approached for permission to exceed the legal speed limits posted on the roads outside and leading to the cities of Kyoto and Osaka. The police ruled out a daytime race on the grounds that it posed a hazard to daily traffic. The only alternative was to hold the race at night.

Once the details were hammered out, "K" selected the Express Number 11, which ran between Nagoya and Osaka, and set the start for 4:37 A.M. on August 7. The local paper ran a brief story about the scheduled event.

At the first hint of dawn on the morning of the seventh, car and train were ready to race. Both Toyota's slammed into gear and the race was off. The SC Toyopet was driven by Toyota's senior and most experienced driver, Heiichiro, and the back-up vehicle was driven by one of the younger drivers.

The Toyopet dashed down the highway alongside the railway track, and when it passed Sekizekibara at 5:45 A.M., it was already twenty-one minutes ahead of the train. At 6:07 A.M., it arrived at Yonebara, went through the Kusatsugawa Tunnel, and arrived in Kyoto at 7:37 A.M. Even though it had slowed to the city speed limit through Kyoto, it was still ahead of the train by 37 minutes. When it reached the paved sections of the Kyoto-Osaka Highway, it was able to increase its speed from 46 to 50 miles per hour. It arrived at the Osaka city limits precisely at 8:12:30 A.M., and from there drove to the finish line without a sputter.

Waiting at the finish line, the Osaka stationmaster clocked the car's arrival time at 8:37 A.M. The train's scheduled arrival time was 9:23 A.M. -- a difference of 46 minutes. The Toyopet had made the trip between Nagoya and Osaka in exactly four hours. That set a record for a small car and is a worthy accomplishment signifying the revival of Japan.

With newsprint in short supply, the "M" Newspaper had little room to spare, but it still gave the race front page coverage, complete with a large photo. The three-column headline for the August 8 edition read:

Small Automobile Wins Over the Express Train - 46 Minute Lead in Nagoya to Osaka Race.

Perhaps by today's standards it was not much of a race. Not only did the "express" train fail to live up to its name, but also the Toyopet was laughably slow compared to today's rail and road vehicles. Back then, however, there was no such thing as the modern high-speed, four-lane Meishin Highway between Nagoya and Kobe, and there was no *shinkansen* -- or "bullet train" -- burning up the tracks.

The Toyopet's victory over the express train, however, made a good story and became a topic of widespread conversation. If nothing else, it helped convince a skeptical public that it didn't have to sacrifice performance to drive a domestically-built automobile.

The morning of the race, after staying up all night to prepare for any possible turn of events, "K" and Yamaguchi joyously toasted each other with cups of coffee when they got news of the Toyopet's victory.

There were no evening newspapers in Japan back then, so the story didn't appear until the following morning. When his morning paper arrived, Kumabe marched it into Kiichiro's office. His huge grin ruined the suspense and drew a smile from his dour boss. Kiichiro read the headline and then dove into the front-page article.

Unfortunately, it was one of the few newspaper items that managed to draw a smile from Kiichiro in those grim, tense, punishing days. Every issue of the newspaper was filled with stories concerning faltering cash flows in business areas, the tightening in the monetary situation, stringent limits on business loans and investment funds, and the inability of firms to generate enough profit or to borrow sufficient funds to modernize. Companies were caught in a financial Catch-22: with loans and investment funds non-existent or in hibernation, retained earnings were the only source of funds for modernizing. But earnings weren't great enough to up-grade facilities and provide an improvement in productivity. There was no way productivity could improve without an up-grade in facilities.

Beginning in March of 1949, a reconstruction program designed to curb inflation and lay the foundation for an independent and self-sustaining Japanese economy was launched under the auspices of GHQ. Named for its creator Joseph M. Dodge, a former Detroit bank president and present financial advisor to GHQ, the "Dodge Line" was a program designed to balance the national budget and set a fixed yen/dollar exchange rate. For the most part, it proved successful in curbing inflation, but in the process it plunged the nation into a sudden and severe depression. The hard times that followed didn't end until the outbreak of the Korean War, which brought a flood of orders that got Japan's industry humming again.

Toyota would ultimately share in that yet-to-come economic bonanza, but in the meantime, the depression triggered by the "Dodge Line" brought the firm to the brink of bankruptcy and dissolution.

At a press conference held on March 7, 1949, to announce GHQ's economic recovery program and to explain its basic principles, Dodge characterized Japan as having a "bamboo-stilted economy." He said:

The United States has disbursed approximately $1.25 billion to Japan for aid and reconstruction. What the United States is requesting -- and is necessary for Japan -- is to end this flow of aid and to enable Japan to rebuild herself on her own.

The domestic policy that exists today in Japan is neither rational nor realistic. The Japanese economy is riding on bamboo stilts. One bamboo leg is American aid, and the other is the mechanism of domestic subsidies. If the bamboo stilts are too high, there is always the danger of falling and breaking one's neck.

It is consequently necessary to reduce this at once. To continue to boost prices through enormous subsidies and foreign aid would not only cause inflation to become worse, but also would create the very real danger of leading the nation to destroy itself.

The balanced budget called for by the "Dodge Line" required that annual revenues for 1950 exceed those for 1949. To achieve that, all loans to industry were to be halted in order to remove the impetus of "inflation caused by currency revival."

To help Japan attain the second objective of building a strong, self-reliant economy, the value of its currency would be stabilized vis-a-vis the dollar. In addition, all export subsidies and subsidies granted to offset price differentials would have to be stopped. On April 23, the official exchange rate was established at 360 yen to the dollar, and subsidies were eliminated. Not long after, the freeze on assets, imposed after Japan's surrender, was lifted.

Without the colonies that had been her supply of natural resources, essentially overnight, Japan was thrown without a life jacket into the stormy seas of international economic competition.

Machine and heavy equipment industries were the hardest hit by the "Dodge Line" measures. Between February, 1949, and March, 1950, there were 1,100 bankruptcies, most of them occurring in the manufacturing arena. The result, as reported by the Ministry of Labor, was a loss of 510,000 jobs.

The automobile makers were faced with economic assaults on all fronts. Restrictions enumerated in the "Dodge Line" made it necessary for customers to pay the full price of automobiles in cash. That effectively killed the demand for motor vehicles and left the automobile industry without a market. Then, as though pouring water on a drowning man, the reduction of subsidies resulted in a 35 percent increase in the price of steel in less than half a year. No market, no money, no materials -- any word describing the state of affairs in the automobile industry would be an understatement.

To cope with the crisis, Toyota began by delaying payment of wages. Soon wage deferments became a normal practice, which led to increased tensions with the Toyota Motor Company Koromo Labor Union.

In the beginning, the labor union was not the hostile, leftist group that many other Japanese manufacturers had to contend with. When it was founded, it even included employees at the section manager level. In March of 1946, the union established a joint management council with the company, and after that, kept informed of the company's situation and was consulted on important matters. As times changed and difficulties arose, the company was still able to rely on the understanding and cooperation of the union. On New Year's Day, 1948, for example, union members came to work to ensure shipping schedules were met. Two days later, the union further demonstrated its commitment by offering to work overtime, if necessary, to achieve the production objective of 601 units.

Then on September 26, 1949, Isuzu Motors laid off 1,271 workers, followed by Nissan's announcement on October 15 that it was letting 1,862 go. The Nissan union called a strike and the Isuzu labor union followed close behind. As would be expected, the Toyota union was on edge but for the moment stayed off to the sidelines.

Shortly after, in an effort to decentralize, Toyota shut down the printing and automobile rebuilding/recycling operations at its Nakagawa factory, while retaining the production of enamel wares there. Attributing the changes to depressed sales and scarcity of materials, Kiichiro insisted "there will be no layoffs." Workers no longer needed at Nakagawa were transferred to the Koromo factory, but while these workers still had jobs, the circumstances the entire work force faced were at best unstable.

With virtually the entire Toyota Motor Company's operations bogged down by slumping sales and rising costs, the Koromo labor union decided to join forces with the Nakagawa union. The ensuing protest centered on the notion that the collapse of the Nakagawa labor union would lead to the total collapse of the Toyota labor movement. Employment rights would be lost and workers would be defenseless against the will of the company. In that sense, it was simply a show of solidarity.

Meanwhile, it took nearly two months for the Nissan strike to be settled. An agreement was signed on November 18. Settlement of the Isuzu strike, signed December 2, also took nearly two months. Both sides in each case had to accept unpopular provisions, but they were able to stave off any layoffs. The hardships endured by striking Nissan and Isuzu union members were a sobering experience for the Toyota workers.

Toyota Motor Company was not the only troubled company in the Toyota group. Except for the Automatic Loom Works, benefitting from the prosperity of the textile industry, all were heavily in debt and faced with labor unrest.

Within the Toyoda group, Risaburo and Kiichiro, in effect, "existed above the clouds;" the next most senior executives were Tojiro Okamoto and Taizo Ishida.

Okamoto, previously the vice president of Toyoda Sangyo up to the time of its break up under the postwar *zaibatsu* dissolution order, was the president of Nisshin Tsusho -- now Toyoda Tsusho -- established in July of 1948. Ishida had been named president of the Automatic Loom Works in November of 1948.

Okamoto and Ishida worked hard to keep Toyoda together and fed. Without the Automatic Loom Works to redistribute income to the sister companies, payroll deferments would have been more frequent and layoffs almost inevitable. As it was, malicious gossip and rumors were making the rounds: "Since Toyota doesn't have any money to pay its employees, it's paying them with miso and soy sauce." The reality was that each company was living day-to-day by producing such sundry items as pots, pans, and various foodstuffs -- all unrelated to their main business.

With each downturn in the recession, Toyota grew that much more financially feeble. In the fourth quarter of 1948, orders for Toyota vehicles had totaled more than ten thousand units; in the same quarter of 1949, orders had fallen to less than five thousand units. As demand plummeted, price ceilings became meaningless and were officially abolished on October 1. Then on October 25, the cap on production of small passenger cars was lifted.

Not only were sales on the skids, but collectibles for credit sales were way behind, leaving the company in the position of paying out a lot more than it was taking in. In September of 1949, for example, there was an outflow of 350 million yen, while collections from sales totaled only about 200 million yen.

As things continued to muddle along, it became increasingly obvious that regardless of how successful the firm was in paring down or streamlining the business operations, a monthly deficit of at least twenty-two million yen would continue to accrue.

Finally, management had to make some hard decisions. With great reluctance, they moved to implement a broad-based wage reduction plan: "(1) Base salaries for Koromo factory employees will be reduced by 10 percent, and the base salary of the branch factories will be reduced by 15 percent. The wage reductions at the branch factories are based on the fact that they have been a greater financial drain to the company; (2) Compensation for city living will be reduced by half; (3) Compensation for families, as well as for commuting and other miscellaneous compensations, will be curtailed; (4) The company will no longer provide free meals and other costly amenities."

The company felt these measures were essential, but did not try to railroad them through the union. A subcommittee of the joint management council was formed to deal specifically with the wage issue and union leaders received information almost as quickly as upper management. Then, without warning, debt began to skyrocket. In November, it totaled 35 million yen, in December, 200 million yen, and double that a month later. Unless the company raised 200 million yen, it would not survive the coming year. The financial peril was acknowledged by the union, and on December 23, it accepted what it could of the wage reduction program but insisted "there will be no personnel reorganization."

Bolstered by the concessions, the company set about procuring the necessary two hundred million yen. Unfortunately, the banks were none too anxious to give what little hay they had to a dying horse. Without Takeo Takanashi, Nagoya branch manager of the Bank of Japan, the company might well have died. Takanashi argued: "The establishment of a viable domestic automobile industry is important for the future. If Toyota Motor Corporation goes bankrupt now, the entire economy of the Nagoya area will collapse." He then formed a consortium of twenty-four banks that included the Mitsui and Tokai banks to mediate financing.

Takanishi's grasp of the situation and understanding of its implications for Japan's future was not the norm. Ichimada, the president of Bank of Japan, also known as "The Pope" because of his arrogance and penchant for autocratic behavior, said coldly, "The domestic automobile industry is a total waste. It's better to just import autos from the United States."

With influential individuals like Ichimada ready to pull the plug on domestic auto makers, Toyota was very fortunate that the Nagoya branch manager of Ichimada's Bank of Japan understood the stakes and followed his convictions. Takanishi's consortium parlayed 188.2 million yen and made the loan to Toyota with one stipulation: "When the new year begins, a clear reconstruction plan must be established."

When the details of this "clear reconstruction plan" became apparent, it proved to be a painful pill for Kiichiro to swallow.

The consortium's conditions stated: "(1) Toyota Motor Company must split off the sales division and create a new company with it; (2) Toyota Motor Company must only produce the quantity of cars that can be sold by the newly formed sales company; (3) excess employees must be discharged."

The first two measures Kiichiro could accept. It was the third which brought deep pain to his heart: "I will not go against my strong belief. I refuse to lay off people. That's a promise I've made to the union and I won't break it."

Kumabe, a pragmatist as well as an academic, came down on both sides of the issue, rejecting it in theory and accepting it in practice: "I also disagree with laying off people. I consider the interests of management and the workers to be the same. Under the circumstances, however, I will accept this condition."

"Why?" asked Kiichiro.

"Why? Because regardless of whatever happens, we can't let the company be destroyed," argued Kumabe. "If it's destroyed, then all of our ideals will be destroyed with it. And if the company goes under, then *everyone* loses their job. That's why we will agree to the reconstruction plan. Besides, in reality, our company does not have unnecessary workers," Kumabe added with a wry smile on his otherwise stony face. "In other words, we do not have *excess employees*."

"Oh, I see," said Kiichiro, also smiling. Kumabe's face softened; they were still both on the same wavelength.

At the round table discussion held the middle of that month, it was quickly apparent that some members of the financial consortium still harbored strong reservations about the ability of domestic auto makers to compete with the U. S.

"Since the domestic automobile industry grew up in the protective environment of a regulated economy, we wonder whether it can stand up to unregulated international competition," expressed one banker.

Another interjected, "It seems that at Toyota, technical matters take priority over financial ones, and we wonder whether the company can survive following that philosophy. How can we be sure our loans to Toyota will be spent in the way we intend them. Maybe the money ear-marked for a financing program to promote sales will be used instead to purchase inventory or finish unit overstocks. In other words, we would like some accountability."

With total candor, the bankers were basically expressing a lack of confidence in the financial management abilities of Kiichiro and Kumabe. Moreover, bank consortium members continued to insist that layoffs would be essential components to the restructuring plan:

"If we give in on these stipulations, we'll undermine the rationale for staking our lives and financial fortunes on the domestic automobile industry that we've worked for."

As they drove back together after the meeting, Kiichiro expressed to Kumabe, "They're right, you know. But what they don't appreciate is that my life is also at stake." He was massaging the back of his head.

Kumabe looked straight ahead with little emotion.

Kiichiro had been through many dark hours, but none darker than the present. He shut himself up in his mountain retreat and thought for several days about the alternatives. There was no peace from the moral dilemma. His blood pressure shot up and headaches would incapacitate him. Still he wouldn't see a doctor. Kiichiro's eldest son, Shoichiro, was now living with him, and provided some comfort, though Kiichiro didn't want to burden him with problems of the business. Shoichiro had just graduated from Nagoya Technical University where he'd studied mechanical engineering. He had also graduated from the First Higher School, after attending Toyko Prefectural Middle School. He had the whole world ahead of him, which was Kiichiro's reason for not pressing Shoichiro into joining Toyota. Carefully remembering his own father's words, Kiichiro explained to his son: "A child should not necessarily follow in his father's footsteps and idle his life away. You should do whatever you feel is your calling. As long as I'm alive, I promise I won't try to force you to work at Toyota."

In his early ruminations about what would happen to Japan in the days after its surrender, Kiichiro had written, "To revive the people and reconstruct this ruined country, we must exert all our efforts on producing food, clothing, and shelter." It was in the spirit of this philosophy that he launched several pursuits while also trying to salvage the automobile business. These included, among many others, the study of prestressed concrete for housing applications and production of various kinds of foodstuffs. Shoichiro had shown great interest in the prestressed concrete housing project and the mechanical production of *chikuwa*, a fish-paste cake shaped like a tube, so Kiichiro had let him work on them both.

Shoichiro supervised construction of a *chikuwa* factory at Wakkanai on the northern shores of Hokkaido and spent six months at the project, gaining practical experience with mixing and utilizing prestressed concrete.

Since he was living with Kiichiro, Shoichiro kept an eye on his father's condition, trying his best to help Kiichiro relax and avoid over-exerting himself. It pained him to see Kiichiro suffering from constant mental anguish, his head heavy from hours of deep concentration, pouring over blueprints and paper work, his face reddened by his high blood pressure. Worst of all were Kiichiro's self-injections with blood pressure medication. As difficult as it was for him to watch, it gave Shoichiro a new and deeper appreciation of the rugged character, great courage, and determination belied by his father's somewhat frail physique.

Although Kiichiro did occasionally go to Tokyo and spend time working at the company, there were more days when he would simply shut himself in his mountain retreat, alternating between recuperating from his illness and losing himself in thought and meditation.

After nearly a month of deliberation, Kiichiro set a course for himself and presented it at the February 28 Joint Management Council meeting:

"I have thought with much humility about the issues raised by the financial consortium. Those things that need to be corrected must be corrected. The financial consortium has expressed its intention to send people to manage Toyota's finances. But I told them I am already making every effort to put our finances in order and to renew their confidence by complying with their wish for Toyota to establish a separate sales company. These things are being done as quickly as possible.

"We will take their advice about not putting technical considerations above financial ones, and we've strengthened the financial group both internally and externally.

"I've spent a lot of time thinking deeply and carefully about this, and have concluded that we must try to resolve this ourselves -- without anyone else's help. We must exert ourselves one more time to do as much as we can ourselves before we turn to others. To overcome this great barrier to the company's welfare, we must regain the confidence of the banks, and fully communicate with the Motor Vehicle Industry Association and with the government.

"As long as management and the workers work together, we can overcome this obstacle. I further believe that each one of your lives will also improve when we achieve this, so I now ask each of you to exert your utmost effort to make this come true. I pledge to you that so long as my body will let me, I intend to watch over the operations of this company and to warrant the trust I am asking you to place in its future."

Although Kiichiro never expressed the point directly, he clearly was determined to reject the consortium's stipulation about lay-offs and their plan to put watchdogs within the company's walls. It was a profoundly courageous stance by Kiichiro, but not a surprising one. In fact, were one to have been present for all of Kiichiro's speeches after the war, a singular theme would emerge with a resounding echo: *never say die in the face of overwhelming odds.* It was his spirit which had been the glue holding the company together through many troubled times and it was worthy of one more try. There would be no lay-offs or watchdogs, but Toyota would make every effort to comply with the rest of the consortium's plan.

Already underway at Toyota was a move to establish a separate sales company. Putting in place a monthly installment program for financing vehicle sales, however, was proving a tough task. Other manufacturers, like Nissan and Isuzu, were also having similar difficulties, nearly all of them related to the "Dodge Line." After a formal complaint was jointly filed by Toyota, Nissan, and Isuzu with the Finance Ministry, an investigation was conducted. The finding simply confirmed what ledgers of the automobile makers had been saying all along. Strict regulation on installment plans for car buyers -- effectively forcing them to pay for cars in full, with cash -- was keeping the automobile industry flat on its back. In September of 1949, that situation began to change somewhat. Through mediation by the Bank of Japan and Ichinaka Bank, as well as pledges of financial assistance, strictures against installment plans were lifted, at least for large trucks. It was a step in the right direction, but capital was hard to come by to buy anything, let alone automobiles.

How splitting sales off from manufacturing could help to improve the stagnant automobile market involved an interesting piece of logic. It must be kept in mind that, in Japan (then, as today), cars were made to order, not inventoried in sales lots. This involved completely different types of buyer psychology and financing arrangements. If a car was paid for in cash when the order was placed, as the "Dodge Line" required, the complete financial onus was put upon the buyer. In an already depression-stricken economy, such a burden was simply too heavy to bear for most prospective buyers. To spread the burden more equally, it was proposed that a sales company, separate from the manufacturer, would act as financial middle-man between bank, buyer, and automobile-maker. When a vehicle was delivered to the sales company's dealership, a promissory note from the dealer would be given to the manufacturer in the amount borrowed by the dealer from the bank. This would provide badly needed capital to the manufacturers, take a substantial portion of the burden off the buyer, and lessen the risk for the bank. In a nutshell, the separation of sales and manufacturing proposed by the banking consortium amounted to a "risk sharing" program.

The depression triggered by the "Dodge Line" unfortunately was stronger than the good intentions of the restructuring plan. At the end of March, Toyota had borrowed 463 million yen to meet operating expenses. When the note matured, Toyota could not pay it off. Nor could it not make payments due on materials or cover the entire payroll.

As bad as things were, they could and did get worse. With Toyota executives trying to cope with the cash shortage, Nippon Denso, the sales operation that had just split off from Toyota Motor Company, announced the layoff of 500 of its 1,500 employees. It was hit immediately with a strike. Convinced Toyota would follow suit, and already sensitized by earlier strikes at Nissan and Isuzu, the Toyota union sent a labor dispute notification to the company on April 7 and went on strike.

On April 3, four days earlier, formation of the Toyota Motor Sales Company had been completed. Four-hundred sixty employees of the old sales division had been transferred to the new company, and Shotare Kamiya was appointed president.

Once the strike got underway, meetings of the joint management committee were suspended, bringing to a temporary end nearly three years of productive communication between company and employees. In its place arose a collective bargaining unit.

Regardless of how deeply the company went into debt, Kiichiro continued to insist that "A debt of one billion or 1.5 billion yen is nothing. That's normal and expected of an automobile company. As soon as we get back on track, we can earn that kind of money in one month." The financial outlook of the company had become so bleak, however, that even those who deeply respected Kiichiro's foresight, courage, and determination could no longer believe the company would survive without taking drastic and painful measures.

At the eighth collective bargaining session, managing director Ono, who headed the company's negotiating team, told the union representatives, "Although the company has been subjected to horrendous financial distress due to the 'Dodge Line,' we have firmly resisted resorting to employee layoffs. As you know, we kept to that position even when our competitors, Nissan and Isuzu, reorganized some six months ago and laid off huge numbers of employees. Unfortunately, our debt keeps on growing. Since there appears to be no end to these economic hard times in sight, we are left with no choice but to reorganize."

The union representatives listened glumly as Ono underscored the company's extreme destitution and then got more to the point: "Consequently, the Shibaura and Kabata plants will be closed, and 1,600 employees at the main Koromo factory will be laid off."

The union representatives responded with understandable anger, given Kiichiro's assurances only a short time earlier. Gesturing for quiet, Kazuo Kumabe stood up and addressed the assembly: "It has always been my highest moral precept to do everything possible to avoid layoffs. But in our desire to protect the welfare of our workers, we have been too optimistic in what we believed we could accomplish." He went on to point out that Toyota had held out against reorganization much longer than any other major manufacturer. The time had arrived, however, where the company either folded -- in which case all workers would be without jobs -- or engaged in selective layoffs. Kumabe closed by saying, "As for the union, I am sure that it will strive to attain the very best livelihood for its union members. For my part, I have prepared myself to accompany the president and share whatever fate has in store for us. I would like to humbly ask for the union's cooperation in these difficult times. I take full responsibility for what has happened and hereby express my intention to resign from the company."

Rising wearily, Kiichiro took the floor: "I worked hard in hopes of getting safely through these stormy seas, but have ended up with but one of two possibilities: either all of us can stay aboard ship and perish when it can no longer stay afloat, or some can go ashore and bring help to those who remain behind. My preference is the first path, to courageously stay our course, come what may. But I also realize that our employees have families to worry about, and so I cannot act upon my preference. We in management bear a heavy responsibility for having brought the company to these dire straits. I do, however, ask for your understanding. We have had to cope with extremely powerful external forces. Because of this, I would like to ask for your cooperation in carrying out the new reconstruction plan.'' Kiichiro had tears in his eyes as he concluded his presentation.

The notes for his speech remain in the Toyoda family to this day. Written on a wide, horizontally-ruled paper, they are penned in very small letters. Sentence after sentence is filled with sadness and regret for the fate of Kiichrio's workers. Not once does he point to anything or anyone other than himself for being to blame.

Whether or not members of the union paid heed to Kumabe's and Kiichiro's pleas for cooperation, the union announced a reorganization plan of its own and spurned the subject of layoffs. When it was rejected, the union walked out, beginning a bitter strike that would last for twenty-four days.

Taizo Ishida, the president of Toyoda Automatic Loom Works, felt a deepening anxiety and irritation as the strike against the Toyota Motor Company dragged on. Up to this point, the Loom Works had already loaned huge sums to Toyota, and were it to collapse, it would bring the Loom Works crashing down with it. In that eventuality, all of the Toyoda companies would topple like dominoes and see *fini* written on their proud histories.

"I cannot let Mr. Kiichiro die,'' Ishida vowed. Since the days of his youth, when Kanesaburo Hatori had committed suicide upon foreseeing the collapse of his company, Ishida had always equated bankruptcy with suicide by the company's president. This was simply what a person of honor and duty did. If he did not, felt Ishida, then he was spineless and despicable. What made Kiichiro's situation a moral dilemma for Ishida were the complexities of modern business.

Kiichiro is a truly great man, mused Ishida. *But he, like Kumabe, is not a business man. That makes him ill-equipped to handle the financial problems that are leading to his company's demise. This is why it would be unfair for him to die. It is also why I must do what I have to do to. Regardless of what people say or how they criticize me, I know exactly what to do. I'll overcome every obstacle and take care of this problem!*

Like Kiichiro, Ishida was strong-willed and given to immediate action, whether it involved rearranging the furniture in his office, hiring new personnel, or spending millions of yen on new equipment. So he marched into Risaburo's office and told him, "Toyota Motor Company will go bankrupt if things continue as they are. We can't let the strike go on like this. We must do something about it.''

"Leave it alone,'' Risaburo replied dourly, as the corners of his mouth dropped and hinted at his displeasure. Now ill and lethargic, and perhaps reluctant to once again cross swords with his headstrong brother-in-law, Risaburo clearly wanted nothing to do with Toyota: "Kiichiro and Kumabe are in charge of Toyota Motor Company. They can do whatever they wish. There's nothing anyone can do about it. If it goes bankrupt, that's just too bad.''

"What on earth are you saying,'' demanded Ishida at the top of his voice, eyes flashing and eyebrows raised in astonishment. "If Toyota Motor Company goes bankrupt, that'll also mean the end of the Automatic Loom Works and the rest of the family companies. Toyoda will be destroyed, and you and Mr. Kiichiro will have to hang yourselves. Maybe it wouldn't bother you to kill yourself, but when you go into the next world, how do you plan to apologize to Mr. Kiichiro and, most of all, to Master Sakichi?! If you're going to be such a pessimist about this, I'll quit Toyoda, wash my hands of the whole affair, and go back to the country."

"Okay, okay, don't get so upset," countered Risaburo, taken aback by the intensity of Ishida's outburst. "But Taizo, even if you say that we can't leave it alone, who will clean up that mess? Can it even be cleaned up?"

"I will! I will clean it up!" Ishida growled, glaring fiercely at the man he had known well since their high school days.

"I'll first blow out the flames of the strike. I owe Mr. Kiichiro a big debt, and he owes me a little one. I will make quick work of restructuring the company, and in that way repay my debt."

"What do you mean by owing each other something?" asked Risaburo.

"A long time ago, when Mr. Kiichiro wanted to start manufacturing automobiles, I tried to stand in his way, as you did. My reasoning was different from yours, but together we provided very strong opposition. I have to say, now, I was wrong and I want to make up for that.

"Mr. Kiichiro is a great man who has done incredible things. However, he does not have the keen business sense needed to save the company. That's where I plan to fit in. I won't stop until the company is back on its feet again."

"Yes, I understand. But what is the little debt he owes you?" asked Risaburo.

"Well, it's just a little one,..." Ishida replied, letting his voice trail off wistfully. He was sending a clear signal he preferred the matter remained private.

"All right then, it's settled," Risaburo responded, breaking a short silence. "I'll be counting on you to follow through."

"Yes, of course," smiled Ishida, taking his leave.

From that day on, Ishida focused on ending the strike, but in such a way that would not take the company further in debt or cause the workers greater hardship. Since the company would need funds once the restructuring was underway, Ishida called on Okamoto at Nisshin Tsusho to do a little preliminary spade work.

"Ah, Mr. Ishida! How good to see you. Mr. Kiichiro was here; he just left," said Okamoto, as he stood up to greet his visitor. "Mr. Kiichiro came here to inform me he's ready to resign. He asked me to look after things and carefully attend to the employees' welfare. As he left here, his spirit seemed crushed and he had tears in his eyes."

"So then," Ishida said, pausing and chewing his lower lip pensively, "you'll be taking care of things."

"Oh, no. Mr. Kiichiro asked me to, but I'm not suited for the job and I told him so. I also told him that you would be well-suited to manage the business during these troubled times. Perhaps I spoke out of turn, but that does not change my feelings. I hope you're not angry that I recommended you to Mr. Kiichiro."

"You don't have to apologize," Ishida replied with self-confidence. He knew he was better equipped to do the company's dealing at this point, and everyone knew it as well. "Forgive me for being so blunt, Mr. Okamoto, but you're both too reasonable, and too gentle-hearted to handle these matters. Let me handle the fights; all I ask is that you back me up from the sidelines. We owe Mr. Kiichiro a debt, so let's you and I quickly wrap up this restructuring so we can pay him back one day sooner," Ishida urged, using the Japanese colloquial phrase similar to "getting it done yesterday."

"You can count on me. I'll do anything I can to help, including sharing with you the necessary financials," Okamoto vowed.

"Okay, let's get started right away," Ishida replied. "I'd like you to tell me about Toyota Motors' current capital picture."

With that, they set about making concrete plans for carrying out the restructuring. Talking with great animation, shoulder-to-shoulder, they resembled a pair of schoolmates working on a term paper, although on closer inspection, the hair on these forty-year-old "students" was already half gray.

Once he and Kumabe had agreed on broad goals, Ishida started aggressively implementing them. As an executive management representative for the labor union, he was on a first-name basis with many if its members and had numerous well-placed connections who owed him favors.

His persuasive technique was simple. He first made a strong case that Toyota's problems were a direct result of the "Dodge Line" depression, and not a company conspiracy to grow rich at the workers' expense.

Then he went on to say: "If the company shuts down, we will all lose. I can understand your feelings but, we must keep Toyota Motor Company operating.

"We must work and earn money. If the company earns a profit, we can improve wages and upgrade facilities. To accomplish that, we have no choice but to be patient at times when patience is required."

Ishida's confidence in his ability to manage the business had been built upon two decades of experience. Among the many tasks he felt certain he could accomplish, resolving the strike was highest on his list. Besides, he'd already had his baptism by fire in a previous strike.

At the end of 1946, about 18 months after the war ended, labor disputes became more frequent at the Automatic Loom Works. Each time they'd been defused and a strike was averted. At least everything looked calm on the surface. The union rank and file were usually satisified with concessions, and work would return to normal. Beneath the surface, however, a maelstrom of discontent was continually being stirred up by younger and more radical groups who felt that compromise was a sign of defeat.

In April, 1947, following the union executive management elections, the radicals made uncompromising demands for extensive wage reforms. Refusing to act hastily, the new union management proposed to discuss the reforms during the next general assembly. The radicals labeled that as a transparent attempt to stall for time and initiated a company-wide strike on June 3.

At the time, the Automatic Loom Works was still in the early stages of reviving its operations, and the strike hurt the company badly. Progress had recently been made in exports to India, and missed deadlines could jeopardize the entire venture.

As managing director, Ishida was not a man to be bluffed or issued ultimatums. He made it clear from the beginning of the strike that Toyoda Automatic Loom

Works had no intention of knuckling under: "If they want to do it, then let them continue. Meanwhile, I'll just take a nap."

At negotiating sessions, he was direct and often caustic: "Each day the strike lasts, the company suffers a loss, and eventually it'll run out of money. When it's all over, we'll only be able to pay you workers, or whomever replaces you, an amount that's lower than your current salary. Keep that in mind as you continue this foolishness."

Ishida was not, of course, napping. Working quietly behind the scenes, he persuaded union moderates to make it clear to all members that the present was a critical time for the company. Gradually, with the strike gaining them nothing but mounting bills, more and more union members began to soften. Within a month of the strike's beginning, the moderate party held sway and the strike ended.

The present strike at Toyota did not present exactly the same situation. It had begun under different circumstances and was waged in a different way. In what amounted to a "partial walk out," workers staged work stoppages on a day-to-day, even hour-to-hour basis -- enough to keep a strangle hold on production without shutting the company down completely. Where output had totaled 992 vehicles during March, it skidded to 619 in April, and then down to 304 in May. Each day the strike went on moved the company 14 million yen further into debt, and its stock continued a steady slide on the exchange. In April, the average price had been twenty-seven yen and ninety sen; in May, it was twenty-five yen and fifty sen.

This put pressure on Ishida to come up with a solution. Though the situation was different from what had occurred at the Automatic Loom Works, his feelings remained the same. Ishida viewed the company as a communal enterprise, where team spirit renewed the individual spirit, and hardships as well as prosperity were shared by all -- management, workers, and investors alike. It was in no one's best interest to allow Toyota Motor Company to go bankrupt, especially the banks'. The key was to turn their thinking around, convince them that they, too, would be victims, and then set their minds at ease about the company's ability to survive and grow. With a vote of confidence from the banks would come an easing of labor tensions. With the easing of labor tensions would come greater confidence from the banks. It was a solid approach and helped along by other factors within the company.

Toward the end of May, the number of voluntary retirements increased. Many employees concluded that early retirement was preferable to riding the company into bankruptcy. Anyway, the Toyota retirement plan was a generous one, consisting of a prescribed pension plus a standard one month's severance, with an additional five thousand yen gratuity for married retirees with families, and three thousand yen for single persons. As the number of retirements increased, the number of mouths to feed daily also went down, which worked in Ishida's favor.

As Ishida was doing his typical behind-the-scenes negotiating, Kiichiro was moving ever closer to resigning. To get a better grasp of the situation and to help clarify his thinking, he called a meeting on Sunday, May 28, at Risaburo's residence. In addition to Risaburo and Kiichiro, Eiji, Tojiro Okamoto, and Taizo Ishida were in attendance.

"Mr. Ishida, I've heard from Risaburo and Mr. Okamoto that you have volunteered to take care of things, but can I really count on you to do that?" asked Kiichiro, a slight quiver in his voice. His noticeable hesitation simply showed the wane in self-confidence that had occurred since the meeting when layoffs were first announced.

"Yes, I make that pledge," Ishida replied without hesitation. "It may be all right for Toyota Motor Company to shut down, but if it does, then the Automatic Loom Works will also have to shut down. When you and Mr. Risaburo travel to the next world, you won't be able to face Master Sakichi.

"Master Sakichi deserves better, but in addition, I have a debt that I must pay back to you. I was stubborn and disagreeable when you wanted to start making automobiles. I won't be satisfied until I redeem myself. I had thought that to oppose automobile manufacturing was in the best interest of Toyoda, but I was wrong. I now believe that it is in the best interest of Toyoda to build automobiles again."

Kiichiro nodded in solemn agreement, and Ishida continued: "Presently, all of our problems are related to money. That's why these problems can only be dealt with by an astute businessman like myself. Unless we lay a solid foundation and do it in a totally pragmatic way, the restructuring won't work. And such things -- please excuse my saying so -- do not play to your or Mr. Kumabe's strengths."

Once again, Kiichiro nodded in agreement. Having Kamabe as his second-in-command was like having two Kiichiro's in the company.

"Mr. Ishida, you're absolutely right. I definitely would like to ask for your help," Kiichiro said, his respectful bow an outward reflection of the bow he felt in his heart for this forty-year-old, outspoken, strong-willed manager. Then, it was decided.

On June 5, Kiichiro, the president; Kumabe, the vice-president; Shohachiro Nishimura, the managing director; and the Board of Directors of Toyota Motor Company announced their intention to resign. At the same time, acting on a motion by Risaburo as chairman of the outgoing board, Taizo Ishida was named acting president. About that time, the number of voluntary retirements suddenly increased to 1,700.

On June 8, a collective bargaining session lasted throughout the night and, on the following day, the union accepted the company's restructuring plan. On the tenth, a new contract was signed, and the two-month-long dispute came to a close.

Stockholder meetings resumed, and on July 8, a formal announcement of the resignations was made to the public. New officers, including Risaburo and Okamoto, were elected by the seven-member selection committee; other officers, excluding the three director-level members, were re-elected and Ishida was elected president. In recognition of the bank consortium, Fukio Nakagawa, managing director of Teikoku Bank, Osaka, was appointed to the newly created post of senior managing director. Ono, Eiji, and Saito were named managing directors. Before the stockholders meeting ended, the newly elected President Ishida paid tribute to the man he was replacing:

"Although President Toyoda has resigned and I have taken his place, we all must take responsibility for the downturn in our business. We also must express heartfelt gratitude to our stockholders and creditors. I, unworthy Taizo Ishida, pledge to do my very best to make this company survive.''

Then, bowing in the direction of Kiichiro, in a voice choked with emotion, Ishida said, ''I would like to ask for your support. Please, help me succeed so that one day I can welcome back Mr. Kiichiro Toyoda as president of this company.''

All of the attending officers and stockholders at this meeting heard this tribute to Kiichiro and saw how Ishida bowed to each person at the meeting, one by one, his cheeks wet with tears.

It was a scene no one in attendance would forget.

Chapter
12

THE ENDLESS SPIRIT

After Kiichiro stepped down from the presidency, he took a much needed rest. It had been nearly twenty years since he started his automobile career, and most of his adult life was spent studying, designing, and working on cars and trucks.

While Kiichiro accepted much of the blame for what happened, he knew in his heart that he'd also been a victim of many adverse circumstances, particularly the severe postwar depression fueled by the "Dodge Line." Still, the toll taken by the emotional and psychological strain of the last few years left him lethargic and physically weak. The family noticed it for several months after his resignation, as Kiichiro tended his garden and spent hours in meditation.

As an inventor and a student of science and the automobile manufacturing industry, he knew his story was not unique. Perhaps among the things he reflected upon as he secluded himself in his quiet mountain retreat, were the ways in which his fate compared with other inventors and automobile industry pioneers -- men such as William Crapo Durant, the founder of General Motors, and Henry Ford, the man whose mass-production methods first put America on wheels.

Durant was a wealthy carriage builder who became the king of the automotive capital of the world, the United States. Like Kiichiro, he had also been forced out of his own company -- in fact, only two years after he founded it. The problems had also been those of debt and dwindling finances. Durant had started with nothing and worked his way into a successful coach-making enterprise. His success was well known, so it was not surprising when he was asked to take the helm of Buick Motor Company and lead it back to prosperity. That was in 1903 and Durant had just turned forty. It didn't take him long to see that Buick's problems stemmed from inefficient production and poor marketing strategy. They had an excellent product, but didn't know how to keep costs down or how to sell it. Under Durant's steerage, Buick did well for all but a brief period during a country-wide depression in 1907. Then in 1908, Durant established General Motors and brought Cadillac, Oldsmobile, and Oakland under its umbrella. In 1910, when the rapidly growing

General Motors ran into financial difficulties, a banking syndicate headed by James Storrow saved the company but forced Durant to resign as president.

Durant wasted no time in joining forces with Louis Chevrolet. With the help of duPont interests, the success of their new venture was so meteoric that they were able to recapture control of General Motors in 1916. Durant was swiftly "recoronated" as president, but faced a rocky reign ahead. As it did many companies during that era, the post-World War I depression brought GM close to financial ruin. The duPont family stepped in again but this time argued that GM's problems were the result of gross mismanagement. Durant was forced to resign and P. S. duPont served as president until the legendary Alfred P. Sloan, Jr., took over in 1923. Still not giving up, Durant founded Durant Motors, a mini-conglomerate that lasted until the Crash of 1929.

It would appear that countrywide and worldwide depressions were the arch enemies of the automobile industry. They staggered GM and finally delivered Durant the knock out punch in the late 1920s. They had hammered Toyota and finally undid Kiichiro after World War II. Hundreds of firms that built the nearly 3,000 different models of automobiles in America came and went on the winds of economic hard times, including firms like the Overland Company, founded by one of the great automobile pioneers, John M. Wiley. Here, in fact, was another story of a man who had built a car manufacturing business with his own blood, sweat, and tears, only to be devastated when the financial road became too rocky. It seemed as though the only firm and family to avoid suffering the fate of a mutiny was Ford. But it faced a host of different problems.

Epitomized by Henry Ford's famous quip, "You can have any color of Ford you want, so long as it's black," it appeared that the company's philosophy then mirrored today's maxim, "if it isn't broken, don't fix it." The Model "T" had enjoyed phenomenal success, and Ford stuck to being the only United States car manufacturer to offer only one model. As it grew overly secure with its own prosperity, Ford began to lag behind General Motors in everything but self-assurance. Style, design, and finally sales lost out to the more aggressive GM.

When Durant's Chevrolet eventually outdistanced them as well, Ford learned the hard way the price one pays for not changing with the times. By then, however, Chevrolet had become the number one best-selling car in America.

Regardless of how one looked at the respective situations of these giants of the American auto industry, their troubles always seemed to be one of two kinds -- poor financial management or poor timing. Rarely were technology or marketing strategy the real culprits.

Postwar Toyota was no different. Perhaps, the challenge to create a mass-production automobile industry was too great for Japan at that time in history. Maybe the scale was too large, the necessary organization too complex, the managerial know-how too inexperienced to meet the demands of this capital-intensive, highly leveraged, and highly competitive new business. The industry required a huge labor force, enormous capital, and shrewd marketing and technical programs. To succeed, companies had to have heroic management and nerves of steel, more than any one man could provide. It required a perfectly coordinated management team to keep the complexities from subtly and steadily undermining the enterprise. It called for *"masterminds,"* not a "mastermind." As steeped as he was in automobile industry lore, Kiichiro doubtlessly was well aware of these dynamics. Perhaps he even took some solace from the recognition that he had expected the impossible from himself. Others like him had tried and faltered -- Durant, Wiley....But that was then, and now he had to again begin considering the welfare of his company, if even from a distance.

Toyota was in good shape technologically. Eiji and Saito had had rigorous technical training, and recently Hanji Umehara, from Tohoku University, had been brought on board. There also were a number of excellent young engineers who had transferred from the aviation and military divisions and had been under Kumabe's direction and tutelage ever since the end of the war. Though equal to its engineering tasks, this staff had no expertise in the main course of the company's problems -- finance. All they could do now was pray that Taizo Ishida, who touted himself as an astute businessman and whom Kiichiro and the others considered to be only a novice manager, would somehow save the company.

Only time would tell, and there was no time to be wasted. After his period of meditation and recuperation, Kiichiro jumped right into several new ventures. As with building automobiles, his vision focused on serving needs rather than making money, so his new activities reflected his often-expressed view: "To the citizens living in this ruined country, food, clothing, and shelter are of utmost importance."

His eldest son, Shoichiro, had already been working on some of Kiichiro's sideline projects, begun right after the war, among them food processing and experimenting with prestressed concrete. Now Kiichiro started working on these himself. He also began working on plans for a passenger car for the general public, a project which would not be funneled through Toyota.

His work on prestressed concrete both fascinated and befuddled him. Through a special process, preformed slabs are made by pouring concrete over a lattice of steel strands, which give the concrete added strength and allows it to expand and contract with changes in temperature without cracking. Although the idea is so familiar to us today as to seem absurdly simple, the technology was just in its infancy when Kiichiro began working on it.

"Reinforced" concrete had been in use for years and consisted of concrete poured over a network of solid steel rods and smaller steel wire mesh. "Prestressed" concrete had only existed in theory. While engineers had surmised for decades that prestressed concrete would be much stronger than simply reinforced material, putting theory into practice was proving extremely difficult. Not until a French engineer named Eugene Freyssinet began using high-strength steel did the mystery seem close to a solution. By the time Kiichiro took a hand in experimentation, several methods for making prestressed concrete were known, if not perfected. The one he focused his efforts on had been pioneered by Hirataka Tanaka, a professor at Tohoku Technical University. Taking all of Tanaka's findings one step further, Kiichiro made several breakthroughs in his work, which was yet another testament to just how many steps Kiichiro stayed ahead of his time. Not until 1964, the year of the Tokyo Olympics, did prestressed concrete come into wide use in Japan. Making it possible to build lightweight bridges, roads, and buildings, the new technology in concrete constituted a major contribution to large-scale architectural schemes.

As Kiichiro moved forward in his own ventures, Toyota Motor Company was moving toward recovery. Controls on production volume, prices, and sales financing had been lifted, and both Japan and the domestic automobile industry had successfully made the transition to a free market economy. Established before the strike began, Toyota Motor Sales Company was now doing well as a separate entity.

Kiichiro's successor, Taizo Ishida, appeared indeed to have been born under a lucky star. Toyota's fortunes got a huge boost less than two weeks after he was named acting president and more than three weeks before he was officially elected to the post. Though no war can be termed a good turn of events, the Korean War, declared on June 25, 1950, turned Toyota around and sealed Ishida's good fate.

As early as July 10, the American military sent requests for bids to Toyota, Nissan and Isuzu, concerning a special order for military trucks. Ishida immediately took the lead in bidding on and accepting orders for military vehicles. On July 31, an agreement was signed which secured the bulk of the initial procurement of 1,000 trucks from Toyota. Shortly after, Ishida secured a second order for an additional 320 units.

On August 29, orders were placed with Toyota for another 2,329 vehicles, and on March 1, 1951, for another 1,350, bringing the total to 4,679 trucks. During the same period, Nissan's orders totaled 4,325, and Isuzu's, 1,276. After North Korea accepted the Armistice on July 1, 1951, vehicle procurements ceased, but orders for parts replacements continued.

In August of 1950, coincidental with orders being placed by the United States, the newly-formed Police Reserve Corps of Japan ordered nearly one thousand trucks from Toyota. As other Japanese industries began to revive under the impetus of the Korean War, they too began buying vehicles. Toyota Motor Company's production lines were humming, and its coffers filled like a dry pond after a long rain. It was a welcome change, but one which seemed like cosmic irony for Kiichiro.

Production had dipped to a mere 304 units during May, 1950, as the strike dragged on. Even during 1945 when the Occupation had brought production to a near halt, monthly output averaged more than that. By August of 1951, not even taking into account military vehicles for the Korean War, production topped the 1,000 mark, totaling 1,096 units.

The financial figures tell the story. When Kiichiro left office in June, outstanding debt totaled 130 million yen. By August, debt had plummeted to a mere 21.5 million yen, and in October, Toyota posted a profit of 42.5 million yen. That was just the beginning. By March, 1951, Toyota's treasury was bulging with a 250 million yen net profit.

Toyota was now able to resume payment of dividends and at a level 20 percent higher than at the time of their suspension in 1948. Even with the increased dividends, the company maintained capital reserves totaling 150 million yen. In

September of 1951, profits rose to 500 million yen, dividends were increased by 30 percent, and internal reserves increased to 240 million yen.

Human fate often is as hard to understand as it is impossible to predict. Only twenty days separated Kiichiro's resignation on June 5 and the start of the Korean War on June 25. By the time he officially left his presidential post on July 18, Toyota had already been notified of the United States military's order. He had overcome incredible odds, endured inhuman stress, devoted several normal lifetimes of work to fulfill a quest, only to miss financial salvation by twenty days.

Ishida may have been fortune's favored child, but he also knew what to do when opportunity presented itself: just as he had promised, he succeeded in bringing fortune to his company. And then he held on tightly to what he gained. He did not, for example, hire more workers when the orders for military vehicles started pouring in. Nor did production dwindle markedly during the strike, when voluntary retirements reduced the work force by over 2,000 workers. By careful redeployment of labor and increases in overtime, Toyota was able to produce and ship all orders on schedule.

Ishida was careful with the firm's money, not miserly. No corners were cut nor funds spared when Eiji requested new machinery, machine tools, and other equipment to replace obsolete or worn-out equipment. He was, however, as shrewd a businessman as he was astute.

Many stories have been circulated regarding Ishida's legendary methods of operation at that time. According to one tale, he gouged the United States military at a critical point during the Korean War. With the Communist forces driving on the Pusan perimeter, the United States was in no position to haggle over the inflated prices Ishida had tacked on for a shipment of military trucks. At war's end, however, the U. S. government lodged a complaint with the Japanese government against Toyota, insisting: "It's impossible for trucks to cost that much! A fair price should be determined and the U. S. duly compensated!"

As the story has it, Ishida caustically spurned the request, responding: "Where on earth does such a person get off telling us to lower our prices after he has already signed a contract, issued payment, and used the merchandise? If that's the way he wants to play the game, then from now on, I'll only pay half of the agreed-upon price for American goods!"

Ishida, of course, categorically denied the story, but that it continued to be told and believed is a pretty good indication of just how formidable, unflappable, and strong-willed Ishida could be.

During the Korean war, when Toyota was turning a tidy profit, Kiichiro was dividing his time between Nagoya and Tokyo. In Tokyo, he lived at his residence in Okamoto-cho, and used the upstairs room of a small renovated warehouse as his office. The downstairs room was occupied by Shisaburo Kurata. Kurata had been involved in designing the Automo-Go at Hakuyosha, and then had later joined Eiji at Kiichiro's Shibaura Laboratory, going on to become design manager at the Koromo factory soon after it opened. A talented as well as veteran engineer, Kurata had amazed everyone with the ease with which he was able to accomplish "impossible tasks."

When World War II broke out, Kurata remained full time in Tokyo as Kiichiro's eyes and ears. As Kiichiro told him, "We must stay in close touch with the military, and be aware of all that is happening in Tokyo." He also conducted special research on such subjects as radar technology and helicopters. When the war ended, Kurata became Kiichiro's private technical aide and remained with him after Kiichiro's resignation.

When Kiichiro was not in Tokyo working with Kurata, he normally was in Nagoya at his mountain retreat. His blood pressure seemed well in check and his physical and mental strength had returned. He was back to his usual, hard-working self, so much so that he set up a place to sleep in the Arakawa Bankin factory in Nagoya, a Toyoda-related company. Whenever he slept where he was doing research on automobile engines and designs, everyone knew he was healthy. It was during this time that Kiichiro also worked intermittently on his food and shelter projects. Having started his eldest son, Shoichiro, and his son-in-law, Nishida, in research and development of prestressed concrete and soft cork, and on the mechanized production of *chikuwa*, Kiichiro began raising quail at his large mountain retreat. The sale of quail eggs had become a flourishing enterprise. He continued his study on artificial breeding of loaches (a fresh water fish resembling catfish) in his large pond, but that did not turn into a business. In addition to these activities, he also ran a porcelain manufacturing company in Tajimi and had begun manufacturing glass tools.

His restless energy, his insatiable hunger for technical and scientific knowledge, and his inability to sit still all helped to account for this potpourri of unique activities. Underneath it all, his heart was ever with the people of his defeated nation and especially with the employees of Toyota. Shortly after the war he'd said: "The occupation forces might take away all of our automobile factories. If that happens, we must think about how we can provide a living for our employees. Let's study all aspects of the necessities of life: food, clothing, and shelter."

After much deliberation, he decided to include these projects as part of Toyota Motor Company's operations. For this reason, Eiji and Saito were often sent to study artificial breeding of fish at the Kyoto University Laboratories, located at the rice paddy ridges of Lake Biwa near Kyoto. The next week might find them in Seto studying the manufacture of ceramics. This was Kiichiro's way of being prepared in the event that the car factory was seized as a war reparation by the Occupation.

As it became apparent the factory would not be confiscated and the automobile business had a chance of survival, these sideline pursuits were continued, but with less urgency. Some of them, including prestressed concrete, soft cork manufacture, and porcelain had already reached the manufacturing stage.

Concerned for all of his employees, not just those involved with automobile production, Kiichiro resisted layoffs across the board. To protect employees engaged in sideline concerns, the smaller companies were split off from Toyota Motor Company to form Kiichiro's private company. This had proved advantageous because it provided Kiichiro with a cushion when he resigned the presidency. Maybe he had seen the future coming, and maybe not. But given his foresight in everything else, chances are that formation of a separate company was no accident.

Kiichiro's mind, it must be remembered, resided most often in the future. And right now the focus of that future was his son Shoichiro. Always putting a premium on education, Kiichiro explained to Shoichiro: "Regardless of whether one is an engineer or a manager, one must think about the big picture on the one hand and details on the other. To study the details, you must go back to school."

When his son agreed, Kiichiro sent him to study at the engineering graduate school of Tohoku University, where Naruse and Nukiyama were now teaching. Shoichiro specialized in jet propulsion under Professor Tanazawa and received his Ph. D. in engineering upon completion of his doctoral research. His father's advice would eventually serve him well when he joined Toyota Motor Company.

As for his own involvement with Toyota, Kiichiro was again engrossed with "the automobile." Not quite a year had passed since his resignation when he told Kurata: "Independent of Toyota, I will capitalize a small company in Tokyo and produce about fifty units a month. There I will manufacture what I think is the ideal small passenger car for the general public."

He then sent Kurata off to Shingawa Sangyo, an automotive parts manufacturer located near Kariya, and had him study engines with Shoichiro. Kiichiro was as unsparing of Shoichiro as of himself: in addition to the young man's graduate work at Tohoku University, Kiichiro had given him major assignments in prestressed concrete, and now research with Kurata on engine technology.

To help him work out the design and plan for production of the new vehicle, Kiichiro asked Eiji to assign a Toyota engineer to help him research his new automobile. The man was Shiro Yamada. A graduate of the military academy, Yamada had a markedly inventive talent, as well as first-rate engineering skills. He was given the task of designing the body and worked at the Arakawa Bankin facility where Kiichiro now had a permanent office. Reminiscent of "the makeshift days" of the first pilot automobile facility in the Kariya plant, a large chicken coop was brought from Kiichiro's mountain retreat and installed on the Arakawa Bankin lot. When fully equipped, this served as the new automobile research lab.

As his commitments multiplied, Kiichiro was kept busy traveling back and forth between his Tokyo office, Shingawa factory, and Arakawa Bankin to "supervise" the work. Supervision of course, involved getting his hands dirty up to the elbows and trouble-shooting knotty problems, from procurement of equipment to general administration.

Kiichiro was obviously spreading himself very thin, and none of his pursuits received 100 percent of his attention, not even the new automobile project. He let Kurata and Shoichiro do the lion's share of work on the engine project. Likely because Kiichiro was not directly involved from the outset, the project went astray or was at least not to his exacting standards. The order was given to scrap all that had been done and to begin anew, but instead work on the engine was temporarily suspended.

Since his research on the new automobile was never completed, there is no record of how the car was to look. While Kiichiro made copious notes and sketches, most of them were too abstract to get an idea of what he had in mind. However, there was nothing abstract about his objectives, as evidenced by his journal:

(1) Above all, it must be economical. That means it must be small and mass-produced using as few materials as possible. First, to stamp out body panels and component housings, we must design a forming press that will be structurally simple, sound, and adaptable to our many needs. Second, the design must permit us to primarily utilize final-shape metalworking methods. This will minimize machining and other metal-finishing processes. Because automotive engineering in Japan lags behind state-of-the-art metal work elsewhere, we may have to leave implementation of this goal for the future.

(2) Although it is to be a car for the general public, the exterior styling must be modern because that will help sell the car in the long run. That does not mean we can ignore existing styles, because these have already programmed the consumer with a particular expectation. If the design is too radical, potential customers may think it will present maintenance problems or prove impractical in some other way. In addition, we must give careful thought to eliminating potential shakes and rattles. It is especially important that we come up with a maintenance-free engine.

(3) Everyone, including women and young people, must be able to easily and safely drive it. It will be a failure if it takes a lot of time and money to learn to drive it. Among other things, it is most desirable to have the gears in the gearbox also disengage from the drive train when the clutch is disengaged. This will improve handling and reduce drive train wear. We may have to look to foreign manufacturers for this technology.

(4) The car must not be prone to mechanical failures. That's important to all drivers, and it will greatly lessen the anxieties of those just learning to drive.

Perhaps Kiichiro was borrowing from Durant's life history. Like the Chevrolet, Kiichiro's new "people car" might prove so successful that he would be able to redeem his position as president of Toyota Motor Company, as Durant did with General Motors. Though Kiichiro intended to do this unassisted, he did not hesitate to tap Toyota for help. He had petitioned Eiji to provide an engineer on the Toyota payroll to help him develop his designs. Eiji had given him Shiro Yamada, in addition to accepting research and testing expenses, which he routed through Toyota's regular accounting department. Clearly, although Kiichiro had formally resigned and had no legal claim to Toyota Motor Company, informally it was still his "baby." How could it be otherwise, when the heart and blood that created it were his own?

On a rainy afternoon in late fall, Kiichiro accompanied Bunjiro to the grave of his mother, Tami, who was buried in Washizu. Tami had died of old age shortly after the war, at a time when the ills of the business made it impossible for Kiichiro to attend the services. For a long time he had wanted to pay his respects, frequently saying to Bunjiro, "One of these days, we must visit her grave. You'll have to show me where it is."

Autumn hovered over the hill at Kosai, fragrant from the damp earth, the fall colors still sparkling with raindrops. A serene beauty hung in the air as far as the eye could see. Tami's grave was simple and small, surrounded by fall flowers. It was a modest grave befitting such a pure and timeless atmosphere.

Kiichiro offered flowers and incense at the grave. Then he poured water into the flower tube and knelt, his hands pressed together in prayer. Finally he rose and walked slowly around the cemetery, returning one last time to his mother's grave. Not a word was uttered as Kiichiro lifted his eyes from the grave and gazed into the distance, somewhere beyond the horizon.

About a month after that visit to Tami's grave, Ishida's assistant came to visit Kiichiro, finding him in the small laboratory at his Arakawa Bankin offices in the midst of a discussion with Kurata.

Kurata rose as if to leave, but Kiichiro gestured for him to remain seated. He then nodded to the caller that it was all right for Kurata to be present for the conversation. Ishida's assistant bowed and said, "Since the restructuring has been successful and President Ishida thinks everything will be all right from now on, it is his wish that you return as president of Toyota Motor Company."

As he heard this, Kurata stiffened, quickly glancing at Kiichiro's face. Toyota Motor Company's financial fortunes had indeed made a remarkable turnaround and there was nothing on the horizon to indicate its situation would not continue to improve. Kurata and Kiichiro had received the September financial statement a few days earlier showing that Toyota had earned a profit of nearly 500 million yen. That was still fresh in their minds. Moreover, while the Korean War had ended, the impetus it had imparted to the revitalization of Japan's industries showed no signs of flagging. Domestic demand continued to grow and with it, the nation's prospects for continued prosperity.

Except for introducing effective financial controls and personnel policies, Ishida ran the company pretty much as Kiichiro had. Trips to the United States for study and growth continued to be a company imperative. No sooner did Eiji, the managing director, return from a three-month visit than Saito left for a two-month visit. Both trips had been planned by Kiichiro and were intended as follow-up studies on current American automobile production methods. With his usual concern for the future of Toyota, Kiichiro had gone ahead with those plans despite the firm's financial problems and the crippling strike. Ishida simply followed through with them, recognizing the value of Kiichiro's policy.

The rationale for Eiji's and Sato's trips was the same as that which prompted Kiichiro to send Oshima, Kan, and Iwaoka to the United States back in the troubled 30's. Like their predecessors, Eiji and Saito spent a great deal of time at the Ford factory. While they respected much of what they saw, they weren't over-awed by the mass-production techniques of the Americans. Under the tutelage of Tohoku University's Naruse, when Toyota had first undertaken automobile manufacturing, they had learned to look, listen, and especially question. Just because

American automobile manufacturers made money did not mean their manufacturing techniques were fail-safe, or necessarily as efficient as they could be. Eiji and Saito were there to learn, not just copy. Thus they placed equal importance on what to avoid and what to carry back to Japan.

Based on these studies made by Eiji and Saito, in the early part of 1951, Toyota adopted its first "Five Year Plan for Modernization of Production Facilities." Ishida had decided to invest 5.8 billion yen -- an enormous sum for the times and not an insignificant one even now. The plan had just entered its first phase when Ishida requested that Kiichiro return and take the helm of his company.

Kurata waited anxiously for Kiichiro's response to the proposal. If his answer was "yes," the work Kurata had put into development of the new engine and various other facets of the project might have a chance of coming to fruition under the company.

Kiichiro just sat perfectly silent for several minutes. Finally the assistant asked, "How do you feel about the proposal?"

Kiichiro did not disguise his brusqueness. Eying the messenger coldly, he said, "You would be better off worrying less about other people's business and more about your own."

"Oh...." muttered the assistant, nonplussed and uncertain of what to do.

Kiichiro remained silent. Feeling he was being turned to stone, the assistant made his way to the door and departed without so much as a single word to carry back with him.

In late February, 1932, Ishida himself came to Tokyo to see Kiichiro. He did not immediately broach the subject, but began by reviewing in detail the developments that had led to Toyota's current prosperity and then the company's prospects for the future.

Even though Kiichiro remained surprisingly indifferent, Ishida finally bowed deeply and made his request, "I've come to redeem the promise I made when I assumed the position of president. I have done my part, so please come back."

"No, I won't do it," Kiichiro replied.

"Why not?" asked Ishida, brows furrowed in puzzlement.

"An automobile company is a company that makes automobiles. So you shouldn't be so proud that you made money on trucks when you can't even make a decent automobile. I **won't** come back," Kiichiro told him, placing heavy emphasis on the "won't."

"I'm asking you to come back so that we can make those automobiles," argued Ishida.

"Make them on your own," retorted Kiichiro.

Ishida responded: "Wait a minute -- you can't say that. I owed you a debt and I have repaid that debt by rebuilding the company. But in case you don't remember, you owe me a debt, and now it's my turn to be repaid!"

"I owe you a debt?" Kiichiro chirped in amazement. "What can that debt possibly be?"

"It goes back nearly twenty years to when I loudly voiced my opposition to your idea about manufacturing automobiles. By chance I happened to see you in the corner of the Automatic Loom Works, and although I'm not faint at heart, I did feel very awkward. So I pretended I hadn't seen you and tried to leave quietly. But then you called out and stopped me, yelling, 'Ishida, Ishida.' "

Kiichiro twisted his neck and head sideways, reflecting as he rubbed the back of his head and desperately tried to remember the incident.

"Since you called," continued Ishida, "I had no choice but to stop. When I walked over to you, you said, 'Mr. Ishida, you presently seem to be against my plan to manufacture automobiles, but please hold off on that judgment. In no time, I will build a splendid automobile and I will give you one free.' And then you said, 'Please wait for that.' "

"Hmm, yes...now I remember. I had forgotten all about that," Kiichiro answered, breaking into a smile.

"But I haven't forgotten," Ishida replied. "I have worked very hard to rebuild the company in anticipation of receiving that one automobile from you. You still haven't given me one."

Kiichiro opened his mouth as if to reply, but paused long enough for Ishida to continue: "I always tell everyone, until they're sick of hearing it, what Master Sakichi said to me long ago in Shanghai."

" 'Taizo, please do a solid job and make money -- make a lot of profit and set aside a big bundle to fund research. Without money, research can't be done.' I'm sure you understand, since you faced financial difficulties when you first began to manufacture automobiles. It's as true today as it was then. But now we have an ample supply of money. Regardless of how much you spend for research, the present Toyota Motor Company will not be strapped for cash. I know how to make money, I don't know how to make cars. So please come back. If you don't wish to be president, that's fine. Anything will do, chairman or whatever you want. I'd like to go back to the familiar surroundings of the Automatic Loom Works. But if you ask me, 'Taizo, please make the company more money,' then I'll be glad to help you in any way I can, even if that means becoming a director. If you think that we can't begin to sell automobiles or build first-rate ones, then please take as many years as you need for research so that we can move into manufacturing. And when you're ready, please make the number one automobile in the world. We have made and saved money for such purposes, and it's no longer necessary to pay attention to how much we spend on research.

"So please pay the debt you owe me. And when you've built your fine new automobile, please give me the one you promised me that day!"

As he finished, Ishida's eyes filled with hot tears.

Kiichiro sat silently musing Ishida's words. His arms were firmly crossed, his eyes looking at the floor. For a long time, the two of them said nothing. Then Kiichiro raised his head and in a hoarse voice, said, "Mr. Ishida, please forgive me. Thank you. I will gladly come back."

When he returned to Nagoya, Ishida immediately called on Risaburo and Okamoto to inform them that Kiichiro had agreed to come back as president. Then he visited influential shareholders one by one, asking for their support in welcoming Kiichiro's return.

Once everyone was in agreement, the board of directors decided that Kiichiro's reinstatement as the President of Toyota Motor Company would become effective as of the July shareholders' meeting.

By the time these arrangements were completed, it was nearly the middle of March. Ishida wasted no time in delivering the good news to Kiichiro, once again in person.

When Kiichiro had finally agreed to Ishida's request to resume the Toyota presidency, he was hesitant to share his good fortune with anyone. The change in leadership was not "official." Now that it *was* official, Kiichiro was like a child again, visiting friends, colleagues, and business associates to give them the news.

On a cold afternoon towards the end of March, Kiichiro was about to leave his office to call upon various colleagues in Tokyo. As he was walking to the car, accompanied by Kurata, he paused for a moment to catch his breath. His face was ashen and he did not appear to be well at all.

"You look very pale," said Kurata. "Are you all right? You shouldn't go out today -- perhaps you should go home."

Massaging the back of his head, Kiichiro replied, "I'm fine. Don't worry." And then he left.

As the car pulled away, Kiichiro seemed momentarily distracted, as though he had forgotten something. Then he leaned forward and informed his driver there had been a change of plans. Their new destination was Tsukiji, a small restaurant-inn operated by an old friend from his university days. Kiichiro liked to do whatever he could to help out friends, even going out of his way to patronize their places of business.

For some time, Kiichiro had been working on his complete memoirs, including childhood remembrances of his father and of Sakichi's inventions, and of course his own quest to manufacture automobiles -- the study and struggles, the momentary triumphs and endless setbacks endured along the way. Whenever he felt the urge to write, he would come to this inn, sequester himself in a private room, and work for hours without interruption. This was the first chance he had had in a while to enjoy his little writing sanctuary. Actually, he had finished the first draft of his memoirs and was into the editing stage, but the work was no less rewarding.

Upon arrival at the inn, Kiichiro walked towards the entrance where a maid was waiting to greet him. Suddenly he was lightheaded and he staggered, as the maid came rushing to his side and lent her arm to Kiichiro and helped him in.

"It's nothing. Everything is okay," Kiichiro assured her. "I just need to lie down. I'll go upstairs for a short while." The maid sensed Kiichiro was being too cavalier about the matter: "But your facial color really looks quite bad. Would you like me to call a doctor? In the meantime, I'll have a bed prepared for you."

"No, honestly, there's no need to worry," Kiichiro told her as she helped him up the stairs. "If something happens, I'll ring the bell."

The maid reluctantly left him alone and went back downstairs. Kiichiro sat down at his writing desk and straightened his manuscript. He had been away from it longer than he thought. Where had he left off? As he began reading pages at random to reorient himself, there was something more bittersweet about the memoirs than before. He could see the distant faces of his youth reeling before him as the pages turned. He could hear the voices, the wind murmurring in the thicket behind the house, the sweet melody of Aiko's presense. He was transported to his father's house in Shanghai. Kiichiro was just departing with Hatako, leaving for Japan so that she could give birth in her homeland. Sakichi was waving. Then Sakichi was speaking about a son not blindly following in his father's footsteps:

"There's no money to be made in inventing or in meddling with machinery. Above all else, one must be involved in business. You must make a serious study of how to make money in the spinning business."

The words of Sakichi came floating back across the broad expanse of time, repeating themselves as they had been oft repeated to Kiichiro as he was growing up. Then they evaporated. Kiichiro was steeped in his drawings of inventions, hived away in the drafting room of Toyoda Spinning and Weaving. He was hungry, he hadn't slept. He was perfecting the automatic loom Sakichi had left unfinished. Momentarily, Kiichiro awoke from the dream triggered by his memoirs:

"That's true. The first thing I really worked on was the automatic loom, not the automobile...."

Then he drifted back into the dream state, to one very special spring day.

For months he had been working on further improving the ingenious automatic shuttle-changing device invented by Sakichi. On this particular day, actually no different than the others before it, Kiichiro was totally absorbed in his work, oblivious to the rest of the world, muttering to himself as he sketched and took notes about the new design.

"Ah hah! I see. Indeed, that is a better way to do it."

These words of the person standing over his shoulder startled Kiichiro. He had been completely unaware that Sakichi was observing him as he sketched. Kiichiro looked up with shock at his father, who had returned from Shanghai unannounced. There he stood in a simple kimono, quietly stroking his chin.

"You are indeed my child. If you like machines so much, then I won't interfere from now on. Go ahead and study machines as much as you can." Having said this, Sakichi sat down next to his son and launched into a discussion of technology, invention, and manufacturing. It went on for several hours.

My career is a mirror image of Father's career. When I was young, I disliked my father, but then one day I realized I am my father's shadow. The memory of his own words was as vivid as the day he thought them. How perfect this match was between the image of the father and the shadow of the son. Kiichiro again drifted deep into his past, to a time when he had been feverishly trying to improve the design of the automobile engine. He now was gazing at his father's unfinished circular loom in the secret room at Toyoda Spinning and Weaving. He had belittled Sakichi's idea of perpetual motion as being an impossible dream. But like other impossible dreams, it had led to practical discoveries that might have otherwise gone unnoticed. That unfinished circular loom had brought Kiichiro's own quest into focus at a critical point in his life. Without the quest for a circular loom, there would have been no quest for an automobile. And Toyota Motor Company would never have been born. A passage in the memoirs Kiichiro was now resting on read:

From parent to child, from one generation to the next -- endlessly....

Suddenly in the present, Kiichiro felt dizzy. The room began to whirl 'round and 'round, and he fell face forward onto the desk.

Oh no! I need a doctor!

He tried to reach the bell to ring the maid, but his hand wouldn't move. A bright red blur passed before his eyes like an ultra high-speed race car headed for the finish line. He was losing consciousness from a hemorrhage in his brain. The faint image of the circular loom returned and faded. The racing car plummeted toward a dark horizon. Kiichiro felt another wave of dizziness, much stronger than the first. He never regained consciousness.

From Kariya, Kiichiro's friend and doctor, Yoshiharu Nomura, hurriedly took the night train to Tokyo and came to his bedside. He remained there for several days, joining with the family and friends to watch over him day and night.

Dr. Kakinuma, a leading neurosurgeon from Tokyo University, was called in, but there was very little that could be done. Kiichiro remained in a coma until 9:10 A.M. on March 27, 1952. At that moment, the quest for the dawn came to an end.

Kiichiro's funeral services were held at Tokyo and Nagoya as a combined ceremony of some ten Toyoda companies. Taizo Ishida made the arrangements in Tokyo. On April 1, more than a thousand people attended the service at Tsukijihongan Temple. In Nagoya, a funeral service organized by Tojiro Okamoto was attended by more than three thousand.

Due to his bad heart, Risaburo could not leave his residence in Nagoya. In the prime of their lives, they had quarreled fiercely with each other over automobile manufacturing, but as they aged, their relationship had warmed, especially after the war. By the time of Kiichiro's death, the two had become brothers. Badly shaken by Kiichiro's untimely death, the sixty-seven year old Risaburo took a sudden turn for the worse and passed away just a few months later, on June 3.

Although Kiichiro was gone, Toyota Motor Company kept his life-long dream alive. Led by Taizo Ishida, managing director and chief executive officer, and Eiji, managing director of design and manufacturing, Toyota finally came up with the world-class passenger car that Kiichiro aimed to build.

With a team of engineers Kiichiro himself had recruited, Eiji orchestrated the development of the Crown. A far cry from the Model A1, the pilot car that was held together only by the sheer will of its creators, the Crown embodied the principles of economy, durability, ease of handling, and low sticker price that Kiichiro had viewed as essential elements of a passenger car produced for the common man. Kiichiro did not live to see it, but his grand spirit, inhuman endurance, and courageous twenty-year uphill battle made it possible.

On April 27, 1954, an unveiling ceremony for a bronze bust of Kiichiro took place in the front courtyard of the Koromo factory, about the time the first Crowns were ready to start coming off the assembly line.

The bust of the bespectacled Kiichiro, mounted on a white marble pedestal, was placed directly in front of the elegant, rectangular, cream-colored Toyota Main Building, immediately to the right of the entrance to the first Toyota factory.

In front of the statue was a wide paved road running east and west in the compound. To the left was a main public road running north and south. It was a fitting placement, as Kiichiro had devoted his life to bring his beloved homeland to the crossroads of a modern domestic automobile industry in Japan.

Today, the statue of Kiichiro is surronded by buildings that reflect the growth of Toyota Motor Company since the memorial to its founding father was erected. To one side are two engineering buildings, one a rectangular, three-story building, and the other, a cream-colored, six-story structure. To their right, stands the unique "Design Dome" where tomorrow's Toyotas gestate and are given birth.

On the corner, to the left of Kiichiro's statue, now stands a cluster of buildings, among which is a three-storied, gray structure housing the production control department. Behind these lie the zig-zag-roofed manufacturing compounds that taper in a line as they stretch toward the horizon.

The main road that passes to the left of Kiichiro's statue heads north to Asuke-cho and the city of Seto, and south to Okazaki. Humming with traffic twenty-four hours a day, it is precisely where Kiichiro would want to be. For those who stop to contemplate his visage, an inscription is offered as a tribute from those who knew, respected, and loved him:

TO THE MEMORY OF KIICHIRO TOYODA

As the pioneer of the Japanese automobile industry, he sacrificed his noble life to build this company on these hills of Koromo. To cherish the memory of Kiichiro Toyoda and to honor his virtues and accomplishments; we have built this bronze statue on this land so that we may remember the generosity and kindness of his face.

March 27, 1954
The Employees of the Toyota Motor Company